STRANGE F

'An uncompromisingly rational approach to the question of whether there is such a thing as "race" is taking us in the right direction.'

New Scientist

'Malik is one of the most interesting and perceptive voices operating in the disputed territory where science, culture and politics meet. A stalwart defender of free speech, he is a formidable enemy of fuzzy or wishful thinking.'

Observer

'Malik weaves politics, science and history into a thoughtful and considered argument.'

BBC Focus

'[Malik's] tone is measured and his arguments well grounded. And underpinning his lucid and important book is a fundamental belief in universal human dignity.'

Financial Times

'A nicely provocative and stylish polemic.'

Guardian

'Kenan Malik delivers a withering critique of what he sees as the racial view of the world. In doing so his arguments are a challenge to all those who seek to better understand the continuing debates about race and racism in our changing global environment.'

John Solomos, Head of the Sociology Department, City University, London and author of Race and Racism in Britain *(2003)*

'Stripping away layers of pseudo-science and taken-for-granted prejudices, paying no dues to political correctness, he has written a penetrating critique.'

Adam Kuper, Professor of Anthropology, Brunel University, London

'Kenan Malik's gloriously sharp and combative new book, *Strange Fruit*, cuts through the cant and confusion that so often surrounds this issue.'

Robin Walsh, Culture Wars – On-line reviews for the Institute of Ideas

Kenan Malik is a writer, lecturer, broadcaster, and Senior Visiting Fellow at the University of Surrey, UK. He writes regularly for *The Times*, the *Guardian*, *Prospect*, and *New Statesman*, and has made a number of acclaimed TV documentaries. His books include *The Meaning of Race: Race, History and Culture in Western Society* (1996), and *Man, Beast and Zombie: What Science Can and Cannot Tell us about Human Nature* (2000).

STRANGE FRUIT

WHY BOTH SIDES ARE WRONG
IN THE RACE DEBATE

Kenan Malik

ONEWORLD
OXFORD

A Oneworld Book

First published by Oneworld Publications 2008
Copyright © Kenan Malik 2008
First published in trade paperback 2009

ISBN 978–1–85168–665–0

Typeset by Jayvee, Trivandrum, India
Cover design by Keenan Design
Printed and bound in Great Britain by
Bell and Bain Ltd., Glasgow

Oneworld Publications
185 Banbury Road
Oxford OX2 7AR
England
www.oneworld-publications.com

For Carmen, without whom
I would have written this book much more quickly.
I am very happy that it took me such a long time.

CONTENTS

ACKNOWLEDGEMENTS

My thanks to many of the usual suspects, and a few new ones too: Toby Andrew, David Cannadine, George Ellison, Thomas Hylland Eriksen, John Gillott, David Goodhart, Anthony Grayling, Tiffany Jenkins, Steve Jones, Funmi Kelani, Marek Kohn, Adam Kuper, Janet McCalman, Jonathan Marks, Meera Nanda, Tunde Okome and Ray Tallis have all either read the manuscript or debated the issues over many years. All have shaped my arguments, though not necessarily in a way of which they would approve. I am particularly grateful to those of whose ideas I have been critical in this book but who have nevertheless been generous with their time and comments. I hope we can continue the debate and refine the arguments.

A note on terminology: Proponents of the idea that race is a biological reality often describe themselves as 'race realists'. It is a loaded term, suggesting that only those who believe in the biological concept of race are in touch with reality. As Jonathan Marks, a fierce critic of the race concept, has put it to me, 'I am the race realist, they are the race reifiers'. I agree. Nevertheless, for the sake of simplicity, and because the term has come into common currency in contemporary debates about race, I use the term 'race realist' in this book to describe proponents of the race concept. It comes, however, with a health warning.

FOREWORD:
RACE, SCIENCE AND
JAMES WATSON

'I am inherently gloomy about the prospect of Africa ... All our social policies are based on the fact that their intelligence is the same as ours – whereas all the testing says not really.'

So claimed the Nobel Laureate, James Watson, in an interview in Britain's *Sunday Times* in October 2007. Watson is one of the most eminent living scientists. In 1953, he and Francis Crick unravelled the extraordinary double helix structure of DNA, perhaps the single most important scientific breakthrough of the twentieth century. For forty years he was director of the Cold Spring Harbor Laboratory on Long Island, New York, one of the most prestigious biological research institutions in the world. He was also director of America's Human Genome Project, until he resigned over plans to patent genes, to which he was passionately opposed.

But Watson also has a darker reputation. He has been mired in controversy throughout his life, such as when he claimed a link between skin colour and libido or seemed to suggest that it might be right to abort 'gay' foetuses (he later insisted that his words had been taken out of context). The journal *Science* once said of him that 'To many in the scientific community, Watson has long been something of a wild man, and his colleagues tend to hold their collective breath whenever he veers from the script.'

The *Sunday Times* interview was one of several that Watson had given to promote his autobiography called, perhaps unsurprisingly, *Avoid Boring People*. Despite the title, the book is quite bland. Watson refers to the issue of race only briefly and obliquely. 'There is no firm reason', he writes, 'to anticipate that the intellectual capacities of people geographically separated in their evolution should prove to have evolved identically. Our wanting to reserve equal powers of reason as some universal heritage of humanity will not be enough to make it so.' In the *Sunday Times* interview, conducted by his former student Charlotte Hunt-Grubbe, Watson translated the careful wording of the book into the language of the street. People expect everyone to be equal, he claimed, but 'people who have to deal with black employees find this is not so.'

Censure was swift and universal. Steven Rose, professor of biology at the Open University, condemned the comments as 'scandalous'. The Mayor of London, Ken Livingstone, fulminated against 'ignorant comments' that 'are utterly offensive and give succour to the most backward in our society.' Britain's newly-formed Equality and Human Rights Commission studied the remarks to see if it could bring any legal action. London's Science Museum, at which Watson was to have delivered a lecture, cancelled his appearance, claiming that the Nobel Laureate had 'gone beyond the point of acceptable debate.'

In America, too, the criticism was almost total. The Federation of American Scientists condemned Watson for choosing 'to use his unique stature to promote personal prejudices that are racist, vicious and unsupported by science.' Francis Collins, director of the National Human Genome Research Institute, described Watson's comments as 'racist' and as both 'profoundly offensive and utterly unsupported by scientific evidence.' Cold Spring Harbor Laboratory not only 'vehemently' disowned Watson's remarks but suspended his chancellorship of the institution, forcing him eventually to resign.

The row over Watson's comments shows all that is wrong with the current debate about race. On the one hand, Watson got his facts in a double helix. On the other, the arguments of Watson's critics were equally in a twist. There are certainly real genetic differences between human populations and the scientific study of these differences can help unravel the roots of disease, develop new medicines, unpick the details of deep human history; perhaps eventually even tell us something about the nature of intelligence. Such genetic differences are, however, not the same as racial differences. Race provides a means, not just of categorising humanity, but also of imputing meaning to those categories and of selecting certain ones, based on skin colour, appearance, or descent, as being of particular importance. Racial thinking divides human beings into a small set of discrete groups, sees each group as possessing a fixed set of traits and abilities and regards the differences between these groups as the defining feature of humanity. All these beliefs run counter to scientific views of population differences.

If Watson's arguments seemed to show a disregard for the facts of human differences, many of his critics appeared to be indifferent to the spirit of free inquiry. For the Science Museum, Watson went 'beyond the point of acceptable debate'. But what is acceptable debate? Two years ago, the then Harvard chancellor, Larry Summers, caused outrage by suggesting, in a speech, that evolved brain differences, rather than gender discrimination, may explain why men dominate science. Like Watson, Summers faced condemnation. Like Watson, he had to apologise for his comments. And like Watson, he was forced eventually to resign his post. The evolutionary psychologist Steven Pinker was asked whether Summers had put himself beyond the pale of legitimate academic discourse with his comments. 'Good grief', Pinker exclaimed, 'shouldn't everything be within the pale of legitimate academic discourse, as long as it is presented with some degree of rigor? That's the difference between a university and a madrassa.'

Of course, there was more than a little lack of rigour to Watson's comments. Yet the issue of race, and of the relationship between race and intelligence, remains the subject of legitimate scientific debate. Almost on the same day as *Avoid Boring People* hit the bookshops, so did Craig Venter's autobiography, *A Life Decoded*. Venter is a geneticist, almost as distinguished as Watson. He was one of the driving forces behind the Human Genome Project and the founder of Celera, the private sector biotechnology company without which the unravelling of the human genome would have taken considerably longer. His view on race is the opposite of Watson's. 'The concept of race', he writes, 'has no genetic or scientific basis'. Nor, he suggests, is there any 'basis in scientific fact or in the human gene code for the notion that skin colour will be predictive of intelligence'.

There is, as we shall see in Chapter 2, a growing questioning of the idea that race has no genetic basis and a burgeoning use of racial categories in scientific and medical research. Nevertheless, Venter's argument broadly accords with the current scientific consensus. It certainly accords with current moral and political sensibilities. However, it is as legitimate for Watson to express his opinion as it is for Venter to express his, even if Watson's appears to be factually wrong, morally suspect and politically offensive. As in many controversies about the human condition, the debate about race is less about the facts of human differences than about the *meaning* of these facts. It is only through open debate that we are able to decide which interpretation of the facts is the most meaningful. A scientific debate that is policed to ensure that opinions do not wander beyond acceptable moral and political boundaries is no debate at all and itself loses any meaning.

For many, though, science *is* political. In recent years, there has grown a greater scepticism about the idea that science provides an objective view of the world that is universal and valid across all societies and cultures. Belief in the objectivity of the scientific method and the universality of scientific knowledge developed through the Scientific Revolution of the seventeenth century and the Enlightenment of the eighteenth. It is a belief that traditionally has been associated with progressive thought – but no longer. Where radicals once championed scientific rationalism and Enlightenment universalism, now they are more likely to decry both as part of a 'Eurocentric' project. 'All knowledge systems', the philosopher Sandra Harding has written, 'including those of modern science are local ones.' Western science has taken over the world 'not because of the greater purported rationality of Westerners or the purported commitment of their sciences to the pursuit of disinterested truth' but 'primarily because of the military, economic and political power of European cultures.' Science, Harding concludes, 'is politics by other means.' And if that is the case, then science clearly must be policed for its moral and political rightness. That is why Watson was sandbagged as much by moral outrage as by rational argument.

The irony is that, for all the vitriol directed at Watson, racial talk today is as likely to come out of the mouths of liberal antiracists as of reactionary racial scientists. The affirmation of difference, which once was at the heart of racial science, has become a key plank of the anti-racist outlook. *We're All Multiculturalists Now* observes the American sociologist Nathan Glazer, in the title of a book. Indeed we are. The celebration of difference, respect for pluralism, avowal of identity politics – these have come to be regarded as the hallmarks of a progressive, antiracist outlook and as the foundations of a modern liberal democracy. The paradoxical result, as we shall see, has been to transform racial thinking into a liberal dogma. Out of the withered seeds of racial science have flowered the politics of identity. Strange fruit, indeed.

This book challenges both sides of the race debate. There are three broad parts to my argument. The first two chapters explore the meaning of race as a scientific category. Race, I argue, is a social, not a scientific, category but it is precisely because it is a social category that it may be useful in scientific and medical research. Chapters 3 to 7 examine the rise and fall historically of the idea of race and explain its sublimation into the idea of culture. Chapters 8 to 10 look at the contemporary clash between claims of scientific rationality and those of cultural identity and at how much modern liberal thinking has been infected by a racial view of the world. The final chapter is an afterword on the Watson row, which re-examines the debate over his comments in light of the argument in this book.

Race is not a rational, scientific category. Antiracism has become an irrational, anti-scientific philosophy. The challenge we face is to confront racial thinking while defending scientific rationality and promoting Enlightenment universality. The aim of this book is to do just that.

1

THE PEOPLE'S GENOME

William Jefferson Clinton, President of the United States, was at his loquacious best. On a warm June day in 2000, he was presiding over a ceremony to mark the news that scientists had unravelled the human genome – or at least eighty-five per cent of it, which everyone seemed to agree was as good as the whole lot. 'Nearly two centuries ago, in this room, on this floor', the President told the assembled throng, 'Thomas Jefferson and a trusted aide spread out a magnificent map – a map Jefferson had long prayed he would get to see in his lifetime. The aide was Meriwether Lewis and the map was the product of his courageous expedition across the American frontier, all the way to the Pacific. It was a map that defined the contours and forever expanded the frontiers of our continent and our imagination. Today, the world is joining us here in the East Room to behold a map of even greater significance. We are here to celebrate the completion of the first survey of the entire human genome. Without a doubt, this is the most important, most wondrous map ever produced by humankind.'

If Bill Clinton played the role of Thomas Jefferson that day, two men took on the mantle of Meriwether Lewis: Francis Collins and Craig Venter. Collins was the director of America's National Human Genome Research Institute (NHGRI), the largest of the public bodies funding the Human Genome Project. Venter, beach bum turned

biotech pioneer, was the founder of Celera Genomics, the private cor-
poration that had revolutionised the process of mapping the genome.
They stood on either side of the President. Joining them by satellite
link from London was the British Prime Minister, Tony Blair.

It was clearly a day for fancy phrases and spellbound words. 'It is
humbling for me and awe-inspiring', said Collins, a born-again
Christian, 'to realize we have caught the first glimpse of our own
instruction book, previously known only to God.' It was also a day for
moral truths – and for one moral truth above all others. 'I believe one
of the great truths to emerge from this triumphant expedition inside
the human genome', President Clinton told the world, 'is that in
genetic terms, all human beings, regardless of race, are more than
99.9 percent the same. What that means is that modern science
has confirmed what we first learned from ancient fates. The most
important fact of life on this Earth is our common humanity.'

For Craig Venter, too, the letters of the genome spelt out a moral
message to humankind. Celera had used DNA from three females
and two males who had identified themselves as Hispanic, Asian,
Caucasian or African American. 'In the five genomes', Venter said,
'there is no way to tell one ethnicity from another. Society and medicine treat us all as members of populations, whereas as individuals we
are all unique and population statistics do not apply.'

Once the razzmatazz had died down, other scientists and journalists quickly took up the refrain. The journal *Nature Genetics*
declared that 'there is no biological basis for race'. According to the
New England Journal of Medicine 'race is a social construct, not a scientific classification' and 'instruction in medical genetics should emphasise the fallacy of race as a scientific concept and the dangers inherent
in practicing race-based medicine.' The distinguished *New York Times*
journalist, Natalie Angier, concluded that 'the more closely that
researchers examine the human genome ... the more most of them are
convinced that the standard labels used to distinguish people by "race"

have little or no biological meaning.' Even conservative politicians joined the chorus. 'The Human Genome Project shows there is no genetic way to tell races apart', the former Republican Vice Presidential candidate, Jack Kemp, claimed. 'For scientific purposes, race simply doesn't exist ... Any excuse for racism, bigotry, hatred, theories of ethnic superiority and excuses for treating our brothers and sisters of any race, creed or color differently because of their physical characteristics has been utterly rejected both biologically and genetically.'

In February 2001, some eight months after the White House ceremony, the journal *Nature* published the first draft of the genome. The cover of this special issue comprised a DNA double helix formed by a mosaic of photographs of human faces. Francis Collins explained that the image 'was chosen by us rather specifically to convey a message':

> The message is, of course, this is DNA – you recognise the double helix
> – but if you look closely, this is actually a mosaic, where the tiles of the
> mosaic are made up of the faces of people from all over the world. And
> they are people from every ethnicity, and culture, and form of dress and
> age, and gender that you can think of, and that was really what we
> wanted to say. This is the people's genome.

The people's genome. It is a phrase that might make you want to reach for the sick bucket, but the meaning is clear. The human genome belongs to all of us, undivided by race or ethnicity. Biology permits no divisions. The Human Genome Project has settled once and for all the age-old question of whether races really exist. Except that it hasn't. In a major paper in the journal *Genome Biology*, the geneticist Neil Risch and his colleagues dissented from the party line, arguing that 'from a scientific perspective' there was 'great validity in racial/ethnic self-categorisations, both from the research and public policy points of view.' 'A decade or more of population genetics research', they insisted, 'has documented biological differences between the races.'

Risch is not the only party-pooper. 'Looked at the right way', the award-winning biologist Armand Leroi suggests, 'Genetic data show that races clearly do exist.' For the anthropologist Vincent Sarich, 'there is compelling evidence to support the proposition that race is a valid biological concept.' According to fellow anthropologist George W. Gill, more than half of his colleagues accept 'the traditional view that human races are biologically valid and real'. For such 'race realists', the denial of the concept of race is simply 'political correctness' or 'postmodern' fallacy. 'The people in "race denial" are in "reality denial" as well', Gill claimed in an online debate about the meaning of race.

The Human Genome Project – one of the great scientific missions of the late twentieth century, the biological equivalent of the moon landing – demonstrates that races do not exist. And it demonstrates that they do. Ironically, it seems that the more we find out about human biology, the less certain scientists appear to be about the meaning of race. It is as if after more than a decade of lunar exploration, NASA still could not decide whether or not the moon was made of blue cheese. Why such confusion? One might understand if biologists and sociologists disagreed about their understanding of race but one should surely expect geneticists to have a fairly clear consensus about the meaning of the data thrown up by the Human Genome Project. So why cannot geneticists agree among themselves whether the Genome Project shows racial differences to be a biological reality or a social myth?

To answer this question we need to look beyond the realm of genetics, indeed of science, and delve into the complex relationship between science and politics in the understanding of human differences. This is not because science cannot provide objective data about human variation. The genetics of population differences is a biological reality, but the *interpretation* of such differences is deeply shaped by politics.

Consider, for instance, how, over the past century, scientists have found very different meaning in the distribution of blood groups. In 1901, the Austrian-born biologist, Karl Landsteiner, noticed that when blood from unrelated people was mixed, it often clumped together, forming large clots. The observation led to a series of experiments, and Landsteiner eventually came to realise that there were four basic blood types among humans. Another biologist, Ludwig Hirszfeld, labelled the four groups 'A', 'B', 'AB' and 'O', and demonstrated that they were inherited.

Today, the distribution of the four blood groups among human populations is seen as a sign that racial differences have no biological basis. A key feature of the worldwide distribution of ABO frequencies, the geneticist Richard Lewontin points out, 'is that they do not have any strong geographical consistency.' If we cluster together populations with similar frequencies of a particular blood type, 'each cluster contains some mixture of European, African, Asian and American Indian populations'. Native Americans, for instance, are notable for having very low proportions of blood type B but so, too, are Australian Aborigines and the Basques. As the physical anthropologist Dennis O'Neil puts it:

> Patterns of ABO ... blood type distributions are not similar to those for skin color or other so-called 'racial' traits. The implication is that the specific causes responsible for the distribution of human blood types have been different than those for other traits that have been commonly employed to categorize people into 'races'. Since it would be possible to divide up humanity into radically different groupings using blood typing instead of other genetically inherited traits such as skin color, we have more conclusive evidence that the commonly used [racial classification] is scientifically unsound.

In the first half of the twentieth century, however, blood group distribution was used to demonstrate the very opposite – the biological reality of race. Testing the blood of soldiers during the First World War, Ludwig Hirszfeld noticed varying frequencies of the four blood types among different nationalities. He suggested that the A and B groups represented traces of 'pure' populations of aboriginal humans, each composed entirely of either A or B individuals. The two original races had evolved independently of each other, race A in Europe and race B in the southern hemisphere. These pure races later became mixed, through migration and intermarriage.

Blood type soon became seen as a marker of racial purity. In 1930, Karl Landsteiner won the Nobel Prize for medicine. In the presentation speech, Professor Gunnar Hedren of the Karolinska Institute, chairman of the Nobel Committee for Physiology and Medicine, argued that 'The varying frequency of the individual blood groups in different races points to essential constitutional differences'. Landsteiner's discovery was important because it 'opened up new fields for research on the determination of the racial purity of a people.' Experiments had shown that 'if an alien race is present within a population this race retains its specific blood group characteristics, even if it has lived away from its main and original homeland for centuries', hence demonstrating to Hedren both the importance and permanence of race. Some thirty years later, when the anthropologist Carleton Coon published *The Origin of Races*, the last major work of racial science, he used blood group distribution as evidence that different races were distinct subspecies and had originated independently of each other.

The history of the use of blood types shows how the same facts about human differences can give rise to very different ideas about the biology of race. The concept of race is a complex hybrid of the facts of human differences and the political and philosophical lenses through which we view those facts. When racial difference – and white superiority – seemed a politically undeniable truth, scientists interpreted the facts of human diversity in a racial fashion. In a post-Holocaust age, when biological concepts of race had become politically unacceptable, those same facts of human variation were interpreted as demolishing the race concept.

Science can neither confirm nor disconfirm race as a biological reality, because race is a not a scientific category. To see this more clearly, I want in this chapter to look at both the traditional liberal arguments against the idea of race and the arguments of race realists who insist that racial differences are rooted in our biology. Both sets of arguments are found wanting, because the meaning of race cannot be settled as a scientific issue.

IS RACE A SOCIAL CONSTRUCTION?

The scientific consensus for the past half-century has been that race is meaningless as a biological category. Four main arguments have been used to justify this belief. First, eighty-five per cent of human genetic variation exists *within* populations; less than ten per cent distinguishes what are commonly called races. Second, there is no such thing as a 'pure race'; all humans are mongrels. Third, all human populations merge into each other, meaning that distinctions between races are arbitrary. And finally, *Homo sapiens* is too young a species for racial differentiation to have deep evolutionary roots. Let us look at these arguments in turn.

Eighty-five per cent of variation exists within populations

Imagine that some nuclear nightmare wiped out the entire human race apart from one small population – say, the Masai tribe in East Africa. Virtually all the genetic variation that exists in the world today would still be present in that one small group. That is a dramatic way of expressing the results of a landmark analysis conducted by the geneticist Richard Lewontin in 1972. Lewontin examined variation in human blood types, to see how exactly population differences worked themselves out. His surprising conclusion was that virtually all the differences – eighty-five per cent – occurred between individuals within single populations. A further seven per cent differentiated populations within a race. Only eight per cent of total variation distinguished the major races. Lewontin's paper caused a sensation and, to this day, remains one of the most frequently cited academic works. At a stroke, Lewontin seemed to have demolished any scientific rationale for the idea of race.

Since 1972, other researchers have confirmed that at least eighty-five per cent of variation exists within populations. The results of a 2002 study by Noah Rosenberg and his colleagues were even more striking. They showed that differences among individuals account for a staggering 93 to 95 per cent of all genetic variation. About two per cent is taken up by differences between populations within a race. And race accounts for just three to five per cent of all human difference. The study also found that almost half of the alleles (when a gene can take more than one form, the different forms are called *alleles*) appeared in every major population in the world. Only 7.4 per cent of alleles were exclusive to one region and such alleles tended to be very rare. Rosenberg's study is the largest of its kind and hence the figures are likely to be the most accurate.

It seems undeniable, then, that race has no biological meaning. Virtually all genetic variation is within a population, not between 'races', and very few genes are exclusive to one part of the world. Yet it would still be wrong to conclude that races are necessarily biological nonsense. From a genetic point of view, poodles and greyhounds are almost identical, as are dachshunds and St Bernards. Tiny genetic differences can lead to major bodily and behavioural changes. Humans share about 99.4 per cent of our functional genes with chimpanzees. Yet we are clearly different species. Just fifty of the 30,000 or so genes that humans and chimps are thought to possess may account for all of the cognitive differences between them. The fact that race accounts for only four per cent of genetic variation among humans does not, race realists suggest, necessarily mean that it has no biological validity.

There is no such thing as a pure race

The conventional view of a race is as a discrete group that is distinguished by certain features – skin colour or body shape, say, or even musicality or intelligence – that are unique to that group. But we now know that there are no features that are possessed by one group to the exclusion of all others. There exists, as Stephen J. Gould has put it, 'no "race" gene present in all members of one group and none of another.' As a consequence, the British geneticist Brian Sykes points out, there can be no 'pure races'. Luigi Luca Cavalli Sforza, the doyen of contemporary population geneticists, makes much the same point when he suggests that 'classification into races has proved to be a futile exercise.' Why? Because 'All populations or population clusters overlap when single genes are considered, and in almost all populations, all alleles are present but in different frequencies. No single gene is therefore sufficient for classifying human populations into systematic categories.'

We have seen how the distribution of blood groups does not match the division of the world into races. The various forms (or alleles) of the genes that determine blood types are distributed differently to the alleles that determine skin colour. This is true for most genes: those that influence eye colour, body height, the presence of the sickle cell trait or susceptibility to breast cancer all have unique distribution patterns. The distributions of individual genes are not *concordant*: they do not match up. This has led many critics of the race concept, such as the biologist Jared Diamond, to suggest that it would be easy to carve up humanity into different units, depending upon which genes we decided were important:

> Traditionally we divide ourselves into races by the twin criteria of geographical location and visible physical characteristics. But we could

make an equally reasonable and arbitrary division ... based on any number of geographically variable traits. The resulting classifications would not all be concordant. Depending on whether we classified ourselves by antimalarial genes, lactase, fingerprints, or skin colour, we could place Swedes in the same race as (respectively) either Xhosas, Fulani, the Ainu of Japan or Italians.

These days, though, few race realists believe that races are exclusive groups distinguished by a unique set of genes or physical markers. Rather, they argue, although all races possess all genes, they do so in different proportions. Almost half a century ago, the biologist Ernst Mayr, one of the great scientific figures of the twentieth century, distinguished between 'typological' and 'population' views of race. The typological idea of race, Mayr wrote, 'asserts that every representative of a race conforms to the type and is separated from the representatives of any other race by a distinct gap.' In other words, every race is defined by a set of fixed characteristics that distinguish the one from the other. This was how nineteenth-century biologists had conceived of race. The 'populationist', on the other hand, 'also recognizes races but in totally different terms', no longer viewing them as unchanging categories. 'If the average difference between two groups of individuals is sufficiently great to be recognizable on sight, we refer to such groups of individuals as different races', Mayr concluded. 'Race, thus described, is a universal phenomenon of nature occurring not only in man but in two thirds of all species of animals and plants.'

Members of a race do not all possess a unique common feature or 'essence'. Nor are members of one race entirely distinct from those of another. They simply differ, on average, in certain traits. Modern race realists suggest that races diverge from each other statistically, not absolutely. For Mayr, races are recognisably different from each other. More recently, race realists have stressed not visible differences but variations in gene frequencies. A race, the biologist Alice Brues writes, is 'a division of a species which differs from other divisions by the frequency with which certain hereditary traits appear among its members.' In other words, there may be few genes that are specifically 'black' or specifically 'white', but some genes will be more prevalent within black populations and others more prevalent within white ones. That is sufficient, race realists suggest, to divide the world into races. We know, for instance, that Europeans are more likely than Africans to have blue eyes and more likely to be taller than East Asians. There are also less obvious differences between the races. If you are African, for instance, you are twice as likely to have a twin brother or sister than if you are European. East Asians are half as likely as Europeans to be born as one of a twin. The fact that there are no *pure* races does not *necessarily* mean that there are *no* races.

What of the argument that by privileging different genes or physical traits we can carve up humanity any way we like? It is true, say the race realists, that by arbitrarily choosing fingerprint patterns or lactose intolerance or the sickle cell trait one could define different 'races'. But why should we? If we consider not single genes but many genes, and compute the *overall* genetic similarities between populations, then Swedes fit with the French and the Italians, Koreans snuggle up to the Chinese and Japanese and the Fulani would be grouped with Nigerians and the !Kung San.

Distinctions between races are arbitrary

OK, say the critics, we can all agree that the people of Mongolia look different to those of Egypt. But there is no particular point between Cairo and Ulan Batur at which the race to which Egyptians belong ends and that to which Mongolians belong begins. Since there is 'continuous gradation' in gene frequencies and every population shades imperceptibly into another so, the biologist Joseph Graves argues, the concept of race is meaningless.

Even race realists acknowledge the difficulty of defining races. Jon Entine is an American journalist and a leading advocate of the race concept. 'The precise number and grouping of races will always be somewhat arbitrary', he has written. Dividing humans into races 'is akin to wrestling an octopus into a shoe box: no matter how hard you fight with it, you still have something dangling out somewhere. Modern typologists cannot even agree whether it is more meaningful to lump races into large fuzzy groups or to split them into smaller units of dozens or even hundreds of populations.'

When even a strong proponent of the race concept admits that it is next to impossible to divide humans into a clean set of races, perhaps it is time to give up on the idea. The fuzziness of the boundaries does not, however, necessarily mean that races do not exist. Many real categories have fuzzy boundaries. In their book *Heredity, Race and Society*, the evolutionary biologists L.C. Dunn and Theodosius Dobzhansky point out that 'By looking at a suburban landscape one cannot always be sure where the city begins and the countryside ends, but it does not follow from this that the city exists only in the imagination.' Similarly, just 'because the dividing lines between races are frequently arbitrary' so we should not conclude that 'races are imaginary entities'. Races, they argue, 'exist regardless of whether we can easily define them or not.'

Among many non-human animals, subspecies, and even species, are often separated by a continuous gradation rather than by a sharp boundary. For instance, in Northern Scotland the herring gull (*Larus argentatus*) has a dove-grey back. As you move eastwards around the Arctic, the gull's back gets darker until, by the time you return to Western Europe, it has a charcoal-grey back and is classed as a different species (the lesser black-backed gull, *Larus fuscus*). You therefore have two species but, travelling eastwards, it is impossible to say where one ends and the other begins. Human races, say the race realists, are, like gull species, 'fuzzy sets': groups with imprecise boundaries. In their book *Race: The reality of human differences*, anthropologist Vincent Sarich and journalist Frank Miele suggest a 'simple answer to the objection that races are not discrete, blending into one another as they do':

> They're supposed to blend into one another, and categories need not be discrete. It is not for us to impose our cognitive difficulties upon Nature; rather we need to adjust them to Nature.

Humans, in other words, might want everything neatly parcelled up and clearly labelled. But nature is not like that. And we just have to get used to the messiness of natural divisions. In any case, recent studies suggest that it is possible to divide up humanity into a number of major genetic groups that closely resemble what we call races. Consider, for instance, the study by Noah Rosenberg and his colleagues that showed that the difference between races accounts for as little as 3–5 per cent of total human variation. The same study also showed that it is nevertheless possible – in fact quite easy – to distinguish genetically between races.

Rosenberg and his colleagues studied 377 DNA sequences from 1056 individuals spread across fifty-two populations world-wide, using a computer program called *structure*. *Structure* takes any set of data and attempts to find a rational way of dividing it into as many subsets as required. In this study, *structure* was asked to divide up the populations of the world (represented by the fifty-two DNA samples) into two, three, four and five groups according to how similar or dissimilar their DNA sequences were. When the population of the world was divided into two groups, one comprised DNA samples from Africa, Europe and western Asia and the other samples from eastern Asia, Australia and the Americas. When the DNA data were divided into three, the populations of sub-Saharan Africa were separated from those of Europe and Western Asia. In other words, the three groups were the populations of sub-Saharan Africa, those of Europe and Western Asia and those of Eastern Asia, Australia and the Americas. Asked to form four groups, *structure* created a new unit by dividing the populations of eastern Asia and the Americas. And when asked to break the data into five blocs, *structure* kept all the other groups as they were but separated the populations of Australasia from the rest of Asia.

Two things are remarkable about these findings. First, the program divides the population of the world according to the continent on which they live and as we move from two to five groups, the boundaries of the continents become ever more distinct. Second, when the world's populations are divided into five groups, those five groups correlate closely with what we call 'races': Africans, Caucasians, East Asians, Australasians and Native Americans. And all this from DNA sequences in which only four per cent of total human variation is apportioned among the races. Rosenberg's study seems to suggest that, however small the differences between races, they are, nevertheless, sufficient to pick them out.

Homo sapiens *is a very young species*

Homo sapiens emerged from the East African savannah some 150,000 years ago; in evolutionary terms we are a very young species. The first bands of modern humans did not leave their African home until around 60,000 years ago. Only after that could any differences between races have developed. For many, such as Luigi Luca Cavalli-Sforza, there simply has not been sufficient time for significant racial distinctions to accumulate. The late Stephen Jay Gould agreed. '*Homo sapiens* is a young species, its division into races even more recent', he wrote. 'This historical context has not supplied enough time for the evolution of substantial differences ... Human equality is a contingent fact of history.'

We know, however, of many genetic mutations that have spread rapidly in a short space of time. Consider, for example, the genes that confer protection against malaria. Malaria was not a major problem for human communities until the advent of agriculture around 10,000 years ago. About 7,000 to 12,000 years ago, a dramatic change in the climate of Africa caused increases in temperatures and humidity, creating conditions in which mosquitoes could breed. At about the same time, the development of agriculture in the Middle East and northeast Africa led to the clearing of forests in the Mediterranean region and the creation of mosquito-breeding pools. With a growing population of people living in villages, the conditions were ripe for a more lethal form of malaria to spread quickly.

A research team led by Sarah Tishkoff of the University of Maryland analysed mutations in a human 'housekeeping' gene, *G6PD*, that is usually involved in metabolising glucose but which, when mutated, can confer limited protection against infection by *Plasmodium*, the malaria-causing parasite, though it can also lead to serious forms of anaemia. Tishkoff's study found that two mutations in the *G6PD* gene almost certainly arose as a result of the emergence of malaria and that the spread of the mutation matched the spread of the disease. One of the mutations arose in Africa sometime between 3,800 and 11,700 years ago and the other arose in the Mediterranean region 1,600 to 6,600 years ago. The speed with which such mutations can spread has led some race realists to question the received wisdom that *Homo sapiens* is too young a species for races properly to have developed.

In any case, genetic differences between races are unlikely to be the products solely, or even primarily, of natural selection. They are likely rather to be the consequence of two other evolutionary forces, whose impact is less time-limited: 'genetic drift' and the 'founder effect'.

'Genetic drift' refers to the random changes in gene frequencies that can occur over time, especially in a small population. If you toss a coin enough times, you will end up with roughly equal numbers of heads and tails. But if you toss it only a few times, there is no telling how often it will end up on one side rather than the other. The same is true of genes. Suppose a particular gene appears in two forms (or alleles), A and B, and suppose that there are equal numbers of each allele in the population and that neither has a selective advantage. One would expect that, in a large population, both alleles would appear in equal numbers in the next generation. But in a small population this may not be true. There may, entirely by chance, be a higher than expected frequency of either A or B – just as, if you toss a coin five times you might, just by chance, get five heads. In a large population, such chance effects generally even out but in a small group there may be a 'drift' in gene frequencies away from the expected, which may even become permanent.

The most extreme case of genetic drift is the 'founder effect'. Suppose a small number of people leave their original population to form an entirely new community. Members of the new population are unlikely to have exactly the same genetic profile as those of the original. The smaller the new group, the more likely it is to have a distinct genetic profile. If, by chance, one of the founders of the new community happens to possess a rare gene, that gene may well become much more common in the new group than it was in the old.

The Afrikaner population of South Africa, which is today about 2.5 million strong, is mainly descended from one boatload of Dutch immigrants who landed in 1652. Although there was later immigration, the influence of the early colonists is shown by the fact that almost one million living Afrikaners bear the names of just twenty original settlers. That ship of 1652 contained one man who carried the gene for Huntington's disease. As a result, Huntington's is far more common among Afrikaners than within the Dutch population.

The combination of founder effect and genetic drift may have helped create genetic differences between the major races. All the people in the world today are descended from small bands of Africans who moved out of that continent some 60,000 years ago. These first groups of migrants were very small; perhaps just a few hundred people. Each group would have had a genetic profile slightly different to that of the African population from which they originated, just as the original

Afrikaner migrants had a slightly different genetic profile to that of the Dutch population as a whole. Some genes would have been more common than in the mother population, others less so. Along the way, as they journeyed out of Africa, these small bands of original explorers would have picked up new mutations and, thanks to genetic drift, the genetic profiles of the new and the old populations would have continued to move apart.

Consider the peopling of the Americas. The question of who were the first Americans, and when they originally arrived, is still a matter of controversy that we will explore further in Chapter 9. There is, however, a widespread consensus that the ancestors of today's Native Americans probably came from Siberia around 12,000–15,000 years ago. That first group may not have numbered much more than a few dozen. The diversity present in the aboriginal Americans was a tiny fraction of that present in the Siberian population from which they originated, which in turn was a tiny fraction of that in the original African population. One consequence is a skewed distribution of blood groups among Native Americans, who have a very high proportion of blood group O and a negligible presence of blood group B.

The combination of genetic drift and the founder effect, race realists argue, together with the mutations that these early migrants must have picked up on their journeys, is sufficient to explain the major differences between the races. Humans may be a young species but that does not deny the biological reality of race. Indeed, the anthropologist Vincent Sarich suggests that the youth of *Homo sapiens* makes 'racial differences more significant'. 'The shorter the period of time required to provide a given morphological difference', Sarich argues, 'the more ... functionally important those differences become.' Since humans are a young species, so there must have been greater evolutionary pressures to produce the genetic differences between races and hence those differences must be more meaningful.

IS RACE A BIOLOGICAL REALITY?

The traditional arguments against the race concept do not exclude the possibility that races exist. So, does science really tell us that race is a biological reality? Infuriatingly, perhaps, for those used to science providing straightforward answers to straightforward questions, it does not. While science does not close the door on the idea of race, neither does it open it.

The debate about race is not a debate about whether differences exist between human populations. Jon Entine, a staunch defender of the idea of race, defines race as 'human biodiversity'. That is meaningless. No one, on either side of the debate, would deny that there are myriad differences between different human populations. We can all plainly see that most Kenyans look different to most Inuit. Virtually everyone can distinguish between the physical characteristics of the major racial groups. Many even believe they can tell the difference between an Ethiopian and a Somali, or an Englishman and an Italian, by their physical appearance alone. The real debate about race is not whether there are any differences between populations but about the significance of such differences. The fact that a BMW saloon is a different colour to a Boeing 747 is of little significance to most people. The fact that one has an internal combustion engine and the other a jet engine is of immense consequence if you want to travel from London to New York. However, if you are a Yanomami Indian living in the Amazonian forest, even this difference may not be of that great an import, since it is quite possible that you will be unable – or will not need – to use either form of transport. If we want to understand the significance of any set of differences, in other words, we have to ask ourselves two questions: significant for what and in what context? One of the problems of the contemporary debate about race is that these two questions are too rarely asked.

In the nineteenth and early twentieth centuries, as we shall see in Chapter 5, races were viewed as fixed groups, almost akin to distinct species, each with special behavioural and physical characteristics that distinguished the one from the other. The races could be ranked in an evolutionary hierarchy, with whites at the top and blacks at the bottom. The last major scientific work that argued such a viewpoint was Carleton Coon's *The Origin of Races*, published in 1962. Coon claimed that *Homo sapiens* had independently evolved five times on different continents and that Caucasians were more advanced than Africans, while Australian Aborigines were the least advanced of all. According to Coon, 'Australian aborigines are still in the act of sloughing off some of the genetic traits which distinguish *Homo erectus* from *Homo sapiens*.' Aborigines, in other words, were not true *Homo sapiens* but caught in some kind of time warp.

Today, with a few exceptions, race realists reject (at least in principle) the idea that there are essential, unbridgeable, unchangeable differences between human populations, or that differences signify inferiority and superiority. The change has happened, as we shall see in the following chapters, for both scientific and political reasons. The consequence has been to make race a highly flaky concept. If races are not unchangeable groups with fixed properties, what are they? Most contemporary race realists attempt to define a race in terms of *geography* or *ancestry* or, more commonly, in terms of both. Such definitions fall into three broad types:

Races are geographically and genetically distinct populations

The anthropologist Vincent Sarich argues that 'Races are populations, or groups of populations, within a species, that are separated geographically from other such populations or groups of populations and distinguishable from them on the basis of heritable features.' Races are distinguished from each other not because they possess unique, fixed genetic features but because one differs from another *statistically*, in the frequencies of particular alleles. A race, the biologist Alice Brues writes, is 'a division of a species which differs from other divisions by the frequency with which certain hereditary traits appear among its members.' Africans are more likely to have a particular form of a particular gene than are Europeans. It does not matter which genes differ, or how many, or to what degree, just that some do, to some extent. This is what Ernst Mayr called a 'population' rather than a 'typological' definition of race. The trouble with this definition is that if we were to test for enough genes, we could find a statistical difference between virtually any two populations. As the geneticist Luigi Luca Cavalli-Sforza explains:

> Our experiments have shown that even neighbouring populations (villages or towns) can often be quite different from each other ... The maximum number of testable genes is so high that we could in principle detect, and prove to be statistically significant, a difference between any two populations however close geographically or genetically. If we look at enough genes, the genetic distance between Ithaca and Albany in New York or Pisa and Florence in Italy is most likely to be significant, and therefore scientifically proven.

Cavalli-Sforza adds that while 'the inhabitants of Ithaca and Albany might be disappointed to discover that they belong to separate races', the 'people in Pisa and Florence might be pleased that science had validated their ancient mutual distrust by demonstrating their genetic differences.'

If any population in the world can be defined as a 'race', then the concept becomes meaningless. As Cavalli-Sforza puts it, in his understated way, 'classifying the world's population into several hundreds of thousands or a million different races', is 'impractical'. Vincent Sarich responds that 'it is for Nature to tell us' what is a 'reasonable' number of races. But if the people of Ithaca and Albany are to be treated as distinct races, then Nature is probably telling us to trash this particular definition.

Your race is defined by your ancestors' continent of origin

To define a race, therefore, it is insufficient for two populations to be geographically separate and genetically distinct. We require an additional means of affirming that the peoples of Europe and sub-Saharan Africa are distinct races but those of Ithaca and Albany are not. The second common definition of race suggests that *ancestry* might be the answer. Many race realists suggest that a race is defined by the continent from which your ancestors originated. 'Racial categorisations', the geneticist Neil Risch argues, 'have never been based on skin pigment but on indigenous continent of origin.' This is clearly untrue as historically skin colour has played a major part in racial categorisation. Risch's point is that continent of origin *should* be the basis of any scientific understanding of race. So, Risch explains, Africans are people 'with primary ancestry in sub-Saharan Africa'. Caucasians 'include those with ancestry in Europe and West Asia, including the Indian subcontinent' together with 'North Africans'. Asians 'are those from Eastern Asia including China, Indochina, Japan, the Philippines and Siberia.' Pacific Islanders 'are those with indigenous ancestry from Australia, Papua New Guinea, Melanesia and Micronesia, as well as other Pacific Island groups further east.' Finally, Native Americans 'are those that have indigenous ancestry in North and South America.'

When humans first came out of Africa around 60,000 years ago, they embarked on a series of complex migrations that took them across the globe. The first group of migrants probably set off from the Horn of Africa, along the Arabian coastline – and kept on walking. They followed the coastline of India to southeast Asia. It is thought that a few then cast off in primitive boats, perhaps from what we now call the Indonesian archipelago, eventually to make landfall in Australia. A second major migration took a band of the original Africans to the Middle East and then to the steppes of central Asia. From here, some moved south to the Indian subcontinent; some moved west into

Europe (where they were joined by another group of migrants who had entered Europe via the Middle East); some turned south-east into what is now southern China; while yet another group moved north-east into the hellish climate of Siberia and eventually, by crossing the Bering Straits, began the peopling of the Americas. Other groups, it is thought, made it to the Americas by following the coastline of China and Japan north to Siberia and on to the Bering Straits.

This is, of course, a highly simplified picture of what was an astonishingly complex set of migrations. Some of that complexity is, however, encoded in our genes. Simply by chance, the bands that left Africa on their different journeys across the globe would have had slightly different genetic profiles to those who did not make the journey, as well as to each other. On their voyages, the travellers would have picked up genetic mutations that would have been present in the newly-established populations but not in the original ones from which they came, nor in those that made different journeys. Since people tended to mate with those close to them, rather than form couplings across vast distances, these genetic differences would have been locally preserved and passed on from generation to generation.

Today's humans are a repository of genetic mutations that tell the story of those ancient journeys. Different ancient migrations are acknowledged by different sets of genetic markers. For example, some time between 80,000 and 50,000 years ago, a man living somewhere in northeast Africa – probably in what now constitutes Ethiopia or Somalia – suffered a random mutation on his Y chromosome, a mutation that geneticists, rather unpoetically, call *M130*. That man, or perhaps one of his sons or grandsons, joined the first band that left Africa to follow the coastline into Asia and eventually Australia. The M130 mutation is virtually unknown in populations west of the Caspian Sea but as one travels east, it becomes more common: five per cent of the population in the Indian subcontinent possesses it, as do ten per cent of Malaysians, fifteen per cent of Papua New Guineans and sixty per cent of Australian Aborigines. The mutation can also be found in Mongolia, eastern Siberia and among Native Americans, suggesting that some of that original band – or rather some of their descendants – continued their journey up the eastern coast of Asia and eventually into the Americas.

Defining someone by their continent of origin is really to establish in which of the first major migrations their ancestors took part. For instance, to say that someone has African ancestry is to say that his or her ancestors did not make the journey out of Africa. To describe somebody as a 'Pacific Islander' is to suggest that their ancestors made that very first journey along the coastline of Arabia and Asia and across the sea to Australia. We have seen that about four per cent of total human variation comprises differences between the major Continental groups. That four per cent is a reflection of the genetic differences between the various bands who made those original journeys. Does it transform contemporary descendants of those original wanderers into distinct races? That is not a question that science can answer, because it is a question of how one wishes to interpret that difference.

'Geographical origins do not in themselves constitute races', the philosopher Naomi Zack writes, 'and to assume that they do in the absence of comprehensive supporting human evolutionary data is an egregious bit of flimflam that begs the question of whether or not there are races.' She adds that 'If all the people identified as white had ancestors alive in Europe at the same time that the people who are identified as black had ancestors alive in Africa, to say that these are racial ancestral differences adds no new information to the data on time and place.' Race realists might argue that a Continental group *is* a race: that is how a race is defined. But this is to say something trivial, about which there could be no debate. For the definition of a race to be non-trivial two questions need to be answered. What is it about Continental groups that distinguishes them as races? And why should Continental groups, as opposed to other population groups, be defined as races?

Neil Risch argues that 'genetic differentiation is greatest when defined on a continental basis'. And, he suggests, such differentiation is significant, because many illnesses and diseases appear to be racially distributed. In fact, the greatest genetic differentiation is not between Continental groups but between Africans and non-Africans. A number of studies have shown that Caucasians, East Asians, Native Americans and Pacific Islanders are genetically significantly closer to each other than any of these groups are to sub-Saharan Africans. If, then, we define races simply according to the greatest degree of genetic difference, we would have to conclude that there are just two races: Africans and non-Africans.

At the same time, there is considerable genetic differentiation *within* Continental groups. The original African migrants did not simply trek to the main landmasses of the world. Within each Continent they formed distinct populations. Those who migrated to Europe, for instance, divided into Icelanders and Turks, Finns and Russians, and so on. In medicine, as we shall see in Chapter 2, it is often far more useful to distinguish between these smaller populations than to divide the world into broad Continental groups. Neil Risch himself makes this clear, when he takes issue with an argument put forward by Wilson *et al.*, a group of geneticists working in David Goldstein's lab in London. Wilson's group studied twenty-nine DNA sequences from eight populations (South African Bantus, Ethiopians, Afro-Caribbeans from London, Armenians, Norwegians, Ashkenazi Jews, Chinese from Sichuan in southeast China and Papua New Guineans) that, conventionally, derive from three distinct races: Caucasians, Africans and East Asians. The DNA sequences they studied were 'markers' for genes known to be important in the process of drug metabolism. The study showed that, rather than falling into three races, the eight populations formed four genetic 'clusters'. One cluster comprised Armenians, Norwegians, Ashkenazis, the majority of Ethiopians and a minority of Afro-Caribbeans. A second cluster was made up of Bantus, the majority of Afro-Caribbeans and a minority of Ethiopians. Finally, the Chinese and Papuans each formed their own cluster. Dividing people into such clusters, the authors suggest, would be helpful in determining how they might respond to drugs. But, they point out, such genetic clusters are not the same as racial categories. Not only can they 'be derived in the absence of knowledge about ethnicity (or geographic origin) but they are also more informative than commonly-used ethnic labels.'

Risch criticises this conclusion on two main grounds. First, he argues that the genetic clusters uncovered in the Wilson study are really racial groups by a different name: Africans, Caucasians, East Asians and Pacific Islanders. The genetic clusters appear distinct from races only because of the peculiarities of the group's methodology. Wilson *et al.* chose to sample the DNA of Ethiopians and Afro-Caribbeans, both of which are groups with mixed African and European ancestry; hence both groups are split between Caucasians and Africans. In choosing to sample Ethiopians and Afro-Caribbeans, Risch suggests, Wilson's group was loading the dice against the race realist argument. Had they chosen virtually any other African population it would have shown uniquely African ancestry and fallen neatly into the same group as the Bantus. It is also loading the dice to suggest that Chinese and Papua New Guineans belong to the same race; most geneticists, Risch points out, would call Chinese 'East Asian' and Papuans 'Pacific Islanders'. It is not surprising that they fell into distinct genetic clusters: they belong to distinct races.

If Risch's first criticism seems to lend credibility to the idea of race, his second criticism undermines it. It is better, Risch suggests, to group people according to the racial labels they themselves ordinarily use than to divide them up into artificial genetic clusters. In the Wilson study, three populations – Armenians, Norwegians and Ashkenazi Jews – fell into a single genetic cluster. Risch suggests that lumping these three populations into a single category does not make sense because 'numerous genetic studies of these groups have shown them to differ in allele frequencies' for a variety of medical conditions. Take, for instance, hemochromatosis, a genetic disorder that causes the body to absorb too much iron, resulting in arthritis, liver disease, heart abnormalities, damage to the pancreas and thyroid gland and even death. It is caused by one of two mutations to the *HFE* gene, responsible for regulating iron absorption. One of the mutations, C_2B_2Y (the name refers to the position that the mutation occupies on the gene), has, as Risch points out, a 'frequency of less that one per cent in Armenians and Ashkenazi Jews but of eight per cent in Norwegians'. He concludes that 'self-defined ethnicity provides greater discriminatory power than the single genotype cluster.' In other words, Wilson *et al.*'s genetic cluster is too broad a category to be of much use in analysing who might be most at risk from this particular form of hemochromatosis.

If this is the case, then it is equally true of Continental groups. Risch's preferred racial category 'Caucasian' includes not just Norwegians, Armenians and Ashkenazi Jews but everyone from Icelanders to Egyptians and Spaniards to Sri Lankans, making it even more difficult to discriminate between those who might be at greater risk of hemochromatosis and those who are less likely to possess the defective gene. As geneticist Jurgen Naggert puts it, 'These big groups that we characterise as races are too heterogeneous to lump together in a scientific way. If you're doing a DNA study to look for markers for a particular disease, you can't use "Caucasian" as a group. They're too diverse.' Or, in the words of anthropologist Loring Brace, 'There is no organising principle by which you could put five billion people into so few categories in a way that would tell you anything important about humankind's diversity.'

Each Continental group possesses a genetic profile slightly distinct from other Continental groups, the consequence of different early human migrations. But Continental groups represent neither the greatest degree of genetic differentiation within humankind, nor necessarily the most useful way of dividing up human populations. It is, therefore, an arbitrary choice defining Continental groups as races. Earlier in the chapter, we came across the argument that races are arbitrary constructions because populations blur into each other, making it impossible to divide humans into a clean set of races. It was an argument that, I suggested, did not particularly damage the race concept. Blurred boundaries do not necessarily make races unreal. Here, I am suggesting that races are arbitrary in a different and more fundamental sense. There is no scientific reason to call Africans or Caucasians, rather than, say, Nigerians or Armenians, a race. Distinctions between Continental groups are real – but why define those distinctions as racial?

One reason might be that each Continental group approximates to what we popularly call a race: Africans, Caucasians, East Asians, Native Americans and Australasians. This allows researchers and clinicians to use ordinary social categories as the basis for research or treatment. This, as we shall see in the next chapter, is why many medical and scientific papers make use of the idea of Continental groups. But this is a *social*, not a scientific, rationale for defining Continental groups as races. We call Continental groups races not because that is a natural way of dividing up humanity but because it approximates to the social practice of classifying human beings.

A race is an extended family

As a result of these problems in defining a race, some race realists have bitten the bullet and accepted that race is effectively genealogy. 'Roughly defined', the philosopher Max Hocutt argues, 'a member of race R is an individual whose forebears were members of race R. Thus an animal is a coyote if it is descended from coyotes, or it is a dachshund if it is descended from dachshunds. A human being is an

Afro-American if she is descended from Americans whose forebears were Africans.' He adds that 'we cannot say with precision how big, how cohesive or how closed a breeding group must be or even how long it must last to count as a distinct race.' But this is immaterial, he claims, for what he calls the 'workaday definition of race'.

Steve Sailer, founder of the self-styled Human Biodiversity Institute (which, despite its grand title, is not an academic centre but a website and e-mail discussion group), puts it in a more informal way when he suggests that 'a race is an extended family that is inbred to some degree'. Like Hocutt, he claims that there is 'no need to say just how big the extended family has to be or just how inbred'. Basques, Icelanders and Africans, Sailer suggests, all constitute races.

British Jews are 'an extended family and inbred to some degree.' So are French Jews. Similarly, people from Sylhet in Bangladesh who have migrated to Britain and those who have migrated to Canada each form a distinct and somewhat inbred extended family. Presumably then, British Jews and French Jews are separate races, as are British Sylhettis and Canadian Sylhettis. The philosopher Naomi Zack points out that 'there is no coherent explanation of what makes one population, such as inhabitants of sub-Saharan Africa, a race, while another breeding group, such as Protestants in Ireland, would fail to be considered a race.' For Steve Sailer that is no problem: Northern Ireland Protestants, he argues, *are* a distinct race!

Once again we come back to the old problem: when virtually any group can be a race, then the concept of race becomes meaningless. Some race realists dismiss such criticism as simply 'semantics'. For the philosopher Michael Levin, 'The argument about which groups, if any, to call "races" looks like a purely verbal question, on par with which ground elevations are high enough to call hills.' But if anything from the compost heap at the bottom of my garden to Mount Everest is a 'hill', then it is not semantics to suggest that the category 'hill' tells us little that is interesting or useful about the real world. If you have to wonder whether you need crampons and oxygen to visit the compost heap or if you believe that you can turn up on Everest in shorts and sandals, then something is clearly wrong with your classification of 'ground elevations'. Similarly with the classification of 'race': if everything from the British royal family to the entire human population can be considered a race (because each is an 'extended family inbred to some degree'), then the category has little value.

Many categories we often use, race realists respond, are equally vague. Take 'society'. 'No one', the philosopher Max Hocutt observes, 'can say exactly how many societies exist; a count that serves one purpose might not serve another. This looseness, however, does not render worthless the concept of society. Indeed, cultural anthropologists can scarcely do without it.' Instead of thinking of races as 'abstract classes – such as numbers or molecules – having timeless essences that can be captured in precise formulas', we should conceive of them as 'historical entities, like societies and social classes.' Nobody assumes, though, that societies, or social classes, are natural entities, or that there is a natural way of carving up the world into societies and classes. They are 'historical entities' because they have been created through human activity. They are, in other words, social constructions. That, of course, is exactly the notion of race against which race realists seek to argue. 'Race', Steve Sailer insists, 'is a natural, omnipresent potential fault line in human affairs'. The attempts to reconcile the insistence that race is a natural category with the acceptance that they are socially-constructed, historical entities often leads to contortions at which Houdini might have blanched. Max Hocutt acknowledges that 'the workaday concept of race is too crude either to have much value for the science of molecular biology or to serve as the basis of preferential government policies' but believes that 'it does not follow and it is not true that the concept of race is either meaningless or devoid of objective basis.' The concept of race, he suggests, is something 'Population geneticists can do without; social scientists and the rest of us cannot.'

A race is a 'historical entity' that molecular biologists and population geneticists 'can do without'. It is also a natural category with an 'objective basis' in human biology. Curiouser and curiouser, as Alice might have said.

The problem for race realists today is the very opposite of that for nineteenth-century racial scientists. Then, racial scientists 'knew' the significance of race but could find no way of defining differences. 'Race in the present state of things is an abstract conception', wrote Paul Broca, the leading physical anthropologist of the late nineteenth century, 'a conception of continuity in discontinuity, of unity in diversity. It is the rehabilitation of a real but directly unobtainable thing.' Even the staunchest advocates of racial science despaired of establishing race as a real, physical entity. Every 'scientific' measure of racial type, from head-form to blood group, was shown to be changeable and not exclusive to any one group. As racial scientists searched desperately for more and more trivial manifestations of race, the biologist W. J. Sollas noted, apparently without a hint of irony, that 'it is on the degree of curliness or twist in the hair that the most fundamental divisions in the human race are based.'

Today, as numerous genetic studies reveal, we can clearly define differences between populations. But the significance of such differences no longer seems clear. Race only appears to have any validity if we are willing to be deliberately vague as to what constitutes a race and what racial differences mean. Such vagueness may have little consequence in everyday discussion about race but it is not a virtue in science or medicine. Imagine what might happen if a doctor thought a heart was 'any organ in the body' or a biologist defined a gene as 'a little bit of DNA'. Yet it is in medicine, in particular, that race appears to have most meaning. In the next chapter I want to explore in greater detail why that might be so.

2

SHOULD SCIENCE BE COLOUR-BLIND?

A white American waits, on average, twenty-two months for a kidney transplant. A black American waits almost four years. Why? Because there are insufficient African American donors and hence insufficient numbers of compatible organs. Three out of five Hispanics who receive stem cell transplants for leukaemia die within three years; more than half the white patients survive. Diabetes is five times as common among African-Caribbeans and South Asians living in Britain as it is in the general population. Women from the Indian subcontinent have a fifty per cent greater chance of having heart disease than white British women. Tay-Sachs disease is found particularly among Ashkenazi Jews. Sickle-cell anaemia predominantly afflicts African Americans.

Illness appears to be colour-coded. Does it not make sense, then, for doctors to take race into account when diagnosing and treating ailments? America's Food and Drugs Agency certainly thinks so. In June 2005, an FDA advisory panel recommended that the government grant a licence to a drug, BiDiL, which helps treat congestive heart failure. When BiDiL was first tested, it had appeared ineffective; so much so that in 1996 the FDA refused to grant it a licence. NitroMed, the pharmaceutical company that in 1999 obtained property rights to the drug, re-analysed the data, saw that African Americans appeared to benefit more than did white patients, and conducted a second trial solely with black subjects. The new trial showed that among African Americans BiDiL appeared to cut death rates from heart failure by forty-three per cent. Armed with this new data, NitroMed successfully applied for both a new patent and an FDA licence for the use of BiDiL specifically as an African American drug.

BiDiL was the first racially-targeted drug to receive official blessing, transforming at a stroke the relationship between race and medicine, and opening the way, in the words of one medical journal, to 'a new era of race-based therapeutics'. Little wonder that it generated a heated debate about how physicians and researchers should approach racial categories. Critics denounced the BiDiL trials as flawed and suggested that NitroMed's main concern was profit, not health. The original patent for BiDiL was due to expire in 2007; re-labelling the drug as race-specific won NitroMed a new patent, to last until 2020. 'BiDiL became an ethnic drug through the interventions of law and commerce as much as through medical understanding of biological differences that correlate with racial groups', claimed ethicist Jonathan Kahn. By marketing BiDiL as a black drug, the *New England Journal of Medicine* warned, 'racial categories are at a heightened risk of being reified as biologic'. In other words, labelling BiDiL as a black drug also helps label 'blackness' and 'whiteness' as real, natural phenomena. Supporters of the drug (which include the Association of Black Cardiologists) dismiss such criticisms as so much political correctness. Three-quarters of a million black Americans suffer from congestive heart failure; what could be more ethical, they ask, than developing a drug that could help save their lives?

The BiDiL debate goes to the heart of one of the most explosive issues in current medicine. Does race matter? Or should medicine be colour-blind? It is a debate that has become more urgent as, in the wake of BiDiL, other race-based medicines have begun to appear. In

2006, for instance, the pharmaceutical company Schering Plough organised a clinical trial for a hepatitis C drug from which African Americans were, controversially, excluded.

According to the *New England Journal of Medicine* 'race is biologically meaningless' and 'instruction in medical genetics should emphasise the fallacy of race as a scientific concept and the dangers inherent in practicing race-based medicine.' Taking into account a patient's race, the journal declared, 'is of no proven value in treating an individual patient.' A paper in *Nature Genetics* argued that 'commonly used ethnic labels are both insufficient and inaccurate.' An editorial in the same journal concluded that 'there is no biological basis for "race"'.

Others beg to differ. The geneticist Neil Risch argues that 'there is great validity in racial/ethnic self-categorisation both from the research and public policy points of view.' He warns that 'Erecting barriers to the collection of information such as race and ethnic background ... will retard progress in biomedical research and limit the effectiveness of clinical decision-making.' In a widely-reported essay in the *New York Times,* the psychiatrist Sally Satel admitted that 'In practicing medicine I am not color-blind. I always take note of my patient's race. So do many of my colleagues. We do it because certain diseases and treatment responses cluster by ethnicity.' She added that 'When it comes to practicing medicine, stereotyping often works.' At the Washington drug clinic where she practises, Satel prescribes different amounts of Prozac to black and white patients. She begins African Americans on a lower dose because 'clinical and pharmacological research show that blacks metabolise antidepressants more slowly than Caucasians and Asians. As a result, levels of medication can build up and make side effects more likely.'

Who is right in this debate? As with much else in the controversy over race, the answer is both and neither. Different populations exhibit distinct risk profiles for diseases and disorders but we should be wary of suggesting that this establishes the reality of race. According to

Sally Satel, forty per cent of African Americans metabolise anti-depressants more slowly than Caucasians. This means that the majority of black Americans respond in the same manner as Caucasians. While Satel does not provide the figures, there is likely to be a proportion of white Americans who also metabolise anti-depressants slowly. Similarly with BiDiL. One of the dangers of marketing it as a black drug is that it may be given to African Americans who won't respond to it but denied to non-blacks who might benefit. It remains a moot point, therefore, whether black and white patients should be treated differently when it comes to anti-depressant intake or whether such differences tell us anything significant about the biology of race.

We know that all but a tiny proportion of genetic variation exists within a population. Ideally, doctors would like to genetically map (or 'genotype') every individual within a population and hence be able to predict the medical problems they may face and how each might respond to any particular drug. Such a procedure may well become as commonplace in the future as, for example, vaccinations are today. Currently, however, individual genotyping is both unfeasible in practice and too costly. Therefore, doctors often resort to using surrogate indicators of an individual's risk profile, such as his or her race. The ultimate purpose of racial research in medicine, Satel writes, 'is to understand differences between *individuals*, not between races or ethnic groups.' Nevertheless, knowing the population from which an individual's ancestors originally came can provide clues as to what genes that person might be carrying. It is what Satel calls a 'poor man's clue'.

But a poor man's clue may be as reliable as an intelligence dossier from the British secret service. We all know, for instance, that sickle cell anaemia is a black disease. Except that it isn't. In the USA, the presence of the sickle cell trait can help distinguish between those with, and without, African ancestry; but not in South Africa. In South Africa, neither blacks nor whites are likely to possess the trait. Sickle cell is not a black disease but a disease of populations originating from areas with high incidence of malaria. Some of these populations are black, some are not. The sickle cell gene is found in equatorial Africa, parts of southern Europe, southern Turkey, parts of the Middle East and in much of central India. Four distinct types of sickle cell genes have been discovered. One, the so-called 'Senegal haplotype', is found on the Atlantic coast of West Africa, in southern Europe, southern Turkey and parts of the Arabian peninsula (a 'haplotype' refers to a combination of linked genes). The 'Benin haplotype' is found in central West Africa, especially Ghana, Nigeria and the Ivory Coast. The 'Bantu haplotype' is widespread in Zaire, the Central African Republic, Angola and Kenya. The 'Asian haplotype' occurs in the Eastern province of Saudi Arabia and in central India. African Americans, as you might expect, mainly possess the Senegal or Benin haplotypes.

Given the diversity of populations suffering from the sickle cell trait, why do we think of sickle cell anaemia as a black disease? Because most people know that African Americans suffer disproportionately from the trait. Given popular ideas about race, they automatically assume that what applies to black Americans applies to all blacks – and only to blacks. It is the social imagining of race, not its biological reality, that turns sickle cell into a black disease.

We see a similar picture in the debate about race and diabetes. In the USA, ten per cent of Hispanics have Type II diabetes – twice the figure for whites. This has led to considerable concern among health professionals. It has also led to race realists suggesting that, once more, the differences reveal the importance of race.

'Hispanic', however, is not a biological category. The Hispanic population is made up of three Continental groups: Caucasian, African and Native American. It has become a distinct group only because of the peculiarities of immigration into the USA. If we break down the Hispanic population into three main sub-groups by country of origin – Mexicans, Puerto Ricans and Cubans – we see that the incidence of diabetes is much lower in Cuban Americans than in the other two groups (Table 1). Some have suggested that this is because Cuban Americans have a lower proportion of African and Native American genes than Mexicans or Puerto Ricans and that both Africans and Native Americans have a greater predisposition to diabetes. However, if we look at the genetic origins of the three main Hispanic groups we find that Cuban Americans and Mexican Americans have similar degrees of Native American ancestry, while when it comes to their African heritage Cuban Americans stand in between the two other groups (Table 2).

It is difficult, in other words, to explain the lower incidence of diabetes among Cuban Americans in terms of a distinct racial ancestry. If a race is defined as a Continental group, then the incidence of diabetes among Hispanics is not related to race. If a race is defined as a 'slightly inbred group' then Mexican Americans, Cuban Americans and Puerto Ricans may, perhaps, all be thought of as races but it also becomes meaningless to suggest that diabetes is linked to race. All it says is that some populations have a higher incidence of diabetes than do others – not a particularly revealing or informative comment or one that tells us much about either diabetes or race.

Table 1 **Percentage of Hispanic American populations with diabetes** (adapted from NIDDK, National Diabetes Information Clearinghouse, *Diabetes in Hispanic Americans* [www.niddk.nih.gov/health/diabetes/pubs/hispan/hispan. htm#1])

	% of total Hispanic population	Year of study	% with diabetes aged 20–44	% with diabetes aged 45–75
Mexican Americans	64.3	1982–1984	3.8	23.9
Mexican Americans	64.3	1988–1994	—	26.2
Puerto Ricans	10.6	1982–1984	4.1	26.1
Cuban Americans	4.7	1982–1984	2.4	15.8

Table 2 **Percentage of genes of different Continental populations in the three Hispanic American populations** (adapted from NIDDK, National Diabetes Information Clearinghouse, *Diabetes in Hispanic Americans* [www.niddk.nih.gov/health/diabetes/pubs/hispan/hispan.htm#1])

	Caucasian	African	Native American
Mexican Americans	31	8	61
Puerto Ricans	18	37	45
Cuban Americans	18	20	62

Population differences are clearly important in medicine but we should not confuse these with *racial* differences. The boundaries of a population, and the differences that matter, vary depending on the question we are asking. Do we want to know about sickle-cell anaemia, diabetes or Tay-Sachs disease? Are we concerned with population differences in Britain or the USA? Are we seeking to understand the influence of genes or of the environment on a disease or the interaction between the two? And so on.

Sally Satel called race a 'poor man's clue' in medicine. It is a telling phrase. Race provides a clue, because there are clearly genetic and social differences between population groups that have medical consequences. But it is a poor clue, because the way we divide up society into different groups is not necessarily the most useful way of understanding a disease or disorder. Indeed, even race realists recognise this. The cardiologist, Jay Cohn, was co-author of one of the first studies that revealed differences between blacks and whites in their response to heart drugs and is a champion of treating BiDiL as a racially- specific drug. Nevertheless, he warns that 'Racial categorisation is only a surrogate marker for genetic and other factors responsible for individual responses to therapy' and a 'crude' one at that. 'Racial intermixing', Cohn adds, 'makes genetic distinctions problematic'.

WHAT IS A GROUP? WHO IS MY ANCESTOR?

When we ordinarily talk about human differences, we are often vague about the terms we use. We may confuse races, cultures, ethnic groups and populations. We usually refer to 'whites' or 'Europeans' rather than Caucasians, even though many Caucasians are neither white nor European. We often use the terms 'black' and 'African' interchangeably, even though there are many blacks who are not African. We think of Cathy Freeman, the Australian Aboriginal 400m sprinter, Maria Mutola, the Mozambican 800m runner and Marion Jones, the black American sprinter, all as black athletes, even though each was born on a different continent, and a race realist would probably describe Freeman as Australoid but Mutola and Jones as Negroid. In Britain, we use the term 'Asian' to describe people from the Indian subcontinent and view them as a distinct race, even though they are Caucasian, like indigenous Britons. In America, 'Asian' refers to people from China, Japan, Korea and Indochina – East Asians – though in recent years people of the Indian subcontinent have also been included, despite belonging to a distinct Continental group.

When we are trying to sort out the problems of life over a pint or around the kitchen table such vagueness and confusion generally does little harm. But we would expect a scientist or physician to think with greater precision. Scientists use 'jargon' precisely to ensure that the haziness of everyday language does not seep into their technical discussions. That is why doctors talk about myocardial infarction, rather than heart attack, and biologists often refer to alleles, rather than simply genes. The same is true of the ways in which scientists classify the world. In their book *Sorting Things Out*, Geoffrey Bowker and Susan Star point out that any scientific classification must possess three properties. First, there must be 'consistent, unique classificatory principles in operation'. When biologists order the living world, the rules they use to define humans (*Homo sapiens*) as a species are the same as the rules they use to define chimpanzees (*Pan troglodytes*) as a species. Second, 'categories must be mutually exclusive': a chimpanzee cannot belong to two distinct species. Third, a classification system must be complete and able to absorb even those entities not yet identified. If we discover a new species we can slot it into the system we use to classify all other known species.

Racial classifications possess none of these properties. Races are difficult to define and there are no objective rules for deciding what constitutes a race or to what race a person belongs. People can belong to many races at the same time. You can be white, an Icelander, a European and a Caucasian all at once. In the classification of the natural world, the same animal can be a chimpanzee, a mammal and a vertebrate but the species *Pan troglodytes*, the class Mammalia and the phylum Chordata (which includes all animals with backbones) occupy different levels of the taxonomic hierarchy; each is a distinct classificatory unit. White, Icelander, European and Caucasian, however, are all considered by race realists to be the same kind of classificatory unit – a 'race'. Finally, new races are not 'discovered' and slotted into the existing classification system; they are 'created' by carving up the classification system in a different way. In 1977, for instance, the American government established four racial categories in the census: American Indian or Alaskan Native, Asian or Pacific Islander, Black and White. Twenty years later, the categories were revised by the addition of a fifth race – 'Native Hawaiian or other Pacific islander' – created by splitting the 'Asian or Pacific Island' category into two.

In the absence of a scientific classification of race, medical researchers are forced simply to import the racial categories we use in everyday life. Take, for instance, a much-quoted paper in the *New England Journal of Medicine* that made the case for 'The importance of race and ethnic background in biomedical research and clinical practice'. Published in 2003, the paper tried to demonstrate the ways in which genes responsible for disease vary across races:

Factor V Leiden, a genetic variant that confers an increased risk of venous thromboembolic disease, is present in about 5 per cent of white people. In contrast, this variant is rarely found in East Asians and Africans ... Susceptibility to Crohn's disease is associated with three polymorphic genetic variation in the *CARD 15* gene in whites; none of these genetic variants were found in Japanese patients with Crohn's disease. Another important gene that affects a complex trait is *CCR5* – a receptor used by the human immunodeficiency virus (HIV) to enter cells. As many as 25 per cent of white people (especially in northern Europe) are heterozygous for the *CCR5-delta32* variant, which is protective against HIV infection and progression, whereas this variant is virtually absent in other groups, thus suggesting racial and ethnic differences in protection against HIV...

NAT2 [is] an enzyme involved in the detoxification of many carcinogens and the metabolism of many commonly used drugs. Genetic variants of *NAT2* result in two phenotypes, slow and rapid acetylators. Population-based studies of *NAT2* and its metabolites have shown that the slow acetylator phenotype ranges in frequency from approximately 14 per cent among East Asians to 34 per cent among black Americans to 54 per cent among whites... One of the best known examples of a gene that affects a complex disease is *APOE*. A patient harboring a variant of this gene, *APOE e4* has a substantially increased risk of Alzheimer's. *APOE e4* is relatively common and is seen in all racial and ethnic groups, albeit at different frequencies, ranging from 9 per cent in Japanese populations to 14 per cent in white populations to 19 per cent in black American populations.

What is striking about this passage is the contrast between the tightness and technical quality of the language when the authors are discussing genes, diseases and physiological process and the looseness of the language about racial differences. The paper specifies the genes – or rather the alleles – exactly: factor V Leiden; *CARD15*; *CCR5-delta32*; *NAT2*; *APOE e4*. No geneticist could confuse one with another. Similarly, the descriptions of diseases (venous thromboembolic disease, Crohn's disease), the explanations of the consequence of allelic variation ('Genetic variants of *NAT2* results in two phenotypes, slow and rapid acetylators') and the physiological illustrations ('*CCR5* – a receptor used by the human immunodeficiency virus (HIV) to enter cells') are all specific and use technical language. The descriptions of population differences, however, are entirely non-technical and often vague and confusing. Population groups are variously described as 'whites', 'white people', 'white people (especially in northern Europe)', 'white populations', 'East Asians', 'Japanese', 'Japanese populations', 'Africans', 'black Americans', and 'black American populations'. These are not scientific categories but the language of the saloon bar translated into a scientific idiom.

The categories used in racial studies are often a horrible mish-mash of groups that do not belong with each other. We are told that whites with Crohn's disease possess three alleles of the *CARD 15* gene, none of which are found in Japanese patients. Whites, a group defined by skin colour, are compared to the Japanese, a national group defined by geographic origin. The slow acetylator phenotype that results from a particular variant of the *NAT2* gene 'ranges in frequency from 14 per cent among East Asians to 34 per cent among black Americans to 54 per cent among whites'. Here, the three groups being compared are a Continental group (East Asian), an admixed group that reveals both African and Caucasian ancestry but is socially defined as 'black' (black Americans) and a group with a particular phenotype (whites). These very different categories are treated as equivalent.

Imagine a zoologist studying a particular behaviour, for example hunting. And imagine her comparing the hunting behaviour of dogs, reptiles and hairy animals. The study would yield no useful informa-tion, because the comparison groups are not equivalent. Dogs are a particular species of the class Mammalia; some dog breeds are hunters, other are not. Reptiles form a class, taxonomically equivalent to mam-mals, comprising many species. 'Hairy' is a description of physical appearance that applies to some dogs but to no reptiles. Most people would agree that comparing the behaviour of dogs, reptiles and hairy animals would be a waste of time because they are such different kinds of categories. The same is true of comparisons of diseases between East Asians, white people and black Americans.

Even social scientists, who are generally forced to use concepts more ambiguous than those wielded by natural scientists, would balk at these kinds of comparisons. If an economist compared productivity rates among white populations, black Americans and East Asians, it is unlikely that any reputable journal would publish the study; nor if a sociologist compared attitudes to crime among 'white people (especially from northern Europe)' and 'other racial groups'. Yet such comparisons are common in genetic studies of population differences, studies that one might expect to have a stricter methodology than econometric or sociological surveys. Even what appear to be equivalent kinds of groups in racial studies may not be so. It is impossible to know, for instance, whether 'whites', 'white people' and 'white populations' refer to the same population group; 'white people (especially in northern Europe)' clearly does not. Do 'East Asians', 'Japanese' and 'Japanese populations' refer to equivalent groups? It is difficult to tell. No wonder that one survey of medical papers concluded that 'terms used for race are seldom defined and race is frequently employed in a routine and uncritical manner to represent ill-defined social and cultural factors.'

Not only do racial studies use non-equivalent categories but, as a report in the journal *Science* has observed, the very meaning of the category 'race' often changes within a paper. A proper study of population differences, the report points out, requires 'choosing the right variable and using it consistently'. While 'this might seem obvious', it continues, 'race-related genetics research does not always observe this rule':

> For example, the initial reference to race in an article is often to the racial identity of individual subjects, sometimes described as 'self-assigned' by subjects. A subsequent reference to race might appear in

the classification of genotypes associated with groups of the self-identified subjects. The final one might appear in the discussion section that generalises the findings to different racial groups, i.e. massive racial populations such as Euro-Americans or Asians.

Such confusion is exacerbated by the use of self-identification as a way of assigning racial categories. Many geneticists argue that if someone defines themselves as black, they should be treated as genetically black; if they call themselves Jewish, that should be their genetic classification. In the Schering Plough hepatitis C trial, for instance, self-identified African Americans were excluded but those who possessed African ancestry, yet who did not identity themselves as African American, were included. This raises important questions about what the trial could possibly tell us about the impact of the drug on different populations, especially as representatives of Schering Plough apparently acknowledged that the lack of a biological or other measurable means of defining population groups introduced complications in interpreting and applying any data.

Much research shows that self-identity can be highly unstable. One study compared data from matched birth and death certificates for infants who had died in their first year of life. The overwhelming majority of children who were identified as black or white at birth were identified the same way at death. However, for other populations, there were significant shifts in racial identity. As a result of inconsistencies in racial identification it was possible to compute infant mortality rates for selected racial groups that varied by as much as fifty per cent. Another study revealed that more than one in ten adolescents gave a different answer when asked to define their race at school and at home.

Confusion exists in the definition not only of racial groups but also of racial ancestry. Consider, for instance, African Americans. They form an 'admixed' group, meaning that their ancestry derives from more than one Continental group. Some seventeen per cent of genes among African Americans derive from European ancestors. For some geneticists, the fact that African Americans have mixed ancestry means that they must be treated in a special way. A number of studies have established 'admixture maps', which allow geneticists to see the proportion of genes from the different Continental groups in any population. One such study observed that African Americans and Hispanics both 'have a history of significant gene flow among parent groups', which could affect the result of research into the genetic causes of diseases. It therefore drew up a genetic map of markers from the 'founding populations' of African Americans and Hispanics; that is, of African, European and Native American markers. The map, the study concluded, 'will be useful for studies of diseases, including prostate and breast cancer, diabetes, hypertension, and end stage renal disease, that have large differences in incidence between the founding populations of either Hispanics or African Americans.'

Other geneticists, however, see African American admixture as largely irrelevant. Neil Risch, for instance, while accepting that Hispanics are an admixed group whose different ancestries must be taken into account in genetic studies, believes that 'African Americans remain a largely African group, reflecting primarily their African origins from a genetic perspective.' As evidence, Risch cites a study, by Esteban Parra, of the proportion of Caucasian genes among African Americans. The study showed that in different regions of the USA the proportion of Caucasian admixture ranged from twelve to twenty-three per cent. It seemed to suggest that, rather than being a unified group, African Americans may be better thought of as a series of populations with different levels of admixture. This, however, was not the conclusion that Risch himself drew – a demonstration of how the same data can lead to different interpretations and of how difficult it is to define a 'population' in genetic studies.

While Risch's claim that African Americans should be seen simply as Africans appears to be based on genetic criteria, it is a conclusion

Bloomfield Township
Public Library

1099 Lone Pine Road

Bloomfield Township, MI 48302
(248) 642-5800

Date: 4/9/2015 Time: 2.11.13 PM
Fines/Fees Owed: $0.00
Items checked out this session: 5

Title: Lucy / Universal Studios ; director, Luc Bess
Barcode: 31160090046462
Due Date: 04-16-15
Title: Enjoy the view / Bobby Hutcherson, David
Sanborn, Joey DeFrancesco.
Barcode: 31160090021374
Due Date: 04-30-15

Title: Caustic love / Paolo Nutini.
Barcode: 31160040109857
Due Date: 04-30-15

Title: The essential Wynton Marsalis [sound
recording] / Wynton Marsalis.
Barcode: 31160030165869
Due Date: 04-30-15
Title: The Sergio Mendes and Brasil '66 foursider
[sound recording]
Barcode: 31160030448901
Due Date: 04-30-15

Renew online at www.btpl.org

or by phone at (248) 593-4919

Page 1 of 1

that also has political antecedents. Politically, blacks in America have been defined by the 'one drop rule' – anyone with even the slightest degree of black ancestry is considered black, not white. As the sheriff of Natchez, Mississippi, puts it in *Show Boat*, 'One drop of nigger blood makes you a nigger in these parts'. The one drop rule originally derived from the eugenic campaign against miscegenation. 'The cross between the white man and a negro is a negro', Madison Grant wrote in his 1916 tract *The Passing of the Great Race*, a seminal cry against race mixing. 'When it becomes thoroughly understood that the children of mixed marriages between contrasted races belong to the lower type, the importance of transmitting in unimpaired purity the blood inheritance of ages will be appreciated at its full value.'

While the racist argument against miscegenation has largely (though not entirely) disappeared, the idea that blackness is defined by the 'one drop rule' has become widely accepted, even by anti-racists. The belief that genetically all African Americans should be regarded as African, whatever their Caucasian ancestry, fits neatly into the political view of what constitutes an African American. The notion of ancestry in human genetics, like the definition of what constitutes a group, is ill-defined and, in part at least, shaped by popular conceptions.

SHOULD MEDICINE BE COLOUR-BLIND?

As a result of such confusions, many now argue that medical research should be colour-blind, worried not just that racial categories are impossible to define but also that linking race and disease could foment intolerance. One academic study expressed a fear that 'the identification of correlation between genes and disease' could lead to 'social prejudice', particularly if that disease was identified with a specific population or race. Jewish women have a higher prevalence of a gene associated with some forms of breast cancer. A time might come when 'Breast cancer becomes a "Jewish disease" and Jews become associated with high rates of cancer.' Genetic research on Jews, the study suggested, could have 'dual consequences: stigmatizing the population through the creation of a new racialised disease, while at the same time contributing to the idea that this population is somehow biologically distinct, that it constitutes a separate "race".' The bioethicist Eric Juengst similarly worries that 'a detectable genetic hallmark ... could serve as an indelible "yellow star" marking for oppression those with indigenous ancestry.'

Such fears have led to calls for race and ethnicity to be excluded from scientific and medical research. A paper in the *Yale Journal of Health Policy, Law and Ethics* argued for the development of 'clinical policies and public health interventions that do not rely on racial and ethnic classification'. A survey of racial categories used in medical research recommended that all researchers receiving federal grants should be banned 'from publishing in any form – including internal documents and citations to other studies – claims about genetics associated with variables of race, ethnicity, nationality or any other category of population that is observed or imagined as heritable unless statistically significant disparities between groups exist and description of these will yield clear benefit for public health'. A 'standing committee' must scrutinise all papers and decide whether their use of racial categories is socially acceptable. Editorial guidelines for the journal *Nature Genetics* warned that 'the laudable objective to find means to improve health conditions for ... specific populations must not be compromised by the use of race or ethnicity as pseudo-biological variables.'

Researchers already face a variety of restrictions in practice. The US National Human Genome Research Institute (NHGRI) has established a databank of DNA polymorphisms, or gene variations, based on 450 samples from African, Asian, European, North and South

American and Native American individuals. The samples, however, come without any information about their population of origin or about the individual who provided it. Researchers who want to use the database have to sign the scientific equivalent of the Official Secrets Act. They must promise not to try to determine the race or ethnicity of the people who contributed the DNA or even to cite papers that might have speculated on this.

Concepts of race, and the use of such concepts in medical research, are, as we have seen, highly unsatisfactory. Yet we should be wary of calls to ban such research. One might believe that a particular methodology is fundamentally flawed but that is a reason to challenge the methodology, not ban the research. Scientific papers are subject to peer review but, especially when the concept of race is so contested by scientists themselves, the idea that they must also be scrutinised for their social consequences smacks of placing them on an Inquisitorial Index. Who should sit on the scrutinising committee? Those who deny the validity of race ? Or those who think that the use of racial categories is crucial for scientific and medical advance?

The question of academic freedom may be irrelevant, however, if research into population differences leads to troubling social consequences, such as the stigmatising of certain groups as carriers of particular diseases. There is a long history of the use of science to 'racialise' medical conditions. The designation of sickle cell anaemia as a 'black disease', for instance, was a weapon wielded by colonial administrators in Africa and racist politicians in the USA to brand black people as unhealthy and unclean and to strengthen the arguments against miscegenation. It also led to widespread discrimination. Until the 1980s, both the US Air Force and many commercial airlines banned black pilots with sickle cell for fear of the effects of the disease. Might not associating breast cancer with Jewish women or hypertension with African Americans lead to similar problems for these groups? 'The mistreatment of African Americans with sickle cell trait', Jonathan

Kahn suggests, 'should not be understood as anomalous but as paradigmatic of problems that may develop as genetic knowledge and technologies continue to advance.' Kahn argues that 'as more biological conditions become correlated with race, differential screening of individuals for those conditions and perhaps even outright group-based exclusions from employment, insurance, or other benefits may result.'

Perhaps. The comparison of contemporary genetic research to nineteenth-century racial science or twentieth-century eugenics is, however, overheated. As we shall see later in the book, the meaning of 'race' has changed quite dramatically over the past century, as has the character of genetic investigation. We may want to show that the negative consequences of research into population differences outweigh the positive ones. . We may even want to challenge the motives of those conducting the research. But we should not confuse contemporary genetics with old-fashioned racial science or eugenics. There are many problems with racial research today, but in constantly harking back to the past, critics of such research often miss the real issues that need to be addressed. Much of what can only be called hysteria about the consequences of genetic research is shaped less by the desire to promote racial equality than by politically-driven anxieties about science. The suggestion, by the sociologist Jacqueline Stevens, that population genetics has 'the potential to alter the political landscape of this country and elsewhere with no less force than the Jim Crow laws implemented just about one century ago' is not just over-heated, but has spilled over and scorched the pan.

In any case, censoring scientific research will not necessarily prevent social groups from being stigmatised. Do we really believe, for instance, that had references to sickle cell anaemia as a black disease been banned in the first part of the twentieth century, there would have been less discrimination against African Americans? The problem is not simply scientific research but also its political context. The question we need to ask ourselves is this: what in contemporary society is driving the tendency to stress group differences and group identities and to view identity in genetic terms? The answer, as I will argue in this book, is neither science nor racial science but what now passes for antiracism. We will see that, ironically, critics of racial research are often more responsible for entrenching belief in racial differences than are race realists.

What really needs challenging is not research into population differences but the meaning that researchers and others often impute to such differences. It is a fact that populations differ in their genetic profiles. Understanding such differences can often be important in medical research. Suppose you want to study the impact of a new drug. It is likely that you would want to sample genetically-distinct populations, to be sure that the drug does not produce an adverse reaction in people with particular genetic profiles. Since we cannot sample every population in the world (indeed, given that it is possible to define populations using all sorts of criteria, we cannot even enumerate all the populations of the world), so researchers and drugs corporations often use race and ethnicity as 'proxies' for genetic difference. By sampling every Continental group, or better still, populations from different regions within every continent, one can create a rough and ready approximation of worldwide genetic diversity. Or suppose you are looking to see if a particular condition or disease – perhaps breast cancer or high blood pressure – is linked to specific genes. One way to conduct such 'association studies' is to compare the genomes of people with and without that particular condition. If the two groups are genetically similar, then it becomes easier to spot the genetic difference that might be responsible for producing breast cancer in one group and not the other. In the first example, we wanted to sample as wide a range of human variation as possible; in the second, we want to find populations as homogenous as possible. However, human populations are rarely homogenous, so race and ethnicity, once again, are often used as proxies, this time not for genetic difference but for genetic relatedness.

Ideally, geneticists would like to be presented with what they call 'Mendelian populations'. These are populations clearly distinguished from other populations, with no movement in or out and which are *panmictic* – the geneticists' term for a group in which there is random mating between individuals. Such populations are genetically homogenous and possess the greatest degree of biological relatedness. It is difficult enough to find animal groups that are panmictic but human groups are particularly difficult for geneticists to study, because social forces constantly ensure that they are neither closed nor panmictic. Migration and intermarriage; war and conquest; forced assimilation; voluntary embrace of new or multiple identities whether religious, cultural, national, ethnic or racial; any number of social, economic, religious and other barriers to interaction (and hence to reproduction); social rules for defining populations such as the 'one drop rule' in America – these, and many social other factors, affect the character of a group and transform its genetic profile.

There is no such thing as a 'natural' human population. Yet human groups can act as surrogates, however imperfectly, for biological relatedness. Many of the ways in which we group people socially – by race, ethnicity, nationality, religious affiliation, geographic locality and so on – are not, from a biological point of view, arbitrary. Members of such groups often show greater biological relatedness than two randomly-chosen individuals. They may have been ghettoised by a coercive external authority or have chosen to segregate themselves from other groups. In South Africa, for instance, apartheid laws banned sex between blacks and whites; since the fall of apartheid, social custom and cultural differences have largely kept the two populations apart. Such populations are, in other words, inbred to a certain degree. Many have a distinct history, perhaps deriving from a small founder population or comprising an admixture of other definable groups.

Categories such as 'African American', 'people of Asian descent' and 'Ashkenazi Jew' can be important in medical research not because they are natural races but because they are social representations of certain aspects of genetic variation. They can become means of addressing questions about genetic differences and genetic commonalities. 'In attempting to approximate the range of human genetic variation', the anthropologist Morris Foster observes, 'social categories such as these offer a practical way of approaching the study of that diversity and of defining inclusive criteria for participant recruitment.' This is why race is a 'poor man's clue' in medicine: not because races are natural divisions of humankind but because investigating socially-defined populations provides a practical means of dividing humans into groups that show different degrees of biological relatedness. However, it is a rough and ready process, because there exists only a rough and ready relationship between social groups and natural populations. How rough and how ready depends on the particular group and the particular question we are asking. As we saw earlier, when we were discussing diabetes and sickle cell anaemia, the ways in which society customarily divides populations may not be the most useful in medical research. 'Deciphering the relationships that may exist between social classifications and biological categories', Morris Foster points out, 'is not a simple matter':

> The biological significance that a social distinction may have for one purpose can dissolve when those same social categories are used to answer other biological questions. Thus, it may be appropriate to use social categories as a proxy for biological relatedness (or unrelatedness) in some circumstances but not in others.

An individual can have a number of social identities, some of which may be important to the research at hand, and some of which may be irrelevant. An individual donating DNA might simultaneously be a resident of a particular Indian village in Arizona, a member of the

Hopi tribe, a descendant of a Laguna tribal family, a Native American and someone of Spanish ancestry, as well as an American citizen. Each of these identities, Foster observes, tells a different social story about the individual and leads to a different scientific perspective on genetic variation. Researchers, in other words, should not assume, *a priori*, that the world is naturally divided into a set of 'races'. Rather, depending on the particular questions they are asking, they have to decide which of the socially-given populations are most useful to sample.

The importance sometimes of group differences in medicine does not reveal the reality of race. Indeed, what we popularly call races are generally least suited to genetic research, because the degree of biological relatedness in Continental groups is barely greater than in a randomly-chosen group of people. That is what we mean when we say that just four per cent of total human variation exists between the major Continental groups. Races, however, are socially significant and a major way in which we divide up our societies. It may make *social* sense, therefore, for researchers and clinicians to use race as the basis by which they divide up the population.

To study human genetic diversity – that is, the biological distribution of genetic difference – scientists need socially-defined categories of difference. The danger is that by using socially-defined groups for medical or other scientific research, biologists will endow differences between such groups with greater importance than is warranted. A contingent, pragmatic division of the world into populations useful for medical research can all too easily turn into the argument that science has 'demonstrated' the reality of race. Sally Satel accepts that 'the ultimate goal [of racial research in medicine] is to understand the differences between individuals, not between races or ethnic groups', yet uses such research to suggest that race is a biological reality. Similarly Clyde Yancy, a cardiologist who helped design and carry out the BiDiL trial on African Americans, suggests that while 'racial designations' used in medical research are 'crude and completely arbitrary' nevertheless 'what will hopefully emerge … are exact clinical and genetic descriptors of race that will supersede something as nebulous as skin color.' As Jonathan Kahn observes, 'Yancy's use of the term "genetic descriptors of race" alongside his recognition of racial groupings as crude and arbitrary markers attests to how biomedical researchers may at once acknowledge concerns about the use of race as a biomedical category, while in practice affirming race as an objective genetic classification.'

All this points to the care needed in handling racial categories in medicine. But just because race is not a real biological entity does not necessarily mean that science or medicine should be colour-blind. Population differences are important and can have medical consequences. Even where there is no compelling medical reason to explore genetic differences between populations, research into such differences can be fruitful, helping illuminate, for instance, the history of human migrations, as we shall see in Chapter 9. The investigation of population differences can tell us much about ourselves, both as we are now and as we were in the past. It makes little sense, from a biological point to view, to regard these differences as 'racial' but it also makes little sense to ignore such differences or to ban the use of racial or ethnic categories in research. Whether or not science and medicine should be colour-blind is a pragmatic question, not one rooted in scientific or political principle.

A WORLD GONE DIVERSE

Our ability to distinguish biologically between different groups is better than it ever has been but our ability to understand the significance of those differences has become ever more cloudy. There is no evidence that races exist, in the old-fashioned sense of clearly delineated groups of people each with a special, essential quality. These days, not even all race realists believe that. What 'race' expresses today is a much vaguer belief about the importance of human differences, a sense that what matters are our particular identities and that preserving and celebrating such differences and identities is essential to the healthy functioning of human societies.

Ironically, such a celebration of difference has today become the hallmark not of old-fangled, reactionary racism but of modern, liberal *antiracism*. 'It's good to be different' might well be the motto of our times. The celebration of difference, the promotion of a plural society, tolerance for a variety of cultural identities – these are seen as the hallmarks of a decent, liberal, democratic, non-racist society. As Unesco has put it, 'diversity is the very essence of our identity'.

From this perspective, modern race realism is not a throwback to nineteenth-century racism but an expression of the contemporary embrace of pluralism. To be sure, race realists stress the importance of biological diversity, antiracists of cultural variety. But the real division is no longer between those who see the world though racial eyes and those who see it through cultural lenses. It is between what the anthropologist Leonard Lieberman has called 'lumpers' and 'splitters' – between those who stress the importance of human commonalities and those who stress the importance of human differences.

Lieberman was writing in 1968, in the midst of a heated debate about the meaning of race, a debate that emerged out of new data from studies of the geographical distribution of physical traits such as blood groups and sickle cell – traits that could directly be correlated with genes. 'While the new data were better and more abundant', Lieberman observed, 'they seemed initially to intensify the debate rather than resolve it.' Times, clearly, don't change.

In the sixties' debate, splitters used the new genetic data to show that humanity was divided into distinct units; lumpers suggested that any such divisions were arbitrary. There was more to their quarrel, however, than simply the question of how to interpret genetic data. It was also an expression of deep political and philosophical divisions about what makes us human. Lumpers believed that humans were defined by their commonalities rather than their differences; splitters argued that differences between human groups were the key to understanding human history and social development. It is a quarrel that, ever since the Enlightenment, has shaped much political and philosophical debate – including the controversies over race.

The political debate about race has always involved two distinct arguments: one about equality, the other about universality. The first is a dispute about whether human beings, by virtue of being human, possess a fundamental sameness. The second is a disagreement about whether that which humans have in common is more or less important than their differences. The relationship between these two arguments has changed over time.

In the nineteenth century, most people accepted that races were real entities and that different races were unequal. The main debate was about whether or not they were different species: in other words, were non-whites human? By the beginning of the twentieth century, the key debate revolved around whether races were unequal or just different. In the postwar world most (though not all) anthropologists came to accept that humanity had a common origin and that different races did not express unequal endowment. The debate now became about the validity of the concept of race.

In the nineteenth century, splitters believed in the inequality of races and often claimed that different races had distinct evolutionary origins; lumpers not only believed in a common origin for humanity but also denied that different groups could be ranked on a scale of equality. Lumpers, in other words, believed in both universality and equality; splitters were hostile to both. Today, this clean distinction between lumpers and splitters is no longer easy to make. Nor is there a straightforward association any more between equality and universality. As Lieberman puts it, 'A racist can only be a splitter, a lumper can only be an egalitarian, but an egalitarian has the choice of being a lumper or a splitter.'

If you believe that human groups are fundamentally unequal you must, by definition, be a splitter. If you don't accept that humanity can be divided into distinct, unequal groups, then, again by definition, you must be a lumper. However, a belief in human equality does not necessarily burden you with a belief about how human beings are parcelled up. This shifting relationship has been made more complex by another transformation in the postwar understanding of human differences. Increasingly, people have come to view differences as not so much a function of biology as of *culture*. The denial of the importance of racial divisions has gone hand-in-hand with the acceptance of the idea that cultural divisions are deep, ingrained and necessary. At the beginning of the twenty-first century, as we shall see in Chapter 7, we have come to view cultural differences in much the same way as people had viewed racial differences at the end of the nineteenth.

The emergence of cultural pluralism has helped disconnect the relationship between universalism and equality. For cultural pluralists, all people are equal – but only because every group is different. As the sociologist and feminist Sonia Kruks puts it, 'The demand is not for inclusion within the fold of "universal humankind" on the basis of shared human attributes; nor is it for respect "in spite of one's differences". Rather, what is demanded is respect for oneself *as* different.'

Through such 'identity' politics, the celebration of difference, which once was at the heart of racial science, has become a key plank of the antiracist outlook. More recently, race realists have returned the compliment. Diversity, the concept through which antiracists understand cultural difference, has become central to the race realists' outlook. Jon Entine defines race as 'biodiversity'; Steve Sailer calls his race realist discussion group the 'Human Biodiversity Institute'. As the cultural analyst, Brady Dunkee, neatly puts it, diversity acts as a *'double entendre'*. As a valued liberal standpoint, it gives race realism a political legitimacy; as an expression of genetic variation, it gives political arguments scientific legitimacy. Diversity, Dunkee writes, 'kills two authority birds with one stone and extends the already flexible term "population" to substitute in another way for race.' Even those who might be thought of as holding old-fashioned views of race increasingly portray themselves as pluralists. Charles Murray and Richard Herrnstein, for instance, authors of the notorious *The Bell Curve*, which argued that blacks are naturally less intelligent than whites, claim that they are simply making a case for 'conservative multiculturalism':

> It is possible to look ahead to a world in which the glorious hodgepodge of inequalities of ethnic groups – genetic and environmental, permanent and temporary – can be not only accepted but celebrated ... Each clan will add up its accomplishments using its own weighting system, will encounter the world with confidence in its own worth and, most importantly, will be unconcerned about comparing its accomplishments, line by line with those of any other clan. This is wise ethnocentrism.

As race realists have donned the garb of pluralism, so antiracists have begun to view cultural identity as a biological phenomenon. In 2001, the BBC broadcast the documentary *Motherland*, in which three black Britons tracked their genetic ancestry. A youth worker from Bristol, Beula McCalla, was told that her ancestry traced back to the tiny island of Bioko, off the coast of Cameroon. The next thing, she was off on a plane to be reunited with her long-lost relatives, the Bubis. 'I've found who I am', she sobbed. 'I've found my home.'

Ten years ago, black identity might have been seen as a cultural or a political expression; now, it is increasingly seen as a genetic heritage, inextricably linking race, culture and belonging. According to Joseph Harker, former editor of the *Voice*, Britain's leading black newspaper, genetics provides black people with 'a route to a new identity', a reconnection with 'their own brothers, sisters and cousins' and the possibility of 'a whole new history and culture'.

The genetic adviser on *Motherland* was Peter Forster, a geneticist at the McDonald Institute for Archaeological Research in Cambridge. He has built up the world's largest database of mitochondrial DNA (mtDNA) samples, gathered from 22,000 individuals around the world. (Mitochondrial DNA is DNA contained in organelles called mitochondria that lie outside the cell nucleus; it is normally inherited exclusively from the mother and therefore provides a record of the female line.) In 2003 Forster joined forces with a businessman, Gavin Heys, to set up *Roots for Real*. For a fee of $300, this London-based company will trace your ancestry. 'I wanted to be involved in a business that helped fill a genuine emotional need and there is a growing desire among people to know their history', explained Heys.

Genetic genealogy is an even bigger business in the USA. Rick Kittles is co-director of National Human Genome Centre at Howard University, Washington. He is also the founder of African Ancestry Inc. which, for $349, will trace the ancestry of African Americans. Kittles tracked his own maternal line back to the Hausa tribe in Nigeria. 'I then went to Nigeria and talked to people and learned a lot about the Hausa's culture and tradition', said Kittles. 'That gave me a sense about who I am. In a way, it grounded me.'

Not only African-Caribbeans and African Americans but Jews, Macedonians, Welshmen – everyone, it seems, wants to know who they are and where they come from genetically. They want to find their family, discover their tribe, unravel their race, uncover their heritage. One of the 'pleasures' of race realism, the biologist Armand Leroi has written, 'is a new kind of genealogy'. That is why there is 'an aesthetic factor' in the 'arguments for the importance of race'.

The idea of 'race' clearly means something very different now than it did fifty, one hundred or two hundred years ago. It has become a means of talking not about inferiority and superiority but about identity and ancestry. The distinction between racism and antiracism no longer appears clear-cut and neither does the distinction between racial ancestry and cultural heritage. Science plays an increasingly important role in the contemporary search for identity and ancestry but the relationship between science and ideas of race is very different than it was in the past. While scientific research has helped establish biological differences between populations, the meaning ascribed to such differences has largely been shaped by political and social developments. From the perpective of history, racial interpretations are relatively new. Half a millennium ago, nobody viewed group identity in biological terms or believed that it was immutable. To understand contemporary ideas of race, we need to understand how the concept of race developed and how it has changed over time. The next chapters, therefore, explore the history of the idea of race and of its changing relationship to science.

3

THERE BE MONSTERS

In 1488, Bemoin, a Wolof prince from West Africa, came to Portugal to ask for assistance in a war in which he was engaged. John II, the King of Portugal and the self-proclaimed 'Lord of Guinea', received Bemoin as he would any visiting prince. While in Portugal, Bemoin converted to Christianity and was baptised, with the King and Queen of Portugal acting as his godparents. Four days later he was made a knight. 'In Portugal then', the historian Anthony Pagden observes, 'he had become a noble, a member of the Royal Household and a Christian vassal of the Lord of Guinea. He had, that is, become European in everything but his skin colour.'

Bemoin returned to West Africa with a fleet of ships, men and military equipment to help him prosecute his war. When the fleet had almost reached its destination, however, the Portuguese commander Pero Vaz killed Bemoin, turned his ships around and set sail for home. 'Once Bemoin had slipped away from the mouth of the Tagus', Pagden concludes, 'he had, for all those in Portugal, already lost his identity as the king's *afilhado*':

> He had become part of another world. In the African Atlantic, far from the reaches of the network of kinship and culture which enlaced all men and made them what they were, Bemoin had become nothing but a 'black', a thing, like any other slave who could be tossed overboard to shorten a tedious journey.

Bemoin's story shows how dissimilar the pre-modern view of social difference was to the modern concept of race. We have become so accustomed to looking at life through a racial lens that we often imagine that all societies and all ages have done so. 'Racism is as human as love', as Thomas Keneally, author of *Schindler's Ark*, put it. Yet the ways in which different ages and different cultures have viewed other peoples' differences can be startlingly distinct from our own. In early modern Europe, as we see in Bemoin's tale, the physical limits of the continent appeared to place constraints on social perceptions of difference. An individual could be treated very differently according to his physical relationship to Europe. Despite Bemoin's strangeness of colour, religion, habits and garb he was nevertheless accepted as 'one of us' so long as he was in Portugal. In the course of travelling to Africa, however, he became a stranger and was treated as such.

The late historian, Ivan Hannaford, observed that 'the idea of race does not lie dormant in every society on all occasions and at all times, simply waiting to be discovered.' For most of human history, the concept of race simply did not exist. The Ancient Greeks, for instance, certainly possessed slaves and viewed non-Greeks as 'barbarians'. They also classified the peoples of the world according to skin colour, believing such differences to be the result of living in diverse climates. Yet, Hannaford observed, the Greeks were resistant to a notion such as race, because they possessed a concept of 'politics' and an idea of 'the civic' which 'involved a disposition to see people not in terms of where they came from and what they looked like, but in terms of membership of a public arena.' The Greek political ideal 'inhibited the holding of racial or ethnic categories as we come to understand them in the modern world'. There clearly was 'persecution, cruelty, oppression, and slavery' in Ancient Greece, Hannaford acknowledged, 'but divisions were not in any way based on the premise of race'. Equally clearly, the Greeks recognised physical differences between populations but never viewed such differences as racial. The public view of individuals was rarely coloured by their origins or physical appearance. The key distinction in Greek society was between those who were civilised and those who were barbarians – and race played no part in establishing this.

Understanding how human differences were seen in societies that possessed no sense of the racial can help us understand how those differences eventually came to be racialised. I want, therefore, in this chapter to provide a kind of 'prehistory' of race and to look at how European thinkers, in particular, tried to make sense of human variation before the concept of race emerged.

MONSTERS AND MAGIC

Europe in the Middle Ages was far more restricted in scope than the ancient classical world. It had only limited contact with different places and peoples. Much of the learning of the Ancients had been lost and only eventually rediscovered through the translations of Muslim scholars. There was, in the first half of the last millennium, a complex and often confused view of human nature and human differences. Christian theology still saw all humans as belonging to a single stock; as St Augustine had written of strangers, in the *City of God*, 'No matter what unusual appearance he presents in colour, movement, sound, nor how peculiar he is in power, part or quality of his nature, no Christian can doubt that he springs from one protoplast.' But medieval Europe was also a world of fixed relations and limited experiences. Difference and inequality was an integral part of the medieval consciousness of the social and natural world. The serf, the slave, the peasant, the artisan, the lord, the king – all were allotted their place in the world by divine sanction. Not only human office but natural order, too, was preordained. Until the eighteenth century, Christendom ordered nature according to the *scala naturae* or Great

Chain of Being. The *scala naturae* was an ancient idea that stretched back at least to the Greeks and was central to Christian theology. It described a ladder of ascent from the inorganic world to the Supreme Being, as Sir Richard Barckley described in *A Discourse of the Felicitie of Man*:

> The great God of nature hath tyed together all his creations, with some meane things that agree and participate with the extremities, and hath composed the intelligible, ethereall, and elementarie world, by indissoluble meanes and boundes; as betweene plantes and liuing creatures, hee hath made sponges and oysters, that in part resemble liuing things, and in part plants; betweene the creatures of the earth, and those of the water, Otters, Tortoyses, and such like; betweene those of the water and birds of the aire, flying fishes; betweene brute beastes, and those of a spirituall essence and understanding, which are the Angels, he hath placed man, which combineth heauen and this elementarie world.

Or as Milton put it in *Paradise Lost*:

> The scale of nature set
> From centre to circumference, whereon
> In contemplation of created things
> By steps we may ascend to God.

Just as Jorge Luis Borges' *Library of Babel* contained all the books that could have been written, so God's mind contained all the living forms imaginable, with no perceptible gaps. Every type of difference existed. But in communities that were ethnically homogenous, geographically isolated, technologically backward and socially conservative, prejudice and superstition were often the response to the strange and the unknown. It was an age in which even educated Europeans believed fabulous tales about monsters that lived in the nether regions of the known world and in the interstices between Man and beast in the

Chain of Being. The *cynocephali*, for instance, were dog-headed giants, said to be highly intelligent, savage warriors who ate raw flesh and engaged in cannibalism. St Augustine wrote of them as being the monstrous children of God and descendants of Adam. Marco Polo insisted that 'men with heads like dogs, and teeth and eyes like dogs' were to be found on the island of Andaman in the Indian Ocean. A number of saints, most notably St Christopher, were regarded as cynocephali who had converted to Christianity. Other monstrous races included *sciapods*, people who hopped around on one giant leg. When relaxing, they lay on their backs and used their foot as a parasol to shield their body from the intense heat of the sun. *Blemmyes* were people lacking heads but with faces on their chests. They were considered fearsome but a more cultured race than the sciapodae or cynocephali. The *abarimon* were thought to live in the north and had feet turned backwards. The *amyctyrae* had a lower lip so large that it could be turned up over their heads and used as a protection against the sun. *Atomi* were people without mouths, who could not eat but lived on smells; a bad smell could cause their death.

While the medieval imagination was peopled by a bestiary of monsters, real non-European peoples were rarely viewed as monstrosities. In part, this was because, like the Greeks, the critical distinction for pre-modern Europeans was not physical but social. 'Are they like us?' meant not 'Do they look like us?' but 'Do they act like us? Do they possess a rule of law? Are they governed by a monarch? Do they grow crops and tend animals? Do they believe in God?' And so on. In part, too, it was because Europeans had little contact with the rest of the world. Until the sixteenth century, few Europeans had ever seen a black person in real life. The most common image of a black man was one of the kings in the depiction of the Adoration of the Magi. As a result, the historian Felipe Fernández-Armesto observes, 'Negritude carried associations of regality, wisdom and the privilege of one of the earliest of divine revelations about the nature of Christ.' The maps of the late medieval period 'gleam with Europeans' high expectations of the black world and the civilised habits of its people. Black Africa appears dotted with gilded cities and richly arrayed monarchs.'

As exploration increased Europeans' knowledge of the world, the technological and social backwardness of Africa became increasingly apparent. There was a growing temptation to place Africans, rather than monsters, in the space between Man and beast in the *scala naturae*. The discovery in Africa of beasts – the Great Apes – that seemed half-human encouraged the idea that Africans might be part-beastly. Travellers such as the seventeenth-century English writer Sir Thomas Herbert were led into wild speculation about the relationship between Africans and apes. Herbert believed that baboons 'kept frequent company with the Women' and Africans 'may be said to be descendants of Satyrs'.

Yet while views such as Herbert's became increasingly common during the sixteenth and seventeenth centuries, Europeans by and large resisted the temptation to depict Africans as beasts or monsters, at least until the eighteenth century. There existed in pre-modern Europe neither a sense that personal identity or group membership was rooted in one's biology nor a belief that such identity was immutable. What defined a person was his or her relationship to law and to faith. 'The human body', as Ivan Hannaford has put it, 'could not be detached from ideas of *polis* and *ecclesia*.' It was a view rooted in the great texts of antiquity and Christendom – in particular, Plato's *Republic*, Aristotle's *Politics* and Augustine's *City of God*. For Europeans, until the eighteenth century, a people was bound together and assumed its identity through law and faith, not through biology or history.

When Europeans embarked on the voyages of discovery in the fifteenth and sixteenth centuries, they were struck by the distinct skin colour and physiognomy of Africans. But what really set Africans apart, in European eyes, was their savagery and heathenism, the contrast between known public ways of governance and what appeared to be the barbarity, brutishness and viciousness of African societies. Above all, African societies seemed to lack a public realm, the basis, as Europeans saw it, for any form of civilisation.

The debate about non-European peoples was not about whether they were biologically distinct but about whether they possessed the capacities to be civilised and potentially to be Christians. Through the sixteenth century, for instance, there was considerable controversy in Spain over the morality of the treatment of American Indians by the *conquistadores*. The debate reached its height in 1550, when the king of Spain, Charles V, ordered a *junta*, a group of jurists and theologians, to meet at Valladolid to hear the arguments. On one side was Juan Gines de Sepulveda, a prominent humanist and Greek scholar, who justified conquest and evangelisation by war. On the other was the Dominican priest Bartolomé de Las Casas who had sailed with Christopher Columbus on his third voyage to the New World in 1498. In 1502 he went to Hispaniola as a planter. Eight years later, Las Casas was ordained as a priest and became a fierce defender of Indian rights.

At the heart of the debate in Valladolid was the question of how to interpret the Bible, Aristotle and Spanish law. De Sepulveda argued that Indians were barbarians, infidels and committed crimes against natural law. Like Aristotle, he argued that barbarians were 'natural slaves' because they were ruled by their passions, whereas civilised humans were ruled by reason. So it was moral for the Spanish to seize Indian lands and properties and to enslave them. Las Casas denied that Aristotle's concept of natural slaves applied to Indians, because they possessed reason. 'Being capable of clear, deliberate, and acute understanding', he wrote, 'they are docile and open to good doctrine and apt recipients of our Catholic faith.'

We do not know how the *junta* adjudicated the debate between Sepulveda and Las Casas. What is clear is that issues of law and faith were at stake, not of biology and race. Even those who wished to enslave Indians were not motivated by any concept of biological differences between peoples. Las Casas's argument that Native Americans should be treated as Christians was highly influential. In 1537, Pope Paul III issued his *Sublimus Dei*, a papal bull condemning slavery. It rejected the view inspired by the 'enemy of the human race' (in other words, the Devil) that 'the Indians of the West and the South, and other people of whom We have recent knowledge should be treated as dumb brutes created for our service, pretending that they are incapable of receiving the Catholic Faith.' The Bull insisted that:

> ... the said Indians and all other people who may later be discovered by Christians, are by no means to be deprived of their liberty or the possession of their property, even though they be outside the faith of Jesus Christ; and that they may and should, freely and legitimately, enjoy their liberty and the possession of their property; nor should they be in any way enslaved; should the contrary happen, it shall be null and have no effect.

TOWARDS A SCIENCE OF HUMAN DIFFERENCE

It was the emergence of modernity that provided both the scientific concepts and the political language underlying the idea of race. Between the sixteenth and eighteenth centuries, Europe underwent a series of intellectual and social transformations that laid the basis of the modern world. It was the period in which the modern idea of the self, and of the individual as a rational agent, began to develop; in which the authority of custom and tradition weakened, while the role of reason in explaining the natural and social world was vastly expanded; in which nature became regarded not as chaotic but as lawful and hence amenable to reason; and in which humans became part of the natural order, and knowledge became secularised. The culmination of this process came in the eighteenth-century Enlightenment, which marked in historian Jonathan Israel's words 'the most dramatic

step towards secularisation and rationalisation in Europe's history ...
[and], arguably, of the entire world':

> During the later Middle Ages and the early modern age down to
> around 1650, western civilisation was based on a largely shared core of
> faith, tradition and authority ... By contrast, after 1650, a general
> process of rationalisation and secularisation set in which rapidly over-
> threw theology's age-old hegemony in the world of study, slowly but
> surely eradicated magic and belief in the supernatural from Europe's
> intellectual culture and led a few openly to challenge everything inher-
> ited from the past – not just commonly received assumptions about
> mankind, society, politics and the cosmos but also the veracity of the
> Bible and the Christian faith or indeed any faith.

Traditionally, European scholars had looked to the past as the source
of learning. From the Christian point of view, the Fall had corrupted
the public stock of knowledge. The role of scholars was not to discover
new facts about the world but to restore an uncorrupted view.
Evidence lay in texts: primarily the Bible but also in the works of the
Ancients, particularly Aristotle. Knowledge came through the correct
interpretation of texts and hence through a process of textual disputation. Worldly phenomena counted as evidence only in so far as they
accorded with the authority of the books.

The 'new philosophy' that developed between the sixteenth and
the eighteenth centuries reversed this relationship between observation and authority. The role of scholars was not simply to argue over
books but to open their eyes – and their minds – to the natural world.
As the English philosopher, politician and courtier, Francis Bacon, put
it, from now on 'Books must follow science, not science follow books.'
At the heart of the new outlook was the belief that knowledge came
through a combination of observation, experiment and reason. By
applying reason to observation, the new philosophers argued, it was
possible to establish the laws by which the world was governed.

During the sixteenth and seventeenth centuries, the Aristotelian view of the universe that had long held sway was replaced by new vision that modelled nature on the characteristics of a machine – what came to be called the 'mechanical philosophy'. The Aristotelian universe was 'teleological': full of purpose and desire. According to Aristotle, every object had a natural place it inhabited and an 'essence' that made it behave in its customary fashion. The new mechanical philosophy expunged teleology from the natural world and created instead a clockwork universe. The magical, vitalistic cosmos of old gave way to an inert universe composed of purposeless particles each pursuing its course mindless of others. It was a philosophy in which the view of nature as a machine opened up entirely new questions (and possible answers) about the Earth and its inhabitants – not least human beings.

Humans were now seen as part of the natural order. As the eighteenth-century French naturalist Buffon put it, 'The first truth that issues from this serious examination of nature is a truth that perhaps humbles man. The truth is that he should classify himself with the animals, to whom his whole material being connects him.' The question now arose: how do humans fit into the clockwork universe? Natural philosophers had begun classifying all of nature. How should humans be classified as part of this project? Two questions needed to be answered. What was the relationship between humans and other animals that seemed to resemble them, especially primates? And what was the relationship between different groups of humans that seemed dissimilar? The first broached fundamental issues about human nature and the place of humans in nature, the second about the meaning of human differences. The mechanical philosophy had rendered animals as machines. Were humans also machines or were they special? How were we to understand language, morality, reason – traits that seemed to separate humans from the rest of the natural world? Did all humans possess these qualities and to the same degree or were some individuals – and some groups – better endowed than others? Did physical differences denote mental differences? Were the physical differences between human groups of the same kind as differences between animal species? And so on. As we shall see throughout this book the two sets of questions, one about the place of humans in nature, the other about the meaning of differences between human groups, are closely related. How one understands the relationship between humans and the rest of nature shapes the way that one understands the relationships between different groups of humans.

As explorations brought Europeans into contact with new animals and new peoples, the question, both of humanity's relationship to other animals and of the meaning of differences within the human family, became increasingly pertinent. Perhaps no discovery made these questions more immediate than that of the Great Apes. The first proper description of an ape was provided in 1641, by the Dutch anatomist Nicolaas Tulp (immortalised in Rembrandt's masterpiece *The Anatomy Lesson of Dr Tulp*). The ape cadaver that Tulp dissected resembled a human body so closely that he commented that it would be hard to find two eggs that looked more alike. Tulp thought that the specimen had come from Angola but nevertheless baptised it an 'Indian satyr', adding that local people called it 'orang-outan' (Malay for 'man of the forest'). Tulp also gave the ape a Latin name: *sive Homo Sylvestris*, or 'man of the woods'.

Half a century later, Edward Tyson, the leading anatomist in England, borrowed Tulp's nomenclature when he published a monograph entitled *Orang-Outang, sive Homo Sylvestris: Or the Anatomy of a Pygmie Compared with that of a Monkey, an Ape, and a Man*. Tyson's specimen was neither an orang-utan nor a pygmy but an infant male chimpanzee that had died while being transported from West Africa to England. Like Tulp, Tyson was struck by the similarity between ape and Man. When he tallied up similarities and differences, he found forty-eight ways in which the 'pygmie' more resembled a human than it did a monkey, but only thirty-four ways in which it more resembled a monkey. According to Tyson's biographer Ashley Montagu, Tyson's monograph was the first scientific acknowledgement 'that a creature of the ape-kind was structurally more closely related to man than was any other known animal.'

People had known about monkeys since antiquity and the resemblance between monkeys and humans was well established. Nevertheless, no one could doubt that a monkey was a dumb brute. Not so with apes. Tyson's 'pygmie' appeared so human-like and yet seemed to lack the cognitive functions of a human being. It was, Tyson wrote, 'a Brute, tho' in the formation of the Body, and in the Sensitive or Brutal Soul, it may be more resembling a Man than any other animal.' He was particularly struck by the fact that the ape possessed a voice box yet was incapable of speech. In 'the Chain of Creation', Tyson concluded, the 'Pygmie' was 'an intermediate Link between Ape and Man', tying humans to the rest of nature.

In the seventeenth century, the Great Chain of Being was central to the way Europeans understood the natural world. Over the following century, however, it became discredited, at least in the traditional sense. The diversity of living forms, it became clear, was too complex to be encompassed by a linear scale. In its place emerged a new way of classifying animals and plants, derived from the work of the Swedish botanist Carolus Linnaeus. Born in 1707, the son of a rural clergyman, Linnaeus trained as a doctor. His real love was botany and he eventually became professor of botany at Uppsala University. He was obsessed by the question of classification. Like many eighteenth-century thinkers, Linnaeus believed that nature could be expressed in simple formulae and that all living forms could be fitted into a rational pattern. Referring to himself as the 'second Adam', who, by giving true names to God's creatures, would ensure a faithful representation of the natural order, Linnaeus argued that the task of natural history was to establish an hierarchy of species based on eternal, intrinsic characteristics. He never fully shook off the influence of the Chain of Being, believing that 'all living things, plants, animals, and even mankind themselves, form one chain of universal being from the beginning to the end of the world.' However, he replaced the linear view of nature embodied in the *scala naturae* with a nested hierarchy of species, genera, families, orders, classes, phyla and kingdoms, a system we still use today.

Under Linnaeus's scheme, every organism had to be assigned to a *species*, and every species had to be assigned in turn to a *genus*. The concepts of genera and species originate in Aristotle's work and were linked to his notion of *essences*, the unobservable qualities that made all things what they were. Aristotle's term for 'essence' literally means in Greek 'what-it-was-to-be-that-thing'. During the seventeenth and eighteenth centuries, these concepts were stripped of their metaphysical qualities and remade for a naturalistic view of the world. The English naturalist, John Ray, often regarded as the father of taxonomy, and upon whose work Linnaeus drew, suggested that the species should be regarded as the fundamental unit of life, the individual links in the Chain of Being. A species was a 'group of individuals that breed among themselves', so that 'one species does not grow from the seed of another species'.

Until Ray introduced the concept of the species and Linnaeus formalised its usage, taxonomists were not bound by any common rules. Under Linnaeus's scheme, the description of each species conveyed the details that made that particular organism distinct from all others. Every species and genus had to be defined on the basis of at least one tangible feature or trait. Species were grouped together according to some features that they possessed in common; a genus was defined by the features that its constituent species shared but which were not specific to each as a species. Every organism was defined by a double name, its species and genus – the binomial system. Modern humans belong to the genus *Homo* and species *sapiens*: hence *Homo sapiens*.

Linnaeus's great work was the *Systema Naturae,* which for the first time described and classified animals and plants in a distinctly modern fashion. The first edition, published in 1735, consisted of ten folio pages. It went through numerous revisions and twelve further editions, ending up as a multi-volume work; Linnaeus eventually catalogued some 7700 plants and 4400 animals, virtually everything that was known to Europeans of that time. The binomial system was introduced in the tenth edition, published in 1758, which is regarded as the origin of modern systematics.

Through the various editions and revisions, Linnaeus developed a complex classification system for humans. In the first edition, Linnaeus placed humans, apes, monkeys and lemurs within the order 'Anthropomorpha', a word meaning 'formed like humans' that Linnaeus had borrowed from Ray. Each belonged to its own genus: *Homo* (humans), *Simia* (apes and monkeys) and *Lemur.* By the tenth edition, the term 'anthropomorpha' had transmuted to 'primate'. Linnaeus found it almost impossible to distinguish between humans and apes. 'As a natural historian', he wrote in his book *Fauna Svecica,* 'I have yet to find any characteristics which enable man to be distinguished on scientific principles from an ape.' His difficulty was not eased by the fact that he had to rely on just a few descriptions of the Great Apes, most of which came from anecdotal evidence, travellers' tales and natural history works that mixed fact and fable, such as Conrad Gesner's *Historia animalium* (1551) and Jacob Bontius's *Historia naturalis* (1658). He eventually divided the descriptions of apes into two sorts: those that appeared more anthropomorphic and those that seemed less so. The latter he deposited in the genus *Simia.* The more anthropomorphic apes – such as Tyson's 'Pygmie' – he placed in a special sub-genera of *Homo* which he called *Homo nocturnus* ('night-dwelling Man' – though he sometimes referred to it as *Homo troglodytes,* or 'cave-dwelling Man'). A second sub-genera, *Homo diurnus* ('daylight Man') was reserved for creatures that appeared to be human.

Homo diurnus was, in turn, divided into three species: *Homo sapiens*, *Homo monstrosus* and *Homo ferus*. *Homo sapiens* – a term that Linnaeus introduced into the famous tenth edition of *Systema Naturae* – were humans proper. He subdivided *Homo sapiens* into four 'varieties' (though Linnaeus never called them 'races'): *americanus, europaeus, asiaticus* and *afer*. *Homo sapiens americanus* was 'red, ill-tempered, subjugated. Hair black, straight, thick. Nostrils wide. Face harsh, beard scanty. Obstinate, contented, free. Paints himself with red lines. Ruled by custom'. *Europaeus* was 'white, serious, strong. Hair blond, flowing. Eyes blue. Active, very smart, inventive. Covered by tight clothing. Ruled by laws'. *Asiaticus* was 'yellow, melancholy, greedy. Hair black. Eyes dark. Severe, haughty, desirous. Covered by loose garments. Ruled by opinion'. *Afer* was 'black, impassive, lazy. Hair kinked. Skin silky. Nose flat. Lips thick. Women with genital flap, breasts large. Crafty, slow, foolish. Anoints himself with grease. Ruled by caprice.'

The other two humans species were 'monsters' of various sorts. *Homo monstrosus* embraced a number of hotly-debated human anomalies, such as the Patagonian giant, the dwarf of the Alps, cone-headed Chinese and flat-headed Canadians. *Homo ferus* ('feral man') covered a number of unfortunate individuals whose existence had been well-documented. Distinguished by bestial traits such as muteness, hairiness and walking on all fours, the *Homines feri* listed by Linnaeus include the wolf-boy of Hesse (*Juvenis lupinus hessensis*), Peter of Hanover (*Juvenis hannoveranus*), and the wild girl of Champagne (*Puella campanica*).

The *Systema Naturae* is one of the landmarks of scientific thought, out of which modern biological taxonomy grew. But the work is still peopled by monstrous creatures that stalked the ambiguous frontier between fable and fact. In the first edition of *Systema Naturae*, for instance, Linnaeus mentions as a member of Anthropomorpha a bizarre creature called 'paradoxon', a 'tailed satyr, hairy, bearded, with a human body, gesticulating much, very lascivious'. Elsewhere he depicts the satyr as a chimpanzee drinking a cup of tea; Linnaeus stresses her good manners, noting that she drank daintily, wiping her mouth with her hand, and slept quietly like 'a respectful matron'. Through the creatures that make up genus *Homo* Linnaeus wove new myths from the remnants of the old.

Eighteenth-century biologists celebrated Linnaeus for his astonishing feat in cataloguing all of nature. God had created nature, it was said, but Linnaeus had arranged it. The details of his arrangements, however, were not always to everyone's liking. The two most important critics were the Frenchman, the Comte de Buffon, and the German biologist, Johann Friedrich Blumenbach. Buffon disagreed with Linnaeus's attempt to capture nature within a single classification system. Science, he argued, was not about certitude but about the probability derived from the immense variety to be found in nature. Buffon rejected classification as the goal of the scientific study of nature. Neither species nor races, he believed, could be sharply distinguished from each other. Rather than force nature into a small number of categories, it was better to describe diversity and the complex patterns that such diversity created. Particularly in the study of human diversity, Buffon stressed continuity between groups and the absence of distinct boundaries.

Johann Friedrich Blumenbach is often considered the founder of anthropology. Born in Gotha, Blumenbach studied medicine at Jena and, in 1775, published his MD thesis *De generis humani varietate nativa* ('On the Natural Varieties of Humankind'), one of the most influential works in the history of race. Though he considered Linnaeus to be his mentor, he rejected much of his classification. Linnaeus had made a 'great mistake' in the *Systema Naturae*, Blumenbach wrote, in 'that the attributes of apes are mixed up with those of men.'

Blumenbach rejected the idea of human monsters. His research told him that the various creatures that made up Linnaeus's *Homo monstrosus* were either apes or myths. He studied the reports on the various individuals that Linnaeus had classified as *Homo ferus* and concluded that all were normal humans. He rejected, too, travellers' tales about satyrs and other ape-like creatures mating with humans. Both the evidence of his own dissections and his philosophical inclinations convinced him that the Great Apes were not as similar to humans as Linnaeus had suggested. Humans, Blumenbach believed, were devoid of instinct, whereas animals were devoid of reason. Reason and speech, he argued, took *Homo sapiens* out of the realm of bestiality and into the realm of humanity.

Blumenbach's most lasting legacy was his attempt to clarify Linnaeus's classification of human varieties. The distinction between human varieties had to be understood, he insisted, in strictly physical terms, without the cultural baggage that accompanied Linnaeus's categories. He built up a large collection of skulls from around the world (he possessed some three hundred by the time of his death) and used skull shape and size as the primary means of differentiating between human groups. In the first edition of *De generis humani*, Blumenbach adopted Linnaeus's four geographical races: Americans, Europeans, Asians and Africans. In the second (1781), he refined his categories to form five varieties (though he did not give names to them until the third edition, in 1795): *Caucasians*, consisting of the peoples of Europe, west Asia and north Africa; *Mongolians*, the peoples of East Asia; *Ethiopians*, the peoples of sub-Saharan Africa; *Americans*, the native peoples of the New World; and *Malays*, the peoples of Oceania. The descriptions were entirely physical:

> **Caucasian variety:** Colour white, cheeks rosy; hair brown or chestnut-coloured; head sub-globular; face oval, straight, its parts moderately defined, forehead smooth, nose narrow, slightly hooked, mouth small. The primary teeth placed perpendicularly to each jaw; the lips (especially the lower one) moderately open, the chin full and rounded.
> **Mongolian variety:** Colour yellow; hair black, stiff, straight and scanty; head almost square; face broad, at the same time flat and depressed, the parts therefore less distinct, as it were running into one another; glabella flat, very broad; nose small, apish; cheeks usually

globular, prominent outwardly; the opening of the eyelids narrow, linear; chin slightly prominent.

Ethiopian variety: Colour black; hair black and curly; head narrow, compressed at the sides; forehead knotty, uneven; malar bones protruding outwards; eyes very prominent; nose thick, mixed up as it were with the wide jaws; alveolar ridge narrow, elongated in front; the upper primaries obliquely prominent; the lips (especially the upper) very puffy; chin retreating. Many are bandy-legged.

American variety: Copper-coloured; hair black, stiff, straight and scanty; forehead short; eyes set very deep; nose somewhat apish but prominent; the face invariably broad, with cheeks prominent but not flat or depressed; its parts, if seen in profile, very distinct, and as it were deeply chiselled; the shape of the forehead and head in many artificially distorted.

Malay variety: Tawny-coloured; hair black, soft, curly, thick and plentiful; head moderately narrowed; forehead slightly swelling; nose full, rather wide, as it were diffuse, end thick; mouth large, upper jaw somewhat prominent with the parts of the face when seen in profile, sufficiently prominent and distinct from each other.

Over the next two centuries, anthropologists put forward various racial taxonomies in which the number of races varied from three to several dozen. Blumenbach's five-fold taxonomy, however, and his terminology – in particular the expression 'Caucasian' – became firmly established in both popular and scientific thinking about race and remain so to this day.

WOVEN INTO MODERNITY

By the end of the eighteenth century, scientists had constructed a taxonomy of nature into which humans could be fitted and out of which emerged a taxonomy of race. This has led many recent scholars to argue that modernity itself, and in particular the Enlightenment, gave rise to the idea of race and to the practice of racism. The historian George Mosse, for instance, argues that 'Eighteenth-century Europe was the cradle of racism' because 'racism has its foundations' in the Enlightenment 'preoccupation with a rational universe, nature and aesthetics.' Similarly, the philosopher Emmanuel Chuckwude Eze, in the introduction to a series of readings on *Race and the Enlightenment*, claims that 'Enlightenment philosophy was instrumental in codifying and institutionalising both the scientific and popular European perceptions of the human race' and helped articulate 'Europe's sense not only of its cultural but also *racial* superiority.' In Enlightenment writings on race, he points out, ' "reason" and "civilisation" became almost synonymous with "white" people and northern Europe, while unreason and savagery were conveniently located among the non-whites, the "black", the "red", the "yellow", outside Europe.'

The philosopher David Theo Goldberg suggests that it was not just the outlook of the Enlightenment but the method of science itself that helped generate a racial view of the world. 'Empiricism', he writes, 'encouraged the tabulation of perceivable differences between peoples and from this it deduced their natural differences. Rationalism proposed initial innate distinctions (especially mental ones) to explain the perceived behavioural disparities.' The very means that the Enlightenment *philosophes* developed for understanding the world caused them to divide humanity along racial lines. 'Race', Goldberg concludes, 'emerged with and has served to define modernity' by 'working itself into the threads of liberalism's cloth just as that cloth was being woven.' For such thinkers, the concept of reason and the scientific methods of observation and categorisation gave birth to the monster of race. It is an argument that confuses the process of cataloguing human differences with the creation of a *racial* taxonomy. The act of categorising is not of itself racial: there clearly are differences between individuals and populations. Potentially, science

allows us to have a rational view of human diversity. What is significant is not the attempt to classify human variety but the ways in which
this is done and the meaning that is read into the distinctions between
categories. As we shall see in the next chapter, Enlightenment views
on the meaning of human differences were very different from those of
nineteenth-century racial scientists – or of race realists today.

4

ENLIGHTENED MAN

In Daniel Defoe's *Robinson Crusoe*, the hero discovers that cannibals also inhabit the desert island on which he has been stranded. 'Nor is it possible for me to express the Horror of my Mind', Crusoe remarks, 'at seeing the Shore spread with Skulls, Hands, Feet, and other Bones of humane Bodies; and particularly I observed a Place where there had been a Fire made, and a Circle dug in the Earth, like a Cockpit, where it is suppos'd the Savage Wretches had sat down to their inhumane Feastings upon the Bodies of their Fellow Creatures.' Fleeing the beach, 'I look'd up with the utmost Affection of my Soul, and with a Flood of Tears in my Eyes, gave God Thanks that had cast my first Lot in a Part of the World, where I was distinguish'd from such dreadful Creatures as these.'

Shortly afterwards, Crusoe rescues from the cannibals a man whom he names 'Friday'. Reflecting on the nature of such a 'savage', Crusoe observes 'with wonder' that God, 'has bestowed upon them the same Powers, the same Reason, the same Affections, the same Sentiments of Kindness and Obligation, the same Passions and resentments of Wrongs, the same Sense of Gratitude, Sincerity, Fidelity, and all the Capacities of doing Good, and receiving Good, that he has given us; and that when he pleases to offer them Occasions of exerting these, they are as ready, nay, more ready to apply them to the right Uses for which they were bestow'd than we are.'

Savages were uncivilised and barbaric and yet they possessed the same reason and emotions as did Crusoe himself. What distinguished Crusoe and Friday was not their God-given nature but that each belonged to a different part of the world and that only Crusoe had been able to put his faculties to the right use. This was an attitude that ran though the Enlightenment, in particular through what the historian Jonathan Israel has called the 'Radical Enlightenment'. Enlightenment thinkers were less interested in the biological differences between human groups than in the distinction between civilisation and savagery. As we shall see, it was to history, rather than race, that Enlightenment thinkers generally turned to understand this distinction.

The Enlightenment was the intellectual wind of change that swept through eighteenth-century Europe. It was the harbinger of intellectual modernity. The *philosophes* of the Enlightenment saw their job as sweeping aside the ignorance and prejudice that had characterised the medieval world. For the intellectuals of the Enlightenment, Irving Zeitlin writes, 'philosophising became something different from what it was before'. Philosophy was 'now no longer merely a matter of abstract thinking; it acquired the practical function of criticising existing institutions to show they were unreasonable and unnatural. It demanded that such institutions and the entire old order be replaced by a new one that was more reasonable, natural and hence necessary.' The Enlightenment, in Jonathan Israel's words, 'not only attacked and severed the roots of traditional European culture in the sacred, magic, kingship, and hierarchy, secularising all institutions and ideas, but (intellectually and to a degree in practice) effectively demolished all legitimation of monarchy, aristocracy, woman's subordination to man, ecclesiastical authority, and slavery, replacing these with the principles of universality, equality and democracy.'

There were, in fact, two Enlightenments, as Israel points out in his wonderful two-part history of the period, *Radical Enlightenment* and *Enlightenment Contested*. The mainstream Enlightenment of Kant, Locke, Voltaire and Hume is the one that we know and that provides its public face. But the heart and soul of the Enlightenment came from the radicals, lesser-known figures such as d'Holbach, Diderot and Condorcet. If such Godless men could be said to have had a patron saint it was Benedict de Spinoza, the seventeenth-century Dutch Jewish philosopher, whose atheism, monism and uncompromising political views made him the driving force of the Radical Enlightenment.

The two groups divided on the question of whether reason reigned supreme in human affairs, as the radicals insisted, or whether reason had to be limited by faith and tradition, the mainstream view. The mainstream 'aspired to conquer ignorance and superstition, establish toleration and revolutionise ideas, education and attitudes by means of philosophy but in such a way as to preserve and safeguard what were judged as essential elements of the older structures, offering a viable synthesis of old and new, of reason and faith.' By contrast, the Radical Enlightenment 'rejected all compromise with the past and sought to sweep away existing structures entirely'.

This distinction shaped the attitudes of the two sides to a host of social and political issues such as equality, democracy and colonialism. The attempt of the mainstream to marry traditional theology to the new philosophy, Israel suggests, constrained its critique of old social forms and beliefs. By contrast, the radicals were driven to pursue the ideas of equality and democracy to their logical conclusions because, having broken with traditional concepts of a divinely-ordained order, there was no 'meaningful alternative ... to grounding morality, politics and social theory on a systematic, generalised radical egalitarianism extending across all frontiers, class barriers and horizons.'

The moderate mainstream was overwhelmingly dominant in support, official approval and prestige but in a more profound sense it proved less important than the radical strand. Historically,

Israel writes, the modern world has been shaped by the contest between the two Enlightenments and still more by that between the Enlightenment as a whole and various forms of counter-Enlightenment, from eighteenth-century clerical reaction to contemporary postmodernism. Yet, at a deeper level, the 'package of basic values' that defines modernity – toleration, personal freedom, democracy, racial equality, sexual emancipation and the universal right to knowledge – derives principally from the claims of the Radical Enlightenment.

Perhaps the most deeply felt, most far-reaching, and yet most contested idea of this package was that of equality. Today, belief in equality might seem self-evident; in the eighteenth century, it was startlingly novel. 'In a Europe long dominated by kings, princes and nobles, saturated in the culture of courts and courtiers', Israel observes, 'to speak of fundamental equality and the unity of man ... must have seemed to almost everyone, aside from the radicals, to be going against the grain of reality, to be lost in chimeras.' True, Christianity, with its doctrine of the immortal soul, came close to the idea of equality, but to Christians the world was still divided between those who believed and those who did not, between those who were saved and those who were condemned to eternal damnation. The Church was also rooted in a deeply hierarchical view of society and nature, a view best expressed in the Great Chain of Being. For Enlightenment thinkers, equality meant something fundamentally different. The very idea that reasoned debate could help establish a better society required acceptance of the notion that all participants in such debate were in principle equal, for otherwise it would not have been possible to examine, judge and resolve intellectual and political differences objectively on the basis of reason. For the radicals especially, reason, progress and equality were inseparable.

The starting point for the *philosophes* was the belief, held by all to a lesser or greater degree, that humans were by nature rational and sociable and hence different from other animals. Buffon, as influential as Linnaeus in the eighteenth century, believed that 'the first truth' that emerges from a scientific examination of nature is that Man 'should classify himself with the animals, to whom his whole material being connects him.' But he also argued that 'Man is a reasoning being; the animal is totally deprived of that noble faculty.' Hence 'man's nature is entirely different from that of the animal.' Reason was made manifest in two principal ways: speech and sociability. 'The savage and the civilised man have the same powers of utterance; both speak naturally and are equally understood', Buffon observed. 'Animals are denied the faculty of speech ... [and] the power of reflection, even in the slightest degree.' Speech allowed 'Man [to augment] his own powers and his knowledge by uniting them with those of his fellow creatures ... Man commands the universe solely because he has learned to govern himself and to submit to the laws of society.' Finally, Buffon argued that 'man in every situation and under every climate tends equally towards society'; the capacity to form societies, in other words, was universal.

The *philosophes* did not just hold that all humanity was sociable and rational. Many also believed, as David Hume observed, that there existed a common human nature:

> It is universally acknowledged that there is a great uniformity among the acts of men, in all nations and ages, and that human nature remains the same in its principles and operations ... Mankind are so much made the same, in all times and places, that history informs us of nothing new or strange in this particular. Its chief use is only to discover the constant and universal principles of human nature.

'Should a traveller, returning from a far country, bring us an account of men wholly different from any with whom we are acquainted', Hume suggested, 'men who were entirely divested of avarice, ambition, or revenge; who knew no pleasure but friendship, generosity and public spirit; we should immediately, from these circumstances, detect the falsehood, and prove him a liar, with the same certainty as if he had stuffed his narration with stories of centaurs and dragons, miracles and prodigies.'

So pervasive were the radical ideas of political equality and human unity that even a figure as doggedly mainstream and deeply conservative as Hume was forced to acknowledge their importance. It was a concept of a universal human nature distinct from the Christian idea of a common humanity. In Christian theology, the unity of humankind meant the possibility of common fellowship in the body of Christ; Enlightenment *philosophes* viewed it, on the contrary, as a common set of attributes rooted in physical being. Human nature was therefore amenable to be both understood and improved by science. But if human nature was so uniform, why did humans differ so markedly across the globe? This was a critical question for eighteenth-century thinkers. The answer, for most *philosophes*, was 'climate', by which they meant not simply the weather (though they considered this important) but more generally a people's environment, including their history. Montesquieu, for example, wrote that the laws and customs by which different peoples lived were related to 'the physical aspect of the country; to the climate ... to the properties of the terrain, its location and extent; to the way of life of the peoples ... to the degree of liberty that the constitution can sustain, to the religion of the inhabitants, their inclinations, their wealth, their number, their commerce, their mores and their manners.'

It was Buffon who was most influential in advocating an environmental view of differences. In his *Histoire Naturelle*, he described the lives of many human groups and tried to demonstrate the material basis for the differences. 'Every circumstance', he wrote, 'concurs in proving, that mankind are not composed of species essentially different from each other'. On the contrary, 'there was originally but one species, who, after multiplying and spreading over the whole surface of the earth, have undergone various changes by the influence of climate, food, mode of living, epidemic diseases, and the mixture of dissimilar individuals'. According to Buffon, 'the heat of the climate is the chief cause of blackness among the human species': 'When the heat is excessive as in Senegal and Guinea, the men are perfectly black; when it becomes somewhat temperate, as in Barbary, Mogul, Arabia, etc., the men are only brown; and lastly when it is altogether temperate, as in Europe and Asia, the men are white.'

Perhaps typically for a Frenchman, Buffon also stressed the importance of food. 'Coarse, unwholesome and ill-prepared food', he wrote, 'makes the human species degenerate. All those people who live miserably are ugly and ill-made.' The mode of living defined a people, too. Why, Buffon asked, were Tartars darker than Europeans when both lived at the same latitude? The difference, he believed, 'may safely be ascribed to the Tartars being always exposed to the air; to their having no cities or fixed habitations; to their sleeping constantly on the ground; and to their rough and savage manner of living.' Similarly, the Chinese were fairer than the Tartars because 'they are more polished; because they live in towns and practice every art to guard themselves against the injuries of the weather.' The size of a population also helped determine the character of a civilisation. 'The want of civilisation in America', Buffon suggested, 'is owing to the paucity of its inhabitants.'

Buffon clearly saw a link between skin colour and civilisation. The lighter the skin, the more civilised a person was likely to be but, paradoxically, this was not a racial argument. Non-Europeans were not naturally, or permanently, inferior or even different. The most striking aspect of Buffon's argument is his insistence on the plasticity of human varieties. A savage tribe transported to Europe and fed on European food, he suggested, would gradually become not only civilised but white. Buffon had no doubt about the superiority of European civilisation but he saw it, not in biological, but in historical and social terms.

This was a motif that ran through the Enlightenment – the superiority of European civilisation coupled with a belief in a common human nature and the plasticity of human varieties. Even in discussions of Australian Aborigines, who were generally seen as among the least-civilised of peoples, there was little inclination to view their inferiority as racial or permanent. In 1793 the English naval Captain, Watkin Tench, published *A Complete Account of the Settlement of Port Jackson*, which provided a detailed report on the Aborigines of New South Wales. 'Considered as a nation', he wrote, Aborigines 'certainly rank very low even in the scale of savages.' He was certain that 'the natives of New South Wales possess a considerable portion of that acumen, or sharpness of intellect, which bespeaks genius'. So why could they not display that genius? Because, Tench suggested, 'all savages hate toil, and place happiness in inaction: and neither the arts of civilised life can be practised, or the advantages of it felt, without application and labour.'

This was a typical Enlightenment argument. Civilisation was the product of hard labour and application, savagery the consequence of indolence. However, the distinction was not between people who by nature were hard-working and those who were instinctively slothful. Europeans were civilised because the conditions in Europe forced people to work hard and to create the institutions of government, commerce, science and art; the conditions of the tropics rendered civilisation unnecessary. 'What is the reason', David Hume asked in his essay *Of Commerce*, 'why no people living between the tropics could ever yet attain to any art of civility, or even reach any police in their government, and any military discipline; while few nations in the temperate climates have been altogether deprived of these advantages?' His answer was that:

> ... the warmth and equality of the weather in the torrid zone, which renders clothes and houses less requisite for the inhabitants and thereby remove, in part, the necessity which is the great spur to industry and

invention ... Not to mention, that the fewer goods or possessions of this kind any people enjoy, the fewer quarrels are likely to arise amongst them, and the less necessity will there be for a settled police or regular authority, to protect and defend them from foreign enemies or from each other.

Or, as the naval surgeon and Australian settler, Peter Cunningham, put it, 'Civilisation depends more upon the circumstances under which man is placed than upon any innate impulse of his own.'

Watkin Tench concluded his survey of Aborigines with a plea for understanding from Europeans:

> Children of the same omniscient paternal care, let them recollect that by the fortuitous advantage of birth alone, they possess superiority: that untaught, unaccommodated man, is the same in Pall Mall, as in the wilderness of New South Wales: and ultimately let them hope, and trust, that the progress of reason, and the splendour of revelation, will in their proper and allotted season, be permitted to illuminate, and transfuse into these desert regions, knowledge, virtue and happiness.

To speak of a society as 'savage' was, for most Enlightenment thinkers, and especially for the radicals, less a moral condemnation than a scientific description. Savagery was a stage in the development of human society, at the summit of which was civilisation. Europeans had once been savages but had now become civilised. In his lectures on jurisprudence, given at Glasgow University in 1752 and 1753, Adam Smith argued that societies pass through four stages, each dominated by what Smith's contemporary William Robertson called a particular 'mode of subsistence': hunting, shepherding, farming and commerce. The stages are like steps on a vertical ladder of progress, leading inexorably towards a 'more advanced state of society'. Government, Smith believed, begins in the second stage and towns begin to be built half-way through the third. From these follows the gradual increase of industry, wealth, law, order, humanity, philosophy and the arts and sciences.

Smith's argument was highly influential, both within the Scottish Enlightenment and, more broadly, within late eighteenth-century European thought. 'Conjectural history', as Smith's contemporary, the Scottish moral philosopher Dugald Stewart, described it, drew into a unified intellectual enterprise the idea of human nature, the belief in progress, the search for material causes for human affairs, the wisdom of the ancient world and the new knowledge acquired from European voyages of discovery. To twenty-first-century eyes such conjectural histories can appear racist. Not only did such histories give systematic form to the European assumption of its superiority, but eighteenth-century thinkers also saw their contemporary savage societies as windows to the past. History, Sir James Mackintosh wrote, 'is now a museum, in which specimens of every variety of human nature may be studied.' Adam Ferguson said of American Indians that 'in their present condition ... we are to behold, as in a mirror, the features of our own progenitors.'

Such arguments have led critics like the American writer Roxann Wheeler to describe the four stage theory as 'racial ideology'. It is true, as we shall see, that some eighteenth-century thinkers were inclined to see social inferiority as permanent, an inclination that became stronger as the century wore on. What motivated most Enlightenment thinkers, however, especially the radicals, was not the belief that non-Europeans were innately or irrevocably backward but a desire to understand the material causes of human variety, including cultural, social and political diversity. The question that mesmerised them was why, if all humans possessed a common nature, they appeared so different, not only physically but socially, culturally and intellectually, too. Their answer was rarely that human groups were racially distinct but rather that environmental differences and accidents of history had shaped their societies in different ways.

Diderot echoed the views of many eighteenth-century thinkers when he pointed out that habits 'are not African or Asiatic or

European. They are good or bad.' There are slaves 'under the Pole where it is very cold' and slaves 'in Constantinople where it is very hot'. But, Diderot wrote, 'everywhere a people should be educated, free and virtuous.' Diderot was drawing a distinction between *peoples* and *cultures*. People were potentially equal but cultural forms were not. Today, such a view is itself often seen as racist. Equality, as we shall see in Chapter 7, has come to be defined as equality of groups and cultures, not just of individuals. This redefinition of equality is one of the reasons that the Enlightenment is seen by many today as the source of racial thought.

MADE BY MAN OR NATURE?

The Enlightenment was marked by a passion for classification and for the bringing of order to the seeming chaos of the world. It was also characterised by belief in the universality of human nature and in the power of progress. These two key aspects of Enlightenment thought seemed to pull in different directions in the debate about the nature of human differences. On the one hand, there was the urge to create a racial taxonomy of humankind, evident in the work of Linnaeus and Blumenbach; on the other, the insistence on the plasticity of human varieties and the possibility of a common civilisation. For much of the eighteenth century, most thinkers did not perceive a contradiction. In large part this was because of the way Enlightenment thinkers understood the meaning of classification: Linnaeus was celebrated for having established a system through which to perceive God's order but many remained sceptical of the philosophy that underpinned it.

The Scientific Revolution that made Linnaeus's work possible emerged from a conflict with the Aristotelian world view yet it was Aristotle himself who breathed life into Linnaeus's *Systema Naturae*. For Aristotle, knowledge rested upon knowing the essence of things, the inner character that expressed the true nature of everything. The essence of a species was present in each member of that species, and was what made it a member. To classify nature in an Aristotelian sense was to arrange species according to their essential characteristics. Aristotle himself never attempted such a taxonomy and indeed doubted whether it would be possible ever to discern the true essence of a species. In early modern Europe, natural philosophers explored new ways of establishing an Aristotelian classification, particularly of plants. In 1694, the French botanist Joseph de Tournefort suggested, in his *Eléments de Botanique*, that all plants could be classified according to the characteristics of their flowering parts. The Creator, he insisted, must have provided us with a simple method of recognising the essence of species so we could perceive the rational order that He had imposed upon the world. Since the reproductive system was the most important part of a plant, so the structure of the flowers must naturally be a sign of a plant's essence. Linnaeus followed Tournefort, both in believing that a small number of characteristics was sufficient to elucidate the essence of a species and in viewing sex as the window to the Creator's mind. 'The flowers' leaves', he wrote in 1729, 'serve as bridal beds which the Creator has so gloriously arranged, adorned with such noble bed curtains, and perfumed with so many soft scents that the bridegroom with his bride might there celebrate their nuptials with so much the greater solemnity.'

In Linnaeus's system, the concept of species was defined by four attributes. First, a species consisted of similar individuals sharing in the same essence; each individual embodied the essence of the species. Taxonomy was the science of arranging beings with respect to the essence. Second, each species was separated from all others by a sharp discontinuity; there were no gradations between species and no doubt as to which species any individual belonged. Third, each species remained constant through time. Almost no eighteenth-century biologist accepted the idea of evolutionary change. Every organism had been created by God and had remained unchanged since the Creation. After all, without such constancy, how could classification be possible? Finally, Linnaean taxonomy imposed severe limits to the possible variation of any species. Since each species was defined by its essence, it could not wander too far from its predetermined form.

In the nineteenth century, as we shall see in the next chapter, these four attributes came to define the concept of a 'racial type'; a race as a fixed and immutable group. In the eighteenth century, though, many objected to the very idea of a system of classification rooted in Aristotelian philosophy. In his influential *Essay Concerning Human Understanding*, John Locke argued that it is not possible to have knowledge of 'real essences'. All we can know are the qualities or appearances that present themselves to our senses: what Locke called the 'nominal essence' of an object. From these we can use our powers of abstraction to create categories. Such categories, Locke wrote, 'are *made by the mind* and not by nature'. Nominal essences, in other words, are not in things, as real essences, but are characteristics chosen by us, on the basis of social needs and systems of meanings, to help us define objects we wish to classify.

For Locke, *genus* and *species* were no more than abstract ideas that enabled actual things to be sorted out more sensibly. Humans, he declared, possess no knowledge of the 'precise Boundaries set by Nature, whereby it distinguished all Substances into certain *Species*.' Instead we create the boundaries ourselves, through the process of classification. Classification is simply a means of arranging nature for human convenience. Hence there is no *a priori* reason to assign a greater importance to one set of attributes (such as the reproductive parts) than to any other in a taxonomy. We should 'quit the common notion of Species and Essences', he concluded, and embark instead upon an empirical enquiry about natural forms, considering them 'as they exist, and not by groundless fancies that have been taken up about them.'

Locke's ideas shaped the work of many botanists and zoologists. John Ray, for instance, dismissed the possibility that animals and plants could be classified according to one or two characteristics; scientists should seek to describe the living form as fully as possible rather than fit animals and plants into predetermined pigeonholes. Buffon similarly criticised Linnaeus's taxonomy as abstract and artificial, because it was rooted in the mind, not in nature. 'It is impossible', he wrote, 'to give a general classification, a perfect systematic arrangement' of the living world because 'Genera, Classes and Orders exist only in our imagination.' For Buffon, a species was defined not by its place in an abstract pattern of creation but by its reproductive history: two individuals belonged to the same species 'if by means of copulation they perpetuate themselves and preserve the likeness of the species.' The essence of the species was embodied not in its form but in its history.

Historically, Buffon's criticism of classification systems has not fared well (though his concept of a species as a reproductive unit has endured). The Linnaean hierarchical arrangement of the natural world has become the basis of modern biology and, for much of the past two centuries, the basis of racial science, too. In the Enlightenment, however, the arguments of Buffon and Locke proved important to the way that the *philosophes* came to understand the meaning of differences, especially between human groups. Enlightenment thinkers took to heart Locke's belief that categories 'are *made by the mind* and not by nature'.

Locke's argument could be read in different ways in debates about human differences. The idea that there is no common human essence could, in principle, provide support for the claim that certain groups are not fully human. This is one of the reasons that contemporary postmodern rejection of any and all 'essentialism' has potentially dangerous consequences. In the Enlightenment, however, Locke's argument was taken to mean something very different: that the delineation of human varieties represented not a reflection of natural classes but a matter of human convention. Blumenbach's classification of humans into five races remains widely accepted to this day yet Blumenbach himself was ambivalent about the meaning of such a taxonomy:

> Although there seems to be so great a distance between widely separate nations, that you might easily take the inhabitants of the Cape of Good Hope, the Greenlanders and the Circassians for so many different species of man, yet when the matter is thoroughly considered, you see that all do so run into one another, that one variety of mankind does so sensibly pass into another, that you cannot mark out the limits between them.

Blumenbach added that 'There is no single character so peculiar and so universal among the Ethiopians, but what it may be observed on the one hand everywhere in other varieties of men'. This, as we saw in Chapter 1, is the argument of many contemporary antiracists. Blumenbach thought it important to divide humanity into distinct categories for the purposes of scholarship but did not believe that such categories were fixed or immutable. It was an argument widely accepted in the Enlightenment. As Samuel Stanhope Smith, the best-known of early American writers on anthropology, put it in his *Essay on the Causes of the Variety of Complexion and Figure in the Human Species*, 'The conclusion to be drawn from all this variety of opinion is, perhaps, that it is impossible to draw the line precisely between the various races of men, or even to enumerate them with certainty; and that it is itself a useless labor to attempt it.'

Historians of science often portray the Enlightenment as an age obsessed with classification. When it came to human beings, however, the question that obsessed eighteenth-century thinkers was not so much how to classify human groups as why they were so diverse. Contrast this with nineteenth-century attitudes, particularly after Darwin. Darwin's theory of evolution by natural selection provided, as we shall see in Chapter 5, a mechanism by which to understand biological variation. Post-Darwinian anthropologists were, however, obsessed with the minutiae of the classification of human groups. Nineteenth-century thinkers, especially in the second half of the century, took it for granted that humans could be divided into a number of essentially distinct groups. Eighteenth-century thinkers took as their starting point the belief in a universal human nature. Difference was something to be explained, not something that explained everything else. As Samuel Stanhope Smith pointed out, all concepts of morality would be confused if we accepted the idea that human varieties were fixed or immutable:

> The rules which would result from the study of our own nature would not apply to the natives of other countries who would be of different species; perhaps, not to two families in our own country who might be sprung from a dissimilar composition of species. Such principles tend to confound all science, as well as piety ... The doctrine of one race removes this uncertainty, renders human nature susceptible of system, illustrates the power of physical causes, and opens a rich and extensive field for moral science.

Enlightenment thinkers, especially the radicals, viewed equality almost as a scientific concept. Once society had accepted the notion of basic equality, it was also compelled, as Tom Paine observed in his *Rights of Man*, towards the idea of the 'unity of man'. Without such belief in a common humanity there was no way of coherently arguing that humans 'are all of one degree, and consequently that all men are born equal, and with equal natural right.' Enlightenment thinkers were concerned to determine why, given the universality of human nature, human groups differed so markedly. Hence most eighteenth-century thinkers, with the notable exception of Linnaeus, were, in the words of the historian John Greene, 'more interested in explaining the origin of races than in classifying them.'

The debate between *nominalists* and *essentialists*, so important to the Enlightenment, continues to this day. Charles Darwin demolished the idea of the constancy of species. Organisms, he showed, evolved over time through the mechanism of natural selection. Nevertheless, the question of whether there is an essential quality to a species remained unresolved and continues to fuel fierce debate. There is, as we saw in Chapters 1 and 2, an even fiercer debate about whether races are real biological entities or socially constructed categories; whether, in Locke's words, they are made by nature or by the mind. The anthropologist, Jonathan Marks, writes that while the Linnaean system was a triumph for biology, it was a disaster for anthropology. The attempt to confine all human variety into the small number of categories we call races 'has led anthropologists down the blindest of blind alleys'. In contrast to Linnaeus's rigid classificatory scheme, 'Buffon's approach to the problem of human variation was inquisitive, descriptive, analytical, experimental.' Rather than 'carving the species into subspecies', Buffon sought to 'survey the diversity of form and behaviour "out there".' Buffon, Marks notes, 'recognised a pattern of variation in the human species quite different from that promoted by Linnaeus: namely, continuity, the absence of discrete boundaries between any distinct formal categories of humans.' Buffon's approach, Marks suggests, provides not only an alternative to the Linnaean method but also the basis for a non-racist way of understanding human variation.

It is true that in the Enlightenment, the arguments of thinkers such as Buffon and Locke helped restrain the move towards racial categorisation. It is also true that in the nineteenth century, Linnaean taxonomy helped anchor scientific racism. Many contemporary race realists, though, as we saw in Chapter 1, reject both the Aristotelian idea of racial essence and the claim that the Linnaean system is a useful way of categorising races. The philosopher Max Hocutt argues that 'we do not think of races as abstract classes ... having timeless essences that can be captured in precise formulas. Instead we conceive of races as historical entities, like societies and social classes, that have to be identified ostensively by being tied to times and places.' Another philosopher and race realist, Michael Levin, believes that 'the Aristotelian idea of natural types rigidly demarcated' is 'foreign to ... the ordinary conception of race.' Levin even accepts Locke's view that racial classifications are the result of 'the workmanship of understanding'. Today's race realists, in other words, appear to have a nominalist, rather than an essentialist, view of races and to be closer to Buffon's approach to human variety than to Linnaeus's. The debate between Linnaeus and Buffon was central to eighteenth-century biology and Buffon's arguments played an important role in the lack of racial thinking in Enlightenment writings. But contemporary racial arguments cannot be understood in terms of that debate. Today's race realism is very much a product of our times, not of the eighteenth century.

RACE AND VARIETY

'We cannot determine to what height the human species may aspire in their advances towards perfection', Edward Gibbon wrote in his masterpiece *The Decline and Fall of the Roman Empire*, 'but it may be safely presumed that no people, unless the face of nature is changed, will relapse into their original barbarism.' The Enlightenment belief in the plasticity of human varieties was rooted partly in an *attitude*: a fervent faith in progress as the mark of humanity. For most Enlightenment *philosophes*, progress was akin to a law of nature and no people was deprived of the possibilities of self-improvement. Reason and progress, the *philosophes* believed, were the motors of social change, the means by which human divisions and inequalities could be overcome and the common human nature allowed full expression. The German philologist Wilhelm von Humboldt passionately expressed the belief that in the concept of the unity of humankind lay the Enlightenment's most valuable possession:

> If we could indicate an idea which throughout the whole course of history has ever more and more widely extended its empire – or which more than any other testifies to the much contested and still more decidedly misunderstood perfectibility of the whole human race – it is that of establishing our common humanity – of striving to remove the barriers which prejudice and limited views of every kind have erected amongst men, and to treat all mankind without reference to religion, nation or colour, as one fraternity, one great community, fitted for the attainment of one project, the unrestrained development of the psychical powers.

The belief in human plasticity was also rooted in the conviction that empirical data would back up this political attitude. While radical *philosophes* were politically and philosophically wedded to ideas of social equality and human unity, mainstream Enlightenment thinkers remained less convinced by the philosophical arguments and sought confirmation from empirical data. By the end of the eighteenth century, many had become sceptical of the argument that human variety was created by environmental differences. In his *Sketches of the History of Man*, the jurist Lord Kames, a key figure of the Scottish Enlightenment, ridiculed Buffon's claim that the environment created physical differences between human groups. How can climate, he asked, explain the low stature of the Eskimos, the smallness of their feet or the largeness of their heads? How come the Laps are so ugly, when Norwegians, who live in almost the same climate, are so 'tall, comely and well-proportioned'? How can Buffon explain the fact that 'all Americans without exception are of a copper colour, tho' in that vast continent there is every variety of climate'? This fact alone, Kames believed, 'overturns [Buffon's] whole system of colour'.

More worryingly for the *philosophes*, cultural and intellectual differences also seemed ineradicable. David Hume, despite arguing that 'there is great uniformity among the acts of men among all nations and ages' was nevertheless 'apt to suspect the negroes to be naturally inferior to the whites':

> There scarcely was a civilised nation of that complexion, nor even an individual, eminent in either thought or speculation. No ingenious manufactures amongst them, no arts, no sciences. On the other hand, the most rude and barbarous of the whites, such as the ancient Germans, the present Tartars, have still something eminent about them, in their valour, form of government, or some other particular. Such a uniform and constant difference could not happen, in so many countries and ages, if nature had not made an initial distinction between these breeds of men.

Across the Atlantic, Thomas Jefferson entertained similar thoughts. He challenged the arguments of people like Samuel Stanhope Smith who ascribed 'the apparent dullness of the negro principally to the wretched state of his existence first in his original country ... and afterwards in those regions to which he is transported to finish his days in slavery and toil.' If Negroes 'were perfectly free, enjoyed property, and were admitted to a liberal participation of the society, rank and privileges of their master', Smith concluded, 'they would change their African peculiarities much faster.' Jefferson disagreed. Many African slaves, he wrote, 'have been liberally educated, and all have lived in countries where the arts and sciences have been cultivated to a considerable degree.' Still 'never yet could I find that a black had uttered a thought above the level of plain narration; never seen even an elementary trait of painting or sculpture.' He added that 'Misery is often the parent of the most affecting touches in poetry. Among the blacks is misery enough, God knows, but no poetry.' American Indians, 'with no advantages of this kind', nevertheless 'often carve figures on their pipes not destitute of design and merit ... crayon out an animal, a plant or a country, so as to prove the existence of a germ in their minds which

only wants cultivation; and astonish you with strokes of the most sub-
lime oratory, such as prove their reason and sentiment strong, their
imagination glowing and elevated.' Moreover, Jefferson pointed out,
Roman slaves had lived in wretched conditions, yet had often been the
'rarest [of] artists'. They had 'excelled too in science, in so much as to
be usually employed as tutors to their master's children.' Roman
slaves, however, 'were of the race of whites.' This led Jefferson to suggest that 'it is not their condition, but nature, which has produced the
distinction.'

Such scepticism embodied the fundamental philosophical distinction between the radicals and the mainstream. For the radicals,
equality was stitched into their political DNA. Mainstream DNA was
harder to read and harder still to express. Many mainstream thinkers
were caught between the desire they shared with the radicals to overcome ignorant ideas, banish immoral practices and re-found society
on a rational basis (a project that seemed to imply an egalitarian view)
and a fear of undermining traditional concepts, institutions and
hierarchies to which they were still attached, a fear shared with many
critics of the Enlightenment. Mainstream equivocation grew as the
world seemed not to be responding to their entreaties to become less
ignorant, superstitious and unequal.

Doubts about the possibility of overcoming human differences
led to a number of alternative arguments as to the cause of human variety. In his *On the Different Races of Man*, Immanuel Kant, the towering
figure of the Enlightenment, attempted to differentiate between *races*
and *varieties*. Kant agreed with Buffon that since all humans could
interbreed, they formed a single species. All humans, he wrote,
'belong to a single stem, whence they have sprung regardless of difference.' Unlike Buffon, Kant also believed that races were real, natural
categories. A variety was a form that would revert to the common
stock; a race was a type that was irreversible. Races were 'deviations' or
'hereditary differences of animals belonging to a single stock' that

'maintain themselves over protracted generations, and which also generate hybrid young when they interbreed with other deviations from the same stock.' So, Kant suggested, 'Negroes and whites are not different species of humans (for they belong presumably to one stock), but they are different races, for each perpetuates itself in every area, and they generate between them children that are necessarily hybrid or blendings (mulattoes).' Of all human characteristics, only skin colour seemed to be transmitted invariably from generation to generation, reproducing itself in all matings between people of the same colour but creating blends in matings between people of different colours. Moreover, there seemed to be just four skin colours (with all others derived by mixture): the white of the European, the black of the African, the copper of the native American and the olive-yellow of the Indian. Having begun by dismissing taxonomies that seek only to 'bring creatures under a system of labellings', Kant ended up defining races in just this way.

Kant rejected the argument that human races were the products of environmental influences. Not only did this appear empirically false, it also offended his belief that external circumstances could not alter the wise design of nature. Instead, he conceived of the original human stock as having been endowed with a variety of latent powers that could be evoked or suppressed according to needs and circumstances. Racial characters, in particular the different skin colours, 'must have lain in the seeds of the original stem, to us unknown, of the human race, and that, as natural dispositions necessary for the perpetuation of the race ... they must unfailingly appear in succeeding generations.'

Kant's understanding of race as a natural category was highly influential. This pre-eminent philosopher of the Enlightenment, the historian Robert Bernasconi observes, 'played a crucial role in establishing the term "race" as the currency within which discussions of human variety would be conducted in the nineteenth century.' Some eighteenth-century thinkers went a step further than Kant, arguing that different races had separate origins and were distinct species. *Polygenism* – the doctrine of separate origins – made scientifically irrelevant the question of why Europeans were different from Africans. They were different because they were so created. 'There are different species of man as well as dogs', wrote Lord Kames. 'A mastiff differs not more from a spaniel than a white man from a negro or a Laplander from a Dane.' Voltaire was another who defended polygenism and ridiculed the notion that all humans had descended from Adam and Eve. 'The negro race', he wrote, echoing Kames's argument, 'is a species as different from ours as the breed of spaniels is from that of greyhounds.' Thomas Jefferson, too, dabbled with polygenism.

Polygenism, however, like the idea of race itself, remained very much a minority view in the eighteenth century. This was partly because it appeared to question the Biblical account of all humans as having descended from Adam and Eve. But the primary resistance to polygenism was because it cut across the political and scientific temper of the time. Enlightenment thinkers, even mainstream conservative ones, were reluctant to accept theories that suggested that certain peoples were by nature inferior or incapable of progress. With one or two exceptions, such as Voltaire and Kames, most eighteenth-century figures who explored racial arguments did so only diffidently or in passing. Hume's comment about the innate inferiority of blacks appeared in a footnote. Thomas Jefferson conceded that 'the opinion that [negroes] are inferior in the faculties of reason and imagination must be hazarded with great diffidence' particularly 'when our conclusion would degrade a whole race of men from the rank in the scale of beings which their Creator may perhaps have given them.' Twenty years later, he wrote to a French correspondent that he had expressed his opinions 'with great hesitation'. He added that 'whatever their degree of talents, it is no measure of their rights'.

The roots of the racial ideas that would flourish in the nineteenth century can be uncovered, in certain measure, in Enlightenment writing, or rather in the equivocations of the conservative wing of the Enlightenment. Yet eighteenth-century thinkers remained highly resistant to the idea of race. This was partly because the empirical case for a racial view of human differences did not seem sufficiently compelling. More importantly, political attitudes towards progress and human unity left little room for race. The debate about race, as we saw in Chapter 1, is not so much about the facts of human diversity as about how we should understand such facts. Enlightenment views on human nature shaped the *philosophes'* ideas about human variety and made them reluctant to interpret such variety in racial terms. The transformation of Enlightenment attitudes through the course of the nineteenth century helped mutate the eighteenth-century discussion of human variety into the nineteenth-century obsession with racial difference.

5

THE ROMANCE OF TYPE

In March 1800, Captain Nicholas Baudin proposed to the French *Institut National* a journey of scientific exploration to New Holland (as Australia was then known). Baudin, who had already taken part in several scientific trips to the South Seas, thought it important both to settle once and for all the question of whether Australia was a single landmass and to collect information on local peoples, cultures and customs. The *Institut* agreed to sponsor the expedition and asked the newly-formed *Société des Observateurs de l'Homme* for its help in preparing instructions for the study of the 'physical, intellectual and moral' bearing of the indigenous peoples. The *Société* was a shooting star in the firmament of French anthropology; founded in December 1799, as part of the revolutionary fervour for scientific knowledge, it lasted fewer than five years and is now remembered only by historians. Napoleon's rise to power marked both the demise of the *Société* and the silencing of the radical voices that peopled it. Yet it in those five years it attracted some of the brightest minds of the age and hosted many of the most important scientific debates of the time.

The *Société* provided two memoirs of instruction for Baudin's voyage. The first, *Considerations on the Diverse Methods to Follow in the Observation of Savage Peoples*, was written by Joseph-Marie Degerando. The second, *An Instructive Note on the Researches to be Carried out Relative to the Anatomical Differences between the Diverse Races of Men*, was penned by Georges Cuvier. Cuvier was one of the founders of the science of palaeontology and was to become France's most distinguished scientist of the early nineteenth century. Where Degerando was a child of the Revolution, a friend of the radical *Ideologues*, and a great believer in education as a motor of social change, Cuvier was deeply conservative in both his politics and his science. He said of the Revolution that it had allowed 'the most ignorant portion of the population ... to pronounce on the fate of the most instructed and the most generous.' He was a lifelong opponent not only of revolution, but also of evolution, and deeply hostile to the idea that species could change their form. From the space between the respective views of Degerando and Cuvier emerged the nineteenth-century concept of race.

Although it was written at a time when there was little left of the Enlightenment other than the glow of its embers, Degerando's memoir is infused with the optimism and scientific open-mindedness that characterised much eighteenth-century thought. Its aim was to establish a scientific basis for the study of non-European peoples. Scientists, he wrote, must begin by learning the language of the people under study. This would allow them to investigate the kinds of ideas, beliefs and values they possess, beginning with the more concrete forms, such as the understanding of colour, and those moral ideas close to sensory experience, for instance joy or fear, before moving on to more complex, abstract ideas of which 'even savages cannot be utterly deprived'. After studying the individual, the scientist must investigate 'the savage in society', including observations of domestic, political, civil, economic and religious life. The scientist must also study the 'traditions' of savage peoples.

It is striking that in a methodological memoir on anthropological research the word 'race' appears just once. There is no concept of permanent hereditary differences between human groups. Degerando considered it essential to establish a scientific understanding of the differences between 'civilised' and 'savage' people yet he did not for a moment doubt that a commonality existed that bound both together. Like most of his contemporaries, Degerando believed that the highest form of civilisation was European culture. But civilisation, for Degerando, did not belong to Europeans: all humanity could aspire to reach the summit of social development. What more 'touching purpose' could there be, Degerando asked, than 'to re-establish the holy knots of universal society, than to meet again these ancient parents separated by a long exile from the rest of the common family, than to extend the hand by which they raise themselves to a more happy state.'

Cuvier's *Instructive Note* was much shorter than Degerando's memoir. It also belonged to a different world. The *Note* began with a brief discussion of the current state of knowledge of physical anthropology. While Blumenbach's work had helped delineate the major races, Cuvier believed, it was not sufficiently smooth-grained to establish a true racial typology. This was now the task of anthropology and should be a major goal of Baudin's journey. Cuvier gave precise instructions on how to make scientific portraits of any local people they might encounter. But more important than portraits, he insisted, was the collection of actual specimens, especially skulls. When the voyagers witnessed or took part in battles involving savages, they must not fail to 'visit the places where the dead are deposited' to collect bones. The skeletons must be properly prepared: the bones were to be boiled for several hours in a 'solution of soda or of caustic potash' to 'rid them of their flesh'. Once prepared, the bones were to be put in bags, labelled and sent back to Europe, where they would be reassembled. It would also be useful to bring back some skulls with flesh attached. These were to be soaked in a corrosive sublimate and set out to dry, a process that would render the heads as tough as wood, with the facial forms perfectly preserved. Cuvier warned that some sailors might view all this as barbarous but, he insisted, 'in an expedition which has as its end the advancement of science, it is necessary for the leaders to allow themselves to be governed only by reason.'

Degerando did not think it necessary to discuss the issue of race; the very title of Cuvier's note proclaimed its central importance. Degerando thought that human beings were best understood through a study of their thoughts, beliefs, history and society; Cuvier was transfixed by their anatomy. Degerando was sure that common bonds could be re-established between savage and civilised man; Cuvier insisted that racial differences were deep and ineradicable. Degerando's memoir harked back to what the eighteenth century had promised; Cuvier's note looked forward to what the nineteenth century was to proclaim.

Sixty years after Baudin's journey to New Holland, Thomas Huxley published his essay *Emancipation: Black and White*. Huxley was a leading liberal of his age, a staunch rationalist and the foremost champion of Darwinism. His essay was an attack on slavery and a defence of women's rights; yet in his understanding of racial differences, Huxley was heir to the conservative Cuvier rather than the radical Degerando. 'It is simply incredible', he wrote, 'that, when all his disabilities are taken into account, and our prognathous relative has a fair field and no favour, as well as no oppressor, he will be able to compete successfully with his bigger-brained and smaller-jawed rival, in a contest that is to be carried out by thoughts and not by bites.' Huxley added that 'The highest places in the hierarchy of civilisation will assuredly not be within the reach of our dusky cousins, though it is by no means necessary that they should be restricted to the lowest.'

At the time that Degerando and Cuvier wrote their respective memoirs, Degerando's view held sway. By the time Huxley penned his polemic against slavery, Cuvier's insistence that racial differences were permanent had displaced the belief that all humans belonged to a common family. Towards the end of the eighteenth century, as we saw in the previous chapter, there emerged a conflict between a belief in the plasticity of human varieties and a recognition of the difficulties in eradicating social and intellectual differences between human groups.

This conflict became far more pronounced during the course of the nineteenth century.

The Victorian age worshipped progress no less than had the Enlightenment but what in the eighteenth century had been an article of faith became, in the nineteenth, a practical reality. Eighteenth-century Europe was a ramshackle muddle of feudal fiefdoms and absolute monarchies, all held in the immovable grip of the church. It was rural and parochial, a continent barely touched by industry. In the nineteenth century, Europe – or parts of it, anyway – became decisively modern. This was the age of Isambard Kingdom Brunel and Baron Hausmann, of the Eiffel Tower and the Crystal Palace, of railways and sewage systems, of pasteurisation and the anaesthetic, of *War and Peace* and *The Fighting Temeraire*, of *Das Rheingold* and *Middlemarch*. In science and technology, architecture and art, education and literature, European thinkers and European nations (not to mention American thinkers and the American nation) seemed to have broken free from the shackles of the past. The English historian, G. R. Porter, opened the first volume of his *Progress of the Nation* by announcing that the present generation had witnessed the 'greatest advances in civilisation that can be found recorded in the annals of mankind.' Tennyson's response to his first train journey ('let the great world spin forever down the ringing grooves of change') summed up the exuberant confidence in progress that infused the Victorian age.

Enlightenment *philosophes*, such as Degerando, believed that social progress would heal the divisions between social groups. Nineteenth-century thinkers discovered that, in reality, progress seemed to exacerbate such differences, revealing ever more sharply the vast gulf that existed not just between Europe and America and the rest of the world but also within Europe itself. The nineteenth century was the great age of nation-building, from which countries such as France, Italy and Germany emerged as fully-fledged nations; but the very process by which nationhood was constructed was also the process that revealed the deep divisions within each nation. The historian Eugene Weber has shown, for instance, the extraordinary modernising effort that was required to unify France and her rural populations and the traumatic and lengthy process of cultural, educational, political and economic 'self-colonisation' that this entailed. These developments created the modern French nation and allowed for notions of French (and European) superiority over non-European cultures but they also reinforced a sense of how socially and anthropologically alien was the mass of the rural, and indeed urban, population. In an address to the Medico-Psychological Society of Paris in 1857, the Christian socialist, Phillipe Buchez, considered the meaning of social differentiation within France:

> Consider a population like ours, placed in the most favourable circumstances; possessed of a powerful civilisation; amongst the highest ranking nations in science, the arts and industry. Our task now, I maintain, is to find out how it can happen that within a population such as ours, races may form – not merely one but several races – so miserable, inferior and bastardised that they may be classed below the most inferior savage races, for their inferiority is sometimes beyond cure.

The dilemma faced by a man like Buchez – or like Huxley, for that matter – was that, like many of his class and generation, he had a deep belief in equality, a belief that he had inherited from the Enlightenment *philosophes*. Buchez was a disciple of the Utopian socialist, Henri de Saint-Simon, and an advocate of workers' associations. Like eighteenth-century *philosophes*, Buchez trusted in progress and assumed that, potentially, all human beings could develop into a state of civilisation. In practice, however, social divisions seemed so deep and unforgiving that they appeared permanent, as if rooted in the very soil of the nation. France was a highly-civilised nation, whose scientists, engineers, philosophers and novelists were the envy of the world. Yet sections of French society seemed trapped in their own barbarism, apparently unwilling to, or incapable of, progress. They seemed, in fact, more barbarous than the savages of Africa, Asia, Australia or the Americas, because the barbarity of the home-grown savages seemed 'incurable'. How could one rationally explain this?

As they wrestled with this dilemma, many prominent thinkers came to the conclusion that certain types of people were, by nature, incapable of progressing beyond barbarism. They were naturally inferior. This idea, tentatively suggested by men like Thomas Jefferson in the eighteenth century, became, by the end of the nineteenth, the principal means of making sense of the world. For Enlightenment radicals, the unity of Man was the logical consequence of their belief in equality. For mainstream thinkers, the reality of inequality had raised questions about such unity. Such questioning became more insistent in the nineteenth century. The idea of race developed as a way of explaining the persistence of social divisions in a society that had proclaimed a belief in equality. From the racial viewpoint, inequality persisted because society was by nature unequal. The destiny of different social groups was shaped, at least in part, by their intrinsic properties. Science, many came to believe, would both elucidate and explain those intrinsic properties.

The process by which Enlightenment humanism was degraded to a racial view of the world was hastened both by increasing pessimism about the possibilities of social change and by a growing fear of such change. These changing attitudes to social transformation were framed by two revolutions: the French Revolution of 1789 and the revolutions of 1848 that swept across much of Europe. For radicals the overthrow of the *ancien regime*, in 1789, represented both the practical embodiment of reason and equality and a concrete expression of social progress. For more conservative thinkers, the French Revolution was an illustration of the darker side of reason and of the dangers of social progress. The social and political upheaval caused by the Revolution, an upheaval that was exported across much of

Europe in the Napoleonic Wars, created a backlash against many Enlightenment beliefs. This backlash can be seen in the writings of men like the Irish philosopher Edmund Burke, the founder of modern conservatism, Romantics such as William Wordsworth and Samuel Coleridge in their later years, and French Catholic reactionaries such as Louis de Bonald and Joseph de Maistre. Wordsworth had at first hailed the Revolution: 'Bliss was it in that dawn to be alive /But to be young was very heaven'. Increasingly, however, he grew fearful of its consequences, declaring by 1805 in *Ode to Duty*:

> Me this uncharted freedom tires;
> I feel the weight of chance desires:
> My hopes no more must change their name,
> I long for a repose that ever is the same.

The differences between the arguments of men like Wordsworth, Burke, de Bonald and de Maistre were important. Wordsworth and Burke were mainstream supporters of Enlightenment beliefs who despaired of the more radical consequences of those beliefs; de Bonald and de Maistre had always lined up with the reactionary opponents of the Enlightenment. But the similarities were also significant. The more conservative Enlightenment thinkers were increasingly drawn to many of the arguments of the counter-Enlightenment.

The disorder and anarchy observed after 1789 led many to decry change and progress and to stress order and stability, tradition and authority, status and hierarchy. They longed for the safe anchor of ancient traditions, of personal faith and of a universe that spoke to them through its myths and symbols. For opponents of the Enlightenment, the altar and the throne, rather than parliament and the ballot box, had always been the twin pillars of a healthy society. This belief now found an echo within the ranks of Enlightenment believers; so did the conviction that prejudice, rather than reason, was the best inoculation against revolution. 'The bulk of mankind', Burke argued, 'have neither leisure nor knowledge sufficient to reason right; why should they be taught to reason at all? Will not honest instinct prompt and wholesome prejudices guide them much better than half-reasoning?'

If the French Revolution had catalysed a conservative reaction against the Enlightenment, the revolutions of 1848 had a similar impact on liberal opinion. In that year, a series of revolts and insurrections swept across the length and breadth of Europe, largely in response to political tyranny and economic immiseration. The revolutions were quickly crushed, often brutally. Liberals, who had initially helped man the barricades, were shocked by the violence and instability the uprisings unleashed and many turned their backs on the very idea of radical change. In the response of the English liberal, Walter Bagehot, to the events of 1848, we find an echo of Burke's fears after 1789. 'The first duty of society is the preservation of society', Bagehot wrote, 'To keep up this system we must sacrifice everything. Parliaments, liberty, leading articles, essays, eloquence, all are good, but they are secondary.' The 'vicissitudes of revolution', the historian Daniel Pick observes, 'seemed to call into question the very terms of liberal progressivism'. Pessimism, Pick adds, 'began to colonise liberalism'; many came to the conclusion that democracy was no more than 'turbulent decadence'.

The story of Richard Wagner encapsulates this shift. We now think of Wagner as a Romantic reactionary and a venomous anti-Semite. The young Wagner was, on the contrary, a Utopian socialist, deeply influenced by the young Hegelians – the group of radical thinkers from whose number Karl Marx emerged – and in particular by Ludwig Feuerbach, whose atheism scandalised mainstream opinion. In 1848, Wagner stood on the barricades in Dresden as the revolutionaries attempted to overthrow the monarchy. Forced into exile after the rebellion was crushed, Wagner's approach to politics, art and life was transformed. He abandoned the optimistic, humanist outlook of Feuerbach for Arthur Schopenhauer's misanthropic philosophy of renunciation. For Schopenhauer, wretchedness was the way of the world and the only solution would come when recognition of this all-pervading misery led people to renounce every shred of desire for existence and gratification. Wagner's philosophical transformation is evident in the libretto for the *Ring* cycle, in which the humanist affirmation of Siegfried gives way to the Schopenhauerian pessimism embodied in Wotan and in Brünnhilde's self-immolation. Wagner abandoned politics and the pursuit of social progress for myth and the embrace of racial identity.

Others responded to 1848 not through an acceptance of myth but by a turn to science. In Ivan Turgenev's novel *Fathers and Sons*, the young doctor, Bazarov, scorns faith and idealism in favour of a blunt, almost brutal, materialist view of the world. 'You and I are just like frogs', he tells a patient, 'except that we walk on two legs'. Barazov was a nihilist, someone who 'does not bow down to any authority, who does not accept any principle on faith, however much that principle may be revered.' The only truth for Bazarov was scientific truth, the only cure a world built according to scientific principles.

Nihilism was never much more than a fringe philosophy. What Barazov welcomed – the rejection of all authority – others feared. 'The supreme dread', Harriet Martineau wrote, 'is that men should be adrift for want of anchorage for their convictions.' Martineau was an English journalist and novelist, the daughter of a textile manufacturer, a friend of Charles Darwin and a tireless propagandist for liberal and scientific causes. She was very much the picture of the new middle-class liberal and her anxieties spoke for a class and a generation. The old sources of authority – the Bible, the Church, the gentry – were in disarray and no new source had emerged to replace them. The result was intellectual turmoil – and the fear that intellectual turmoil could lead to social disorder. As the historian, John Burrow, has observed, 'Anarchy – social anarchy as a fear, intellectual anarchy as a fact – is a word that constantly occurs [in intellectual debates] in the eighteen-forties and eighteen-fifties.' The events of 1848 only served to sharpen such trepidation.

While liberals like Martineau rejected Barazov's nihilism, they too looked to science to resolve the problem of authority. Science, they felt, would have to supplant religion, and Nature replace God, as the guarantors of intellectual truth, moral fulfilment and social peace. Once human history had been turned into a science, the English jurist Henry Maine wrote, 'it must teach that which every other science teaches – continuous sequence, inflexible order, and eternal law.' This vision of the relationship between science and society came to be called 'positivism'. The concept of a 'positivist' science was formulated by the French scholar, Claude Henri Saint-Simon, to describe a science from which metaphysics, or the search for final cause, had been eliminated. It is Saint-Simon's erstwhile secretary, Auguste Comte, with whom the ideas of nineteenth-century positivism are most associated. Like Saint-Simon, Comte distrusted politics and believed that science held the key to solving social and moral problems. He aimed to reconstruct the 'science of Man' on the lines of natural science. To this new science, which would lay bare the natural laws of society, Comte gave the name *sociologie*. Comte's sociology was, paradoxically, a *biological* discipline. 'The subordination of the social sciences to biology is so evident', he wrote, 'that no one denies it in statement, however it may be neglected in practice.' Since society was governed by natural laws it could not be any other way. As Harriet Martineau put it in her introduction to the English translation of Comte's *Positive Philosophy*, positivism restored a sense of order to Man's place in nature. Thanks to positivism, she wrote, 'we find ourselves not under capricious and arbitrary conditions ... but under great, general, invariable laws.'

The growing, and seemingly unbridgeable, gulf between peoples, both those within Europe and between European and non-European peoples; pessimism about, and fear of, social change; the view of society as a natural order; the embrace of science as a replacement for religion – through these developments, Degerando's vision of the universal human family gave way, in the course of the nineteenth century, to Cuvier's concept of fixed racial types. They catalysed a shift from a view of human beings as primarily social creatures, governed by social laws, to a view of human beings as primarily biological entities, governed by natural laws. They also brought about a shift, as the historian Nancy Stepan observes, 'from an emphasis on the fundamental physical and moral homogeneity of man, despite superficial differences, to an emphasis on the essential heterogeneity of mankind, despite superficial similarities.' In Chapter 2 we saw how the modern debate on race has been shaped by a philosophical debate between lumpers and splitters. That debate was given historical shape in the nineteenth century, as Enlightenment lumpers gave way to Victorian splitters.

DIFFERENT STROKES FOR DIFFERENT VOLKS

The tolerance, egalitarianism and optimism that characterised the Enlightenment derived, at least in part, from the relative stability of Europe in the first part of the eighteenth century. This stability gave rise to the classic, liberal, providential view of Man, in which individual aspirations and social needs were seen as totally compatible. As Alexander Pope put it in his *Essay on Man*,

> Thus God and Nature linked the general frame,
> And bade Self-Love and Social be the same.

This argument proved extremely durable among British thinkers. It was at the heart of Adam Smith's political economy, of the utilitarian philosophy of Jeremy Bentham and John Stuart Mill, of natural theology and of the evolutionary ideas of Herbert Spencer. On the

Continent, however, the Providential view of Man began crumbing at the end of eighteenth century, the second half of which saw the rise of new tensions and conflicts, culminating in the epic drama of the French Revolution. Such conflicts made the inevitable correspondence of individual and social needs sound less plausible.

From these changes emerged the Romantic reaction to the Enlightenment. Romanticism is one of those concepts that cultural historians find invaluable but almost impossible to define. It took many political forms – it lies at the root both of modern conservatism and many strands of radicalism – and appeared in different national versions. Romanticism was not a specific political or cultural view but rather described a cluster of attitudes and preferences: for the concrete over the abstract, the unique over the universal, nature over culture, the organic over the mechanical, emotion over reason, intuition over intellect and particular communities over abstract humanity.

The late-Enlightenment thinkers attempted to reconcile the disharmony between the individual and the social through two, seemingly contradictory, arguments. They stressed the idea of an 'inner voice' that spoke uniquely to every individual and guided their moral actions. This led to a preoccupation with individual conscience, helped downgrade the previous stress on reason and elevated emotion and imagination in importance. The Romantic inner voice, as we shall see in Chapter 7, lies beneath many of the contemporary notions of identity that animate modern views about multiculturalism. As well as giving colour to the inner voice, Romantics also emphasised the concepts of community and nation, stressing the importance of the collective over the individual. The cosmopolitanism of the Enlightenment gave way to national loyalties and a more organic view of society.

The stress on the idea of an intuitive, non-rational form of thought and the new regard for group loyalty led many Romantics to propose the notion of an unchanging inner essence within human beings, an essence beyond the reach of history or society. This common essence provided the means of binding together communities by creating a sense of belonging that could overcome the fragmentary effects of capitalist society. The Romantic stress on social cohesion and solidarity led, paradoxically, to an emphasis on social divisions. A 'community' was defined as much by its exclusion of those who did not belong as by its inclusion of those who did. What came to define human essence within the Romantic tradition was that it was not universally constituted; humanity did not possess a common innate nature. The philosopher who best articulated this idea was the German, Johann Gottfried Herder.

Born in Mohrungen in East Prussia, Herder studied at the University of Königsberg (where Kant taught all his life). He became a schoolteacher before being appointed court preacher, first in Bückeberg and then in Weimar. A close friend of Goethe's, Herder became hugely influential in the development of German Romanticism. He rejected the Enlightenment idea that reality was ordered in terms of universal, timeless, objective, unalterable laws, which rational investigation could discover. He maintained rather that every activity, situation, historical period and civilisation possessed a unique character. David Hume had suggested that 'Mankind are so much the same at all times and in all places that history informs us of nothing new or strange.' Man, Voltaire declared, 'was, generally speaking, always what he is now.' Herder, on the contrary, insisted that history (and anthropology) reveals many things new and strange. Mankind was *not* the same at all times and in all places. Man was not always what he is now. Different cultures and ages differed tremendously in their beliefs and concepts, perceptions and emotions. All Enlightenment *philosophes* were intrigued by the phenomenon of diversity but while earlier thinkers had sought to *explain* the presence of diversity, Herder, and many of those who followed him, thought it important to *accept*, and indeed to celebrate, it.

Herder rejected the idea that humanity was composed of distinct physical types. What made each people or nation – or *volk* – unique was not its biological make-up but its *Kultur*: its particular language, literature, history and modes of living. The unique nature of each *volk* was expressed through its *volksgeist* – the unchanging spirit of a people, refined through history. The relationship between the individual and the collective was expressed not through a political contract but a spiritual union. For Herder, a *volk* expressed both a bond between contemporaries and a dialogue across generations. Although Herder was politically and philosophically dissimilar to Burke, nevertheless he believed, with Burke, that the nation was 'a partnership between those who are living, those who are dead and those who are to be born.' For Herder, to be a member of a group was to think and act in certain ways, the ways that were given by the group or *volk*.

The *volksgeist* was conveyed through myths, songs and sagas that, for Herder, carried the eternal heritage of a people, far removed from the ephemera of science and modernity. Like the Romantics, Herder stressed the importance of feeling and expression in human life. 'In the works of the imagination and feeling', he wrote, 'the entire soul of a nation reveals itself most clearly'. Language was particularly important to the delineation of a people. 'Has a nation anything more precious than the language of its fathers?', Herder asked rhetorically. 'In it dwell its entire world of tradition, history, religion, principles of existence: its whole heart and soul.' Language provided the mode of living and the means of thinking. 'Each nation speaks in the manner it thinks', Herder believed, 'and thinks in the manner it speaks.' A foreign language was, for Herder, something alien to the soul: 'I am able to stammer with intense effort in the words of a foreign language; its spirit will evade me.' Artificial, polyglot entities like the Hapsburg Empire were absurd monsters, contrary to nature: 'a lion's head with a dragon's tail, an eagle's wing, a bear's paw [sewn together] in one unpatriotic symbol of state.' For Herder, 'the most natural state' was 'one nation, with one national character'. Nothing 'appears so directly opposite to the end of government as the unnatural enlargement of states, the wild mixture of various kinds of humans and nations under one sceptre.'

For the *philosophes*, the existence of universal laws of human nature suggested that, through the use of reason, one could derive a set of values and beliefs that best promoted human flourishing in whatever context. Morality, as Voltaire put it, 'is the same in all civilised nations' (though, of course, in Voltaire's eyes, not all nations could be civilised). This belief lay at the heart of the distinction between civilisation and savagery. For Herder, though, each *volk* was a self-contained entity, with an individuality and character of its own. 'Every nation', he wrote, 'has its own inner centre of happiness, as every sphere has its own centre of gravity.' The values, beliefs and histories of different peoples were, Herder suggested, *incommensurate*. So, 'a Negro is as much entitled to think the white man degenerate as the white to think the former a black beast.' Civilisation, Herder pointed out, is not simply European; it 'manifests itself, according to time and place, in every people.' He questioned the kinds of judgements necessary to distinguish between civilised and savage people. Every culture was authentic on its own terms, each adapted to its local environment. Each native people 'displays as much understanding as his own way of life afford or require'. The 'grand law of nature', he proclaimed, was 'let man be man. Let him mould his condition according to what he himself shall view as best.' 'Let us follow our own path', Herder beseeched, 'let men speak of our nation, our literature, our language: they are ours, they are ourselves, let that be enough.'

Herder saw himself as swimming against the main current of eighteenth-century thought. 'The general philosophical tone of our century', he wrote, 'wishes to extend "our own ideal" of virtue and happiness to each distant nation, to even the remotest age in history'; but he questioned whether 'one such single ideal can act as an arbiter praising or condemning other nations or periods, their customs and laws.' Herder also questioned what he regarded as the Enlightenment's unhealthy obsession with reason. In a passage that recalls Burke's argument in *Reflections on the French Revolution*, Herder suggested that 'prejudice is good in its time and place, for happiness may spring from it. It urges nations to converge upon their centre, attaches them more firmly to their roots, causes them to flourish after their kind, and makes them more ardent and therefore happier in their inclinations and purposes.' Yet, for all his *Sturm und Drang* Romanticism, Herder remained very much a child of the Enlightenment. At the heart of his philosophy was a deep-seated belief in equality and in universal human capacities. He despised racial theories. 'A monkey is not your brother', he protested, 'but a negro is, and you should not rob and oppress him.' He was particularly harsh towards the degradation brought about by colonialism. 'If there were such a thing as a European collective spirit', he wrote, 'it must feel ashamed of the crimes committed by us, after having insulted humankind in a way that hardly any other group of nations had done.'

Herder occupies an ambiguous role in modern political thought. In the eighteenth century, he saw himself as part of the Enlightenment tradition, but also as someone forced to challenge some of the basic precepts of the *philosophes* – such as their stress on universal law and on the universal validity of reason – in order to defend the cherished ideals of equality. In the twentieth century, his pluralism, ambivalence about reason and celebration of what we now call particularist identities, became the root of much antiracist thinking. In between, in the nineteenth century, Herder's impact was to encourage, albeit unwittingly, a racial viewpoint. In insisting that the key differences between humans were cultural rather than political, and in arguing for the incommensurability of cultures, Herder discarded the common yardstick by which to gauge humanity. The consequence of his belief in difference as the motivating force was to undermine the idea of equality and unity. The consequence of his insistence on the importance of tradition was to loosen the grip of reason. Taken together, they helped encourage a racial view of human differences.

Following Herder, there was a reawakened interest in folk cultures and oral traditions. The Grimm brothers, Jacob and Wilhelm, began their collection of idealised folk tales that they presented as authentically German. Scholars also developed a new interest in history, and in a new kind of history that emphasised not just the actions of great men but also the processes of historical change. It also emphasised racial differences. The German historian Barthold Niebuhr's landmark *Lectures on the History of Rome,* often viewed as the first scientific study of the past, interpreted the struggle between patricians and plebeians as an ancient race war. The *History of Rome* was also a modern racial tale. The genius of the German people, Niebuhr believed, lay in its resistance to Roman conquest and hence to its subsequent repudiation of 'artificial, spiritless Frenchified forms and tastes and ideas'. This idea of the noble, free tribes of the ancient German forests, from which had descended modern Germans, Anglo-Saxons and Scandinavians and which had led the resistance to 'Frenchified forms, tastes and ideas' was very popular – at least outside France. In the first few decades of the nineteenth century, English historians, such as John Mitchell Kemble, rewrote English history as a racial conflict between Saxons and Normans. Robin Hood, who in the past had been depicted as a Norman earl, now became a Saxon hero, defying Norman tyranny. He was a central figure in Walter Scott's *Ivanhoe*, the first novel of race, which portrayed the distinction between Saxons and Normans as racial, rather than social or political. 'Four generations had not sufficed to blend the hostile blood of the Normans and Anglo-Saxons', Scott wrote, 'nor to unite, by common language and mutual interests, two hostile races, one of which still felt the elation of triumph, while the other groaned under all the consequences of defeat'.

Once it was accepted that different peoples were motivated by different sentiments, unique to themselves, it was but a short step to view these sentiments as racial. Herder's *volksgeist* became transformed into racial make-up. The bridge from the one to the other was the biological concept of 'type'.

THE SCIENCE OF TYPE

Biology – both the word and the discipline – is a nineteenth-century invention. It was in Continental Europe, particularly in Paris and in Berlin, that the new science first developed. At the turn of the nineteenth century, the study of the living world was dominated by French scholars, in particular Georges Cuvier, whom some saw as the 'new Aristotle'. Cuvier helped establish both comparative anatomy and palaeontology as scientific disciplines. Not the least of his accomplishments was firmly to establish the extinction of past life forms as a scientific fact. By the mid-century, however, the centre of gravity of biological research had shifted from Paris to Berlin. Where Cuvier's biology was austere and observational, German biology was deeply infused with Romantic or Idealist philosophy. Indeed, nineteenth-century German biology, in its purest form, was called *romantische Naturophilosophie*. To the Idealist, the whole world was a rational plan in the mind of the Creator and Romantic biologists applied this dictum to the study of nature. The material world, they believed, was but the projection of a deeper spiritual reality.

Romantic biologists stressed the unity of nature and, in particular, of the living world. They saw every living form as a concrete manifestation of an ideal *archetype* or *Bauplan* – a basic plan that underlay all organisms despite their diverse forms. Humans were part of the Romantic unity of nature, a view that eroded the strict Christian distinction between Man and beast and lent Romantic biology, for all its metaphysical undertones, a decidedly naturalistic sheen. The unity of nature also meant the erosion of the distinction between the physical and the mental. For many Romantic biologists, the physical form was simply the outer manifestation of the inner spiritual being or mental state, a view that would have immense importance for racial science. Finally, within Romantic biology were the ideas of development and progress and a teleological view of nature. All natural things, Idealists believed, showed a yearning to advance to a higher state of nature; lower beings were 'a preparation for a superior existence.' According to Herder, as nature advances, so 'the powers and impulses of each branch of creation grows more manifold' until finally, 'they all unite in the figure of Man. At Man the series stops.'

Naturophilosophie, with its mystical undertones, did not travel well beyond the borders of German-speaking lands. Hard-nosed Anglo-American and French scholars, brought up in the positivist, empirical or utilitarian traditions and tending to see themselves as down-to-earth purveyors of scientific fact rather than as philosophers with poetic imaginations, often poured scorn on the wild speculative leaps of their German counterparts and espoused a more observational and experimental science. Yet, despite their penchant for metaphysics, *Naturophilosophen* were often good scholars and intermixed with wild speculation were often important ideas about the workings of the material world. The search for nature's underlying plan advanced many areas of biology, including neurology, palaeontology, embryology and evolutionary theory, and in a less concentrated form many of the themes of *Naturophilosophie* worked themselves into the arguments and theories of biologists in France, Britain, America and elsewhere, throughout the nineteenth century. The unity of nature, a teleological view of history, the physical as the manifestation of the mental, the fixity of biological type: these themes became central to nineteenth-century biology and to the emerging science of race. Forged in the furnace of Romantic Idealism, they were, nevertheless, burnished by the hand of positivism. Positivists recognised the importance of these ideas to their ambition of uniting order and progress and of replacing God with Nature.

Perhaps the most important of these concepts was 'type'. As a scientific term, it was both vague and precise, flexible and rigid. The French biologist, W. F. Edwards, noting that it was 'a word which has the same sense in ordinary speech and in natural history', recognised that the concept was useful because it was not tied to any classificatory level and hence could be wielded in a flexible fashion. 'In identifying a combination of well-defined characters as a type', he wrote, 'I avoid all discussion about the rank which a group so characterised will occupy in a general classification, since it suits equally well the distinctions between variety, race, family, species, genus, and other categories yet more general.'

In the eighteenth century, as we saw in the previous chapter, there was considerable debate about what it really meant to classify organisms. Linnaeus's binomial system was hailed as a scientific triumph yet the argument of John Locke that categories 'are *made by the mind* and not by nature' was highly influential. Especially when it came to human varieties, Enlightenment *philosophes* viewed their classification less as a reflection of natural classes than as a matter of human convention. When Blumenbach divided humankind into five races, he tended to view this as an aid to scientific study rather than as a set of groupings given by nature.

The nineteenth-century concept of type signified something very different. A type was characterised not by what John Locke called its 'nominal essence' – superficial characteristics that humans group together by convention – but by its 'real essence'. In the Romantic tradition, that real essence was constituted in the *Bauplan* or archetype of the organism. The concept of type was also central to a very different biological tradition – the observational, experimental biology championed by Cuvier. Indeed, Cuvier was probably the most important nineteenth-century thinker in the popularisation of type.

Cuvier rejected the Romantic idea of ideal forms and the belief in progress and transcendence. He stressed instead the Aristotelian idea that all organisms, and parts of organisms, had been designed to play a particular function within the whole. He used his studies of comparative anatomy to divide all organisms into four basic *embranchments,* or types, each recognised by a common pattern of internal structure: the vertebrates, the molluscs (snails, octopuses, etc.), the articulates (segmented animals including insects), and the radiates (animals with a circular body plan, such as starfish and sea urchins). Each type was divided into classes, orders, families, genera and species, as in the Linnaean system.

An embranchment was neither an idea in the mind of the Creator nor an ideal form from which all organisms derived. Rather, each represented the most efficient form of animal organisation, a basic type of adaptation to life on earth. The four embranchments could not be ranked along a linear scale as higher or lower; they were simply *different*. Cuvier did not understand adaptation in a Darwinian fashion, as a process that constantly transformed a species and, indeed, created new ones. He saw every species as fixed and immutable and opposed the idea of evolution because change, he argued, would destroy the delicate balance that maintained the perfection of its adaptation. Cuvier's opposition to evolution was not simply scientific, nor was it confined to the natural world. Society, like nature, he believed, was built out of parts so closely interwoven into the whole that it could not be otherwise. Change would destroy the harmony of the parts and hence threaten the very being of society.

For the Romantics, form dictated function. An organism's *Bauplan* determined whether it would hunt on the plains like a lion or swim in the sea like a shark. For Cuvier, function dictated form. Every animal was constructed to fill a particular role in the economy of nature and its role determined its construction. A lion possessed sharp eyes, fast reflexes, fearsome jaws and a great turn of speed, because those were the necessary attributes of a carnivore on the African savannah. Racial scientists borrowed from both concepts of type; some viewed human groups as built to different plans, while others adopted a more Cuverian view that different races were differently adapted to different environments. In both views, type came to mean a group of beings, linked by a set of fundamental characteristics and differing from other types by virtue of those characteristics. Each type was separated from others by a sharp discontinuity; there was rarely any doubt as to which type an individual belonged. Each type remained constant through time and there were severe limits on how much any member of a type could vary from the fundamental ground plan by which the type was constituted. Biologists came to think of human types, in other words, as fixed, unchanging entities, each defined by its special essence. The echoes of Herder's concept of *volksgeist* – a group of people linked by their common cultural heritage, or essence, and distinguishable from every other group by virtue of that heritage, which remained constant through time – are unmistakeable. Through the concept of type, Herder's cultural essence took on biological garb.

6

TO MAKE AN ACCOMPLICE
OF NATURE

In Elizabeth Gaskell's *Mary Barton*, the courtroom crowd scruti-
nises Jem Wilson's face at his murder trial. 'I have seen a good
number of murderers in my day', observes one man 'but I have
seldom seen one with such marks of Cain on his countenance'. 'I am no
physiognomist', responds another, 'but I don't think his face strikes
me as bad'. A third is convinced of Wilson's criminality: 'Only look at
his brow, his downcast eye, his white compressed lips.'

There was barely a Victorian novelist who did not make use of the
idea that the face was a window to the soul. From *David Copperfield* to
Germinal, the face told its own story about honesty and criminality,
genius and unsavouriness. The reading of faces was an ancient art that
went back to the Greeks and beyond. It was, however, an eighteenth-
century Swiss theologian, Johann Lavater, who resurrected the idea for
a modern audience. In his two major works, *Essays on Physiognomy* and
One Hundred Rules of Physiognomy, Lavater transformed an art into a science and laid bare the rules of facial grammar. 'An exact relationship
exists between the soul and the body [and] between the internal and
the external of a man', he wrote. According to Lavater, the 'form,
height, arching, proportion, obliquity, and position of the skull, or
bone of the forehead show the propensity, degree of power, thought,
and sensibility of the man.'

It was not just Victorian novelists and courtroom voyeurs who were seduced by the idea that the head revealed all. Scientists, too, became increasingly obsessed by the skull, which they viewed as the best piece of physical data from which to determine an individual's racial type. No one helped foment the mania for skull measurement more than the Philadelphia doctor Samuel Morton. When Morton died in 1851, the *New York Tribune* said of him that 'probably no scientific man in America enjoyed a higher reputation among scholars throughout the world than Dr Morton.' His reputation was built on his personal collection of more than a thousand skulls of different races. 'Nothing like it exists anywhere else', enthused Louis Agassiz, America's leading naturalist of the time. Friends and enemies alike referred to Morton's charnel house as the 'American Golgotha'.

Morton's view of the skull was influenced by Romantic biology and in particular by phrenology. Phrenology – or 'organology' as it was originally called – was developed in the 1790s by the Austrian neurologist, Franz Josef Gall, and his student and collaborator Johann Spurzheim. Gall and Spurzheim claimed that the mind was composed of a number of innate, fixed and distinct 'faculties' or mental characters and aptitudes. These included the instinct for reproduction, love of offspring, courage, vanity, ambition, the tendency to steal, sense of place and space, memory and sense of people, language and speech, kindness, mimicry and religion. The various aptitudes were located in twenty-seven 'organs' on the surface of the brain. The size of the brain organs, Gall and Spurzheim claimed, varied in proportion to the amounts of the particular faculties they contained and since the organs pressed upon the skull, so the phrenologist could make an accurate analysis of character, personality and mental make-up by examining the shape of an individual's head.

Many phrenologists believed that mental exercise and practice could enlarge particular organs of the brain and hence develop certain aptitudes and personality traits. An individual could cultivate and improve his socially-desirable traits and inhibit his vices. In the 1820s, phrenology became particularly popular among working-class radicals and Dissenters, because it suggested a practical way of improving one's lot and of challenging the prevailing social order.

There was, however, a pessimistic and conservative side to phrenology, too, because it also appeared to suggest that mental propensities were fixed and innate. The conservative interpretation of phrenology was given substance by the increasing tendency to view it as a science not of individual characteristics but of group differences. Spurzheim viewed different groups as differently endowed with innate capacities:

> It is of great importance to consider the heads of different nations ... The foreheads of negroes, for instance, are very narrow, their talents of music and mathematics are also in general very limited. The Chinese, who are fond of colours, have the arch of the eyebrows much vaulted, and we shall see that this is the sign of a greater developement [sic] of the organ of colour. According to Blumenbach, the heads of Kalmucks are depressed from above, and very large sideward above the organ, which gives the disposition to covet. It is also admitted that this nation is inclined to steal, etc.

This shift from individual to group characteristics was eased by an ambiguity in the concept of type. On the one hand, phrenological type referred to the basic plan that underlay all brain structures. On the other, it also described the kind of human characterised by a particular form of brain structure. The concept of type embodied both a naturalistic view of the human mind and a mechanism by which this could be used to divide up humanity into distinct groups.

By the 1840s, the popularity of phrenology had waned, as most of its assertions were disproved. But while the conclusions drawn by phrenology were refuted its influence was nevertheless long-lasting, because its fundamental principle – that there is a correspondence between the inner and the outer man – was accepted by most biologists. It was this assertion that gave weight to the repeated claim that some technique – whether the measurement of cranial capacity, facial angle, cephalic index, brain volume or brain weight – would provide a true indication of innate ability and that by such a method the races of humankind would be found to form a scale of being.

Samuel Morton's preferred measure was skull size. He first laid out the fruits of his labour in his 1839 book, *Crania Americana*. Not surprisingly, Morton found that Caucasians were the bigheads, with a mean skull size of eighty-seven cubic inches. Blacks had the smallest heads, with an average skull of seventy-eight cubic inches. In between, in ascending order, came Native Americans, Malays and Mongolians.

In his classic book, *The Mismeasure of Man*, Stephen Jay Gould re-examined Morton's data. Morton's summaries, he concluded, 'are a patchwork of fudging and finagling in the clear interest of controlling *a priori* convictions'. For instance, the 144 Native American skulls that Morton used came from groups with significantly different head sizes. One group, the Peruvian Incas, who had a particularly small stature and hence small heads, made up twenty-five per cent of the sample, biasing the entire collection. The Iroquois, whose heads were larger than Caucasians', contributed only three skulls to the sample. Morton failed to correct for this, ensuring that his figure for the average Indian skull was artificially low. When Gould took sample bias into account, the figure for the average Indian skull rose by nearly three cubic inches. At the same time, Morton eliminated all but three 'Hindoo' skulls from the Caucasian sample because they were 'smaller than those of any other existing nation'. Gould restored the full complement to the Caucasian sample and recalculated; the figure for the average Caucasian skull fell by 2.5 cubic inches. Other biases in Morton's samples stemmed from his failure to control for sex differences. Women, having smaller bodies, tend to have smaller heads; the 'lower' races in Morton's collection just happened to be represented by more female skulls, the 'higher' races by more male skulls.

Gould did not accuse Morton of fraud. He was only able to recalculate the figures because Morton had explained all his procedures and published all his raw data, not something that a conscious fraudster would do. But, Gould suggested, Morton's social prejudices had led to a series of unconscious biases which 'directed his tabulations along preestablished lines.'

Morton was the leading American polygenist of his age, believing that every race had been separately created. He challenged the idea that all races could interbreed. Many inter-racial couplings, he insisted, especially between Caucasians and Australian Aborigines, did not produce fertile offspring. Every race, like every species, represented a 'primordial organic form' – a definition that betrayed his debt to Romantic biology and its concept of the archetype. 'From remote ages', Morton wrote on the opening page of *Crania Americana*, 'the inhabitants of every extended locality have been marked by certain physical and moral peculiarities, common among themselves and serving to distinguish them from all other people.' Cranial capacity demonstrated the capacity for civilisation: the larger the skull, the greater the propensity for civilised life. Hence the difference between Europe and Africa.

When Morton began his skull collection, in the 1820s, there was little enthusiasm in America for the idea that certain races were permanently inferior. We saw in the previous chapter that Thomas Jefferson had tentatively hinted that blacks might be naturally less intelligent and might even be a distinct species. But, the historian George Frederickson points out, while whites commonly assumed the inferiority of blacks, in the first half of the nineteenth century 'open assertions of permanent inferiority were exceedingly rare.' Morton's work was part of a wider movement that came to be called the American School, which made a scientific case for polygenism and became increasingly influential from the 1840s.

According to the American School, each race was adapted to a particular place and a particular climate. Josiah Clark Nott and George Robbins Gliddon laid out the argument in detail in their 1854 book, *Types of Mankind*. The Earth, they wrote, 'is naturally divided into several zoological provinces, each of which is a distinct centre of creation, possessing a fauna and flora and every species of animal and plant was originally assigned to its appropriate province.' The human family 'offers no exception to this general law, but fully conforms to it: Mankind being divided into several groups of Races, each of which constitutes a primitive element in the fauna of its peculiar province.' To buttress their argument, Nott and Gliddon invited Louis Agassiz to write a nineteen-page *Sketch of the Natural Provinces of the Animal World and their Relation to the different Types of Man*. Agassiz was a Swiss-born naturalist and probably the best known scientist in mid-nineteenth-century America. His views were rooted in Idealism and in Romantic biology. He lived long enough to become the most prominent opponent of Darwinism, continuing to the end of his life to believe in the immutability of type. In his *Sketch*, Agassiz distinguished eight global geographical regions, each the source of a race: Arctic, Asiatic, European, American, African, East Indian, Australian and Polynesian. Each was home to a particular type of humankind that had existed since the beginning of time and would continue to exist until Kingdom come. 'History', Nott and Gliddon believed, 'affords no evidence of the transformation of one Type into another, nor of the origination of a new and Permanent Type.' All races 'have their appropriate geographical ranges, beyond which they cannot go with impunity.' Man likes to think of himself as governed by reason but is in fact 'the most unreasonable of animals' because 'he forsakes the land of his birth, with all its associations, and all the comforts which earth can give, to colonise foreign lands – where he knows full well that a thousand hardships must await him, and with the certainty of risking his life in climates that nature never intended him for.'

We have come full circle from the arguments of the Enlightenment radicals. The radicals' certainty about social equality and human unity led them to claim that as people moved across the globe, so their skin colour would eventually come to match their environment. For Agassiz, the biological disunity of humankind demonstrated the folly of such global movement.

With this notion of type, the journey from *volksgeist* to race was complete. For Herder, every people possessed a particular culture that had remained essentially unchanged since its origins, inhabited a particular nation, lived a particular history, and was sharply distinguished from every other people. For Morton, Nott, Gliddon and Agassiz, every racial type occupied a particular geographical range, possessed a specific set of traits that was rooted in its biology and hence unchangeable, and was sharply distinguished from every other type. The journey from *volksgeist* to race captured, however, a significant shift in perceptions of human beings that characterised the middle decades of the nineteenth century, not just in America but in Europe too. Humans were no longer evaluated in terms of their moral or political qualities but were appraised principally according to their physical characteristics. For the Greeks the key division in the world was between civilised people and barbarians. In pre-modern Europe, what defined a people was its relationship to law and to faith. In the eighteenth century, Enlightenment *philosophes* judged people largely according to their moral capacities. By the second half of the nineteenth century, however, biology determined identity and fate. It was, in the words of the historian Nancy Stepan, 'a move away from an eighteenth-century optimism about man, and faith in the adaptability of man's universal "nature", towards a nineteenth-century biological pessimism.'

Eighteenth-century *philosophes* sought to explain diversity. For nineteenth-century thinkers diversity *was* the explanation. Scientists did not seek to discover why humans appeared so different despite their underlying unity but accepted such differences as a fact of life and attempted to analyse their consequences. In that change lie the origins of modern racial thinking.

THE COLOUR OF CLASS

It is tempting to see the strength of American polygenism as the product of a society in which slavery was still legal. The American School, the anthropologist David Hurst Thomas observes, 'gave pre-Civil War America a way to cope with the Jeffersonian dilemma: whereas the Declaration of Independence proclaimed that all men were created equal, black slaves need be considered equal *only* if they were the product of the very same Creation that gave rise to the Caucasian race'. Many, though not all, polygenists supported slavery, but most Southerners, including Southern slave-owners, opposed polygenism. In 1854, the fire-and-brimstone pro-slavery *Richmond Inquirer* declared that the 'doctrine of diversity' might provide an excellent defence of slavery but Southerners could not afford such a defence if the Bible was 'the price it must pay for them'. Morton's fiercest opponent was John Bachman, minister of St John's Lutheran Church in Charleston, South Carolina, a natural historian and supporter of slavery. He insisted that 'the African is an inferior variety of our species' and 'incapable of self-government' but also that the slave was as human as the slave owner. He justified slavery in Biblical, not scientific, terms; slavery was sanctioned by God because blacks were descendants of the 'accursed' Ham, while Caucasians descended from the blessed Shem. As the historian William Stanton has observed, 'when the issue was clearly drawn, the South turned its back on the only intellectually respectable defense of slavery it could have taken up.'

The arguments of the American School appealed less to Southern conservatives than to Northern liberals. At the heart of racial ideology, as we have seen, was the great liberal dilemma: their belief in equality did not seem to be borne out by reality. This was not a problem for conservatives, who had never accepted the idea of equality in the first place. They justified inequality not as a fact of nature but as a custom sanctioned by God or history. As a biological theory, nineteenth-century racial thought was shaped less by the attempts of a reactionary slave-owning class to justify its privileges than by the growing pessimism among liberals about the possibilities of equality and social progress.

In Europe, the liberal dilemma expressed itself in a slightly different fashion than in America. The inequalities that appeared most significant were not, as in America, between Europeans and non-Europeans but were those that cut through the heart of European nations themselves. Today, the notion of race is so intertwined with the idea of 'colour' that it is often difficult to comprehend the concept of race in nineteenth-century Europe and especially in Victorian Britain. For Victorians, race was a description of social distinctions, not of colour differences. In the summer of 1881, King Kalakaua of Hawaii was visiting England and was a guest at a party given by Lady Spencer. Also at the party were the Prince of Wales and his brother-in-law, the German Crown Prince, the future Kaiser. The Prince of Wales insisted that King Kalakaua should take precedence over the Crown Prince of Germany. 'Either the brute is a king', he told his brother-in-law, dismissing his objections, 'or he's a common-or-garden nigger, and if the latter what's he doing here?' This might seem to us an insufferably racist remark but the prince's view also demonstrated that to Victorians, social status was as important, if not more so, than racial difference. The historian, Douglas Lorrimer, has shown that until the middle of the century black people were treated according to their social standing rather than the colour of their skin:

> Like their eighteenth-century forebears, the mid-Victorians accepted an individual black according to his ability to conform to English social conventions. A dark complexion did not necessarily signify lowly

social status ... In spite of theories claiming the Negro was inferior, the variable conduct of the English at this time showed that these racial assumptions had not sufficient support to influence patterns of behaviour. In the absence of any consensus over the significance of racial differences, mid-Victorians simply treated each individual black according to their evaluation of his social standing.

As the notion of the permanence of social hierarchy took hold within liberal circles, however, commentators became increasingly sceptical about the idea of Negroes aspiring to high social status. As a result, observes Lorrimer, 'the conventional norms about the correct bearings towards one's social inferiors, whether black or white, were extended to include all blacks regardless of an individual's character or background.'

In fact, high status blacks continued to be treated as social equals. When Arthur Hamilton Gordon was made governor of Fiji in 1874, he insisted that Fijian chiefs were his equals, possessed of 'undoubted aristocracy'. 'Nurse can't understand it all', Lady Gordon observed with amused condescension, 'she looks down on them as an inferior race. I don't like to tell her that these ladies are my equal, which she is not!' From one perspective, the historian David Cannadine observes, 'the British may indeed have seen the peoples of their empire as alien, as other, as beneath them – to be lorded over and condescended to. But from another perspective, they also saw them as similar, as analogous, as equal and sometimes even as *better* than they were themselves.' Depending on circumstance, Cannadine adds, '*both* white *and* dark-skinned peoples of the empire were seen as superior; or, alternatively, as inferior.'

In the second half of the nineteenth century social inferiors increasingly came also to be seen as *racial* inferiors. A vignette of working class life in the *Saturday Review*, a well-read liberal magazine of the era, is typical of English middle class attitudes of the time:

The Bethnal Green poor ... are a caste apart, a race of whom we know nothing, whose lives are of quite different complexion from ours, persons with whom we have no point of contact. And although there is not yet quite the same separation of classes or castes in the country, yet the great mass of the agricultural poor are divided from the educated and the comfortable, from squires and parsons and tradesmen, by a barrier which custom has forged through long centuries, and which only very exceptional circumstances ever beat down, and then only for an instant. The slaves are separated from the whites by more glaring ... marks of distinction; but still distinctions and separations, like those of English classes which always endure, which last from the cradle to the grave, which prevent anything like association or companionship, produce a general effect on the life of the extreme poor, and subject them to isolation, which offer a very fair parallel to the separation of the slaves from the whites.

This separation of the classes was important because each had to keep to their allotted place in the social ladder:

> The English poor man or child is expected always to remember the condition in which God has placed him, exactly as the negro is expected to remember the skin which God has given him. The relation in both instances is that of perpetual superior to perpetual inferior, of chief to dependant, and no amount of kindness or goodness is suffered to alter this relation.

Class division denoted the relation of 'perpetual superior to perpetual inferior', a distinction that to Victorians was every bit as visible as that between blacks and whites, slaves and masters. We can see here how the gap between an abstract belief in equality and a society built on social distinction had created the space for a racial view of the world. Social rank, for liberal Victorians, was an expression of individual achievement and aptitude. Yet it was clear that individuals largely occupied the same rank as their parents. The son of a factory hand rarely became a factory owner, the daughter of a farm labourer was almost never a philosopher. Differences of class appeared to express hereditary distinctions. As John Stuart Mill was to complain, social commentators 'revolved in their eternal circle of landlords, capitalists and labourers, until they seemed to think of the distinction of society into these three classes as though it were one of God's ordinances.'

Racial theories, as they unfolded in the nineteenth century, were part of a broader development: the use of natural explanations for social phenomena. As the critical outlook of the Enlightenment gave way to the positivist vision of the Victorian age, so the belief in social transformation was replaced by the doctrine of a naturally-sanctioned social order. 'Racial science', Johann Spurzheim claimed, 'will exercise a great influence on the welfare of nations, in indicating clearly the difference between natural and artificial nobility, and in fanning the relations between individuals to each other in general, and between those who govern and those who are governed in particular.'

The typology of racial science included both the lower orders at home and non-European peoples and justified the inferiority of both. 'The lowest strata of European societies', the French psychologist Gustav LeBon wrote, 'is homologous with the primitive men.' He added that, given sufficient time, 'the superior grades of a population [would be] separated from the inferior grades by a distance as great as that which separates the white man from the negro, or even the negro from the monkey.' Francis Galton, the founder of eugenics, believed that 'beside ... three points of difference – endurance of steady labour, tameness of disposition and prolonged development – I know of none that very markedly distinguishes the nature of the lower classes of civilised man from that of the barbarians.' Galton divided both black and white populations into twenty-four grades, from A at the bottom to X at the top and believed that 'classes E to F of the negro may roughly be considered as the equivalent of our C and D'.

Scientific racism helped generate a hierarchy, underpinned by forces beyond the reach of humanity, that justified the superiority of the ruling class both at home and abroad. It proclaimed the fitness of the capitalist class to rule over the working class and of the white race to rule over the black. It did so not in the name of divine will or aristocratic reaction but of science and progress.

DARWIN CHANGES EVERYTHING – AND NOTHING

The scientific development that, more than any other, helped confirm the existence of a racial hierarchy was the publication in 1859 of Charles Darwin's *On the Origin of Species*, in which he laid out his theory of evolution by natural selection. The book is a milestone of modern biology, the theory one of the greatest scientific breakthroughs of the past two hundred years and one that has played an immense role in shaping the modern view of the world, challenging theological dogma and allowing us to imagine a universe designed without a designer.

The traditional view of species presented them as creations of God, each adapted to its particular role in the order of creation and each defined by its essence. To Darwin, on the contrary, species were not fixed but continually changing, by a natural process of variation, struggle and the selection of traits favourable for survival. As a consequence, species were constantly adapting to changing circumstances and new species forever forming out of old. Species were not fixed, essential, entities but a group of interbreeding forms defined by a certain set of characteristics. With Darwin, the typological view of species finally gave way to a populational view.

In theory, Darwinism should have fatally undermined the idea of race – or, at least, the nineteenth-century typological conception of race. Evolution was a theory of continual change that rejected the notion of species as fixed types . Racial scientists were committed to a science of fixed and unchanging essences, to the idea of racial types whose stability allowed humanity to be divided into distinct groups. Yet, far from undermining the idea of race, Darwinism helped buttress it further. Racial scientists were among the most enthusiastic

Darwinists, adapting the theory for their own purposes, often in highly-contradictory fashion. When, as President of the Royal Anthropological Society, John Beddoe gave a series of lectures in 1891 on race, he finished with two conclusions. 'Under normal circumstances', he wrote, 'the physical characteristics of well defined races of men ... are absolutely permanent.' He also believed that 'Natural selection may alter the type'. The two conclusions clearly contradict each other. If natural selection can alter the type, then the physical characteristics of racial types cannot be permanent. The contradiction did not seem to bother Beddoe or any other racial scientist of the time. Racial science had come to develop a 'two-stage' theory of human evolution. Natural selection operated on early humans to establish racial types but beyond a certain point, the human body was no longer subject to evolutionary forces and hence racial characteristics became fixed. Racial scientists could therefore both commit themselves to Darwin's theory of evolution and also view racial types as ancient and permanent.

The founding fathers of evolutionary theory themselves encouraged such speculation. Alfred Russel Wallace, who discovered the idea of natural selection at the same time as Darwin, put forward a highly-influential argument about race formation in a lecture he gave in 1864 to the Anthropological Society of London. The Society had been specifically set up to challenge the humanist outlook of the existing Ethnological Society and to promote a more hard-line, polygenist view of racial differences. Wallace suggested in his lecture that all humans came originally from a single racial stock. As that original group of humans spread out across the globe, so selection worked to modify the body and adapt individuals to their new environments. Hence 'the striking characteristics and special modifications which still distinguish the chief races of mankind. The red, black, yellow or blushing white skin; the straight, the curly, the woolly hair; the scanty or abundant beard; the straight or oblique eyes; the various forms of the pelvis or cranium and the other parts of the skeleton.' Humans, however, unlike other animals, owed their evolutionary survival not to their exquisitely-adapted physiques but to their highly-inventive minds. Once humans became fully-thinking beings, natural selection ceased to operate on the body, because human resourcefulness allowed them to adapt to any environment regardless of physique. Bodily racial traits therefore became fixed. Evolution, however, continued to work on the mind, selecting for traits best fitting a race for survival. Racial competition was the motor of human evolutionary development, ensuring that the white race continued to progress while revealing other races to be mentally less suited to the modern world. 'It must inevitably follow', Wallace believed, 'that the higher – and more intellectual and moral – must replace the lower and more degraded races.' The 'inevitable effects of an unequal mental and physical struggle' was the elimination of weaker races such as the Australian Aborigines and the Native Americans. For Wallace, this was a positive development, as the world would eventually be peopled by a single race 'no individual of which would be inferior to the noblest specimens of existing humanity.'

Later in life, Wallace disavowed his earlier arguments about racial formation. Under the influence of both socialism and spiritualism, he came to reject – or at least to attenuate – ideas of racial inferiority and superiority. This in turn led him to deny that the human mind was subject to selective forces. All humans, whether civilised or savage, had similar mental capacities, Wallace suggested, including such traits as the power of abstract thought, the capacity for language, the understanding of number and the ability to make moral judgements. Yet savage life required 'the exercise of few faculties not possessed in an equal degree by animals.' Since natural selection could not have anticipated the future needs of civilised life, it should 'only have endowed savage man with a brain little superior to that of an ape, whereas he actually possesses one very little inferior to that of a philosopher.'

Wallace suggested, therefore, that the development of the human mind could not have been shaped by natural selection but was instead guided by a special spiritual force that he called 'will force'.

Darwin was appalled at Wallace's rejection of natural selection. 'I hope you have not murdered too completely your own and my child', he wrote. Yet, while Darwin never for a moment doubted that the human mind was the product of evolution, he too developed his own version of the two-stage theory of race formation. Darwin believed that most racial traits – such as skin colour and type of hair – had little selective value as 'Not one of the external differences between the races of man is of any direct or special service to him'. In other words, possessing black skin or white skin, curly hair or straight hair seemed to afford an individual no particular advantage or disadvantage. Such traits could not, then, have arisen through natural selection. Darwin suggested instead that they developed through sexual selection, an idea he developed in his book, *The Descent of Man*, to explain the persistence of traits that had no obvious selective advantage and may even have been burdensome. The classic example is the peacock's tail, which may look striking but makes it harder to escape predators. How did such traits develop? Darwin suggested that in many animal species, one or other of the sexes might take a liking to a particular look and preferentially mate with individuals sporting that look.

Humans too were shaped in this way. According to Darwin, as the original stock of humans spread out across the globe in small bands, each group developed new physical traits through spontaneous variation. In each group, some of these traits – white skin or black skin, curly hair or straight hair – would have seemed particularly attractive to members of the opposite sex. As a result, such traits would have spread through the population and become its defining racial features. 'Of all the causes that have led to the differences in external appearance between the races of man', Darwin wrote, 'sexual selection has been by far the most efficient.'

Natural selection, of course, continued to operate both on the human body and the human mind, making the different races morally and intellectually distinct and continually in conflict. 'When two races of men meet', Darwin wrote in his notebook, 'they act precisely like two species of animals' in that 'they fight, eat each other, bring diseases to each other, etc, but then comes the more deadly struggle, namely which have the best-fitted organisation or instinct (i.e. intellect in man) to gain the day?'. For Darwin, sexual selection ensured that racial traits arose very early in human history, were not adaptive and were relatively fixed. At the same time, natural selection assured the moral and intellectual progress of certain races and helped establish a racial hierarchy in which whites had possession of the summit.

In the end, what racial science took from Darwinism was not anything scientific but the two central metaphors associated with the theory – those of progress and struggle. Progress described the ascent of European Man, struggle the means by which he had achieved supremacy. Both ideas, of course, were part of the racial idiom well before Darwin published his masterwork. Progress had been a central figure in Western thinking since the Enlightenment; as racial theories developed in the nineteenth century, so it increasingly acquired racial connotations. The idea of competition and struggle too had deep roots in European intellectual history. Darwin drew heavily on Thomas Malthus' famous *Essay on the Principle of Population*, in which the misanthropic reverend argued that the central feature of human society was the struggle for existence caused by the pressure of a growing population against the background of limited resources. Darwin translated this idea into the living world to obtain his mechanism of evolution by natural selection. Well before Darwin, it had been widely accepted that racial struggle ensured that only the fittest survived. Indeed, the phrase 'survival of the fittest', so often associated with Darwin, was actually coined by the English philosopher, Herbert Spencer, in 1851.

When it came to race, then, Darwin changed everything – and nothing. Darwinism was not necessary to prove racial differences. The starting point of racial science was the reality of race. Racial scientists simply adapted Darwin's theory to suit their preconceived ideas. The impact of social Darwinism was, paradoxically, to reassert many of the traditional ways in which concepts such as 'survival of the fittest' had been used before Darwin. The struggle for existence was used as a mechanism through which a social and natural hierarchy was preserved, allowing organisms to be distributed within that hierarchy according to their fitness. The idea of fitness tended to be imbued with traditional notions of the desirable and the valuable. Change and evolution became the means by which ultimate order and the realisation of these ideal faculties and types was achieved. Darwinism allowed racial science to create a dynamic concept of hierarchy. The pre-Enlightenment Chain of Being was static; indeed, it was anti-evolutionist. In appropriating the concept of evolution by natural selection, racial science married the idea of a fixed hierarchy to that of progress – those at the top of the hierarchy arrived there on merit, because of their natural superiority in the struggle for existence. Racial theories, as Condorcet had put it a century earlier, made 'nature herself an accomplice in the crime of political inequality'.

THE GUILT OF SCIENCE

As biology became a science, so did race. The 'transition to racial science', Nancy Stepan observes, 'was part of the transition to modern biology itself.' The paradox of nineteenth-century thought is that while 'racial science was more "scientific" by the 1850s, racial science was also more "racist" – in its insistence on the permanency of racial types, and in the existence of a scale of racial worth.' This intimate relationship between the emergence of biological science, on the one hand, and of racial science, on the other, lends currency to the view that the very act of categorising the world, of applying reason to it and of viewing it through a scientific lens inevitably led to a racial perspective. Science bears the guilt of racial science, because without science there could have been no racial science; the birth of science made race possible, indeed inescapable.

Yet the relationship between race and science was far more contingent than this. What gave shape to that relationship was not the intrinsic character of science but the wider intellectual climate of the late nineteenth century. Science became racial science not because science itself was racist but because, in a particular social and political context, the science of human differences could be read – and indeed, to many, it seemed that it could *only* be read – in a racial fashion.

Take, for example, the idea of the 'facial angle', a concept introduced by the eighteenth-century Dutch painter and anatomist, Peter Camper. Camper was interested in developing a system of accurately portraying human diversity. He realised that the angle between a line drawn horizontally from the lower part of the ear to the lips, and one drawn vertically through the most prominent part of the forehead varied according to race. It was greatest among Europeans and smallest in Africans. It was smaller still for apes.

Nineteenth-century racial scientists drew deeply on the concept of the facial angle. Anthropologists distinguished between *prognathous* and *orthognathous* people, the former with protruding jaws, the latter with jaws less prominent, and established an evolutionary ladder, with Europeans at the top and Africans at the bottom, most closely resembling apes. In his influential book *The Races of Man*, published in 1885, John Beddoe, the future president of the Royal Anthropological Society, emphasised that the Irish, Welsh and the lower classes were all prognathous, while all men of genius were orthognathous. Beddoe also developed an 'Index of Nigressence' that demonstrated, among other things, that the Irish were close to Cro-Magnon Man (a prehistoric ancestor of modern Europeans, who died out around 10,000 years ago) and hence must have had links with the 'Africinoid' races.

This has led modern historians to view Camper as one of the true founders of racial science and strengthened the belief that the roots of racism lie in Enlightenment rationalism. According to one author, Camper 'determined that blacks were the missing link between the humans and apes in the great chain of being'. In fact, Camper's aim in deriving the facial angle was to demonstrate the very opposite – not the inferiority of Africans but their true humanity. Africans, he insisted, were fundamentally different to apes and should not be seen as the missing link on the evolutionary chain. 'Hold out a fraternal hand to the Negroes', Camper exhorted his fellow-Europeans, 'and recognise them as the descendants of the first man to whom we all look to as a common father'.

In any case, even in the eighteenth century, many recognised the concept of the facial angle to be shoddy science. 'Not much is to be deduced' from Camper's theory, Blumenbach wrote, because he 'has so arbitrarily and inconstantly used his two normal lines'. But bad science does not mean racial science. In the eighteenth century, Camper's shoddy science aimed to establish the humanity of Africans and to deny their closeness to apes. A century later, in a different political context, the same shoddy science was used to establish a racial hierarchy and to prove notions of racial superiority and inferiority. The question of whether a scientific argument is right or wrong, in other words, is distinct from the question of how it is used and how its results interpreted.

Just as a particular political context allowed Camper's arguments to buttress a racial view of the world, so it is a particular political context that leads many historians today to view Camper himself as standing in the tradition of racial science. We live in an age in which we have grown wary of the claims of science and reason. No age has been more penetrated by science, nor more dependent upon it. Yet no age has been more uneasy about it and felt more that the relationship with scientific knowledge is a Faustian pact. Many today are likely to sympathise with John Donne's sixteenth-century response to the new science of Galileo, Bacon and Boyle, that the 'New Philosophy calls all in doubt', leaving '... all in pieces, all coherence gone /All just supply, all Relation.' Science and reason, which the *philosophes* saw as the solutions to humanity's problems, are now more often viewed as their cause. Against this background, many have come to accept that the roots of racial science lie within the scientific method itself. The next chapters will explore how, and why, science ended up in the dock – and what are the consequences.

7

THE BURDEN OF CULTURE

G
ermany's Memorial to the Murdered Jews of Europe is extraordinary in every way. Most capital cities have monuments to their national heroes: Nelson, Lincoln, de Gaulle. Berlin commemorates its national shame: the greatest crime ever committed. The memorial was not unveiled until May 2005, some six decades after the event. Designed by the American architect Peter Eisenman, it is situated in a vast tract of no man's land between the Brandenburg Gates and the buried remains of Hitler's bunker and above the tunnels used by Goebbels. It is quite unlike what most of us imagine a memorial should look like. The structure consists of 2,711 pillars ranging in height from a few centimetres to almost five metres, forming a dense undulating grid through which visitors can wander. From a distance, the site looks like a dusky, placid ocean. As one descends on uneven, sloping ground into the memorial, the concrete blocks grow more imposing, tilt at irregular angles and street noise fades. The experience is intended to create feelings of unease and loneliness.

For Eisenman, the field of concrete was a metaphor for the Nazi regime and the mad, ordered nature of its genocide. 'The field looks like it's reasonable, lined up', he observed. 'Then you find the stones are not perfectly horizontal or vertical. There is a warping sensation. It's unsettling. It seems reasonable from the outside but when you get into it it's out of control.' According to Eisenman, the memorial 'is a warning against reason. When reason gets turned to excess, when there is too much reason, you get madness.'

'Too much reason'. The very idea that there could be an excess of reason would, for much of the past two hundred years, have struck progressive thinkers as close to madness. Even more so the idea that too much reason was a condition to be feared. But strangest of all would have seemed the notion that the madness of the Final Solution was engineered by a surfeit of reason.

The belief that too much reason is a bad thing finds its origins initially in the debate between the radical and the mainstream Enlightenment and then much more forcibly in the claims of the counter-Enlightenment. While the radical *philosophes* looked to reason to light the path to a better world, more mainstream thinkers sought a role for faith, and defenders of the *ancien regime* placed their faith in wholesome prejudice as the best guide to the good society. Later reactionary thinkers followed through the argument that reason was too dangerous to be left unleashed. In the nineteenth century, racial scientists and social Darwinists viewed instinct as ever triumphant over reason. In the twentieth, with the Nazis, unreason found its apotheosis.

Today, however, the world – not to mention reason – seems turned on its head. The architect of a monument to the abominations of Nazism suggests that, at the heart of the Holocaust, there was too much, not too little, reason. Many agree with him. The Final Solution, the eminent sociologist Zygmunt Bauman suggests, was the product, not the breakdown, of modernity. For more than six decades, Bauman's work has been steeped in the tradition of the liberal Enlightenment. Yet, he maintains, it was 'the rational world of modern civilisation that made the Holocaust thinkable.' For Bauman, 'every ingredient of the Holocaust – all those many things that rendered it possible – was normal ... in the sense of being fully in keeping with everything we know about our civilisation, its guiding spirit, its priorities, its immanent vision of the world.' According to the philosopher Herbert Marcuse – one of the intellectual gurus of the Sixties revolution – 'Concentration camps, mass exterminations, world wars and atom bombs are no "relapse into barbarism" but the unrepressed implementation of the achievements of modern science, technology and domination.'

The experience of Nazism destroyed racial science. The Allies fought the Second World War in defence of democracy against fascism, racism and tyranny. They denounced the Nazis' unspeakable crimes against humanity. In the shadow of Auschwitz, it became nigh on impossible openly to espouse belief in racial superiority. And not just belief in racial superiority. In the postwar period, the American sociologist Daniel Bell noted, the entire conservative project was exiled to the margins. Since 'World War Two had the character of a "just war" against fascism, rightwing ideologies and the individual and cultural figures associated with those causes were inevitably discredited.' After the 'preponderant reactionary influence in prewar European culture', Bell pointed out, 'no single rightwing figure retained any political credibility or influence' in the postwar era.

If the experience of Nazism laid low conservative thought, paradoxically, it also helped unstitch many of the arguments that had been central to progressive politics in the previous two centuries. The postwar world rejected racial and other reactionary theories that had their roots in the counter-Enlightenment but it also grew increasingly uncomfortable with the Enlightenment itself. Why?

Even before the war ended, the victors had turned their attention to the creation of new ideologies and institutions through which to rebuild a bruised and battered world. In 1945, the horrors of the war and the Holocaust gave birth to the United Nations, an organisation that the Allies hoped would bind together the world's nations around a set of sacrosanct principles protecting basic human rights. But many felt a need to go further: not simply to remake international relations but also to transform individual minds. So, a year after the UN was created, the United Nations Educational, Scientific and Cultural Organisation (Unesco) was born. 'Since wars begin in the minds of men', Unesco's founding constitution declared, so 'it is in the minds of men that the defences of peace must be constructed.' It added that 'A peace based exclusively upon the political and economic arrangements of governments would not be a peace which could secure the unanimous, lasting and sincere support of the peoples of the world, and peace must therefore be founded, if it is not to fail, upon the intellectual and moral solidarity of mankind.'

The first job that Unesco set itself was to fashion a new vision of humanity, distinct from that of racial science. It convened a group of scientists, under the chairmanship of the British-born American anthropologist and prominent antiracist Ashley Montagu, and charged it with producing a definitive statement on race. The first Unesco proclamation on the subject was issued on 18 July 1950. 'Scientists have reached general agreement in recognising that mankind is one: that all men belong to the same species *Homo sapiens*', it began. 'Genes responsible for hereditary differences between men are always few when compared to the whole genetic constitution of man and the vast number of genes common to all human beings regardless of the population to which they belong.' Hence 'the likenesses among men are far greater than their differences.' 'For all practical purposes', the report concluded, '"race" is not so much a biological phenomenon as a social myth.'

According to the Unesco report, scientific evidence did not 'justify the conclusion that inherited genetic differences are a major factor in producing the differences between cultures and cultural achievements of different peoples and groups.' The evidence indicated that 'the history of the cultural experience which each group has undergone is the major factor in explaining such differences.' The one trait, the report claimed 'which above all others has been at a premium in the evolution of men's mental characters has been educability, plasticity.' Plasticity of mind is a 'species characteristic of *Homo sapiens*.' Science, the report suggested, supported the dictum of Confucius that 'Men's natures are all alike, it is their habits that carry them far apart.'

Unesco Man embodied the hopes of a generation that had witnessed the most appallingly bestial behaviour that such behaviour would never be repeated. His nature reflected the political aspirations of that generation. Whereas the *Übermensch* of racial science was entirely moulded by the laws of nature, Unesco Man was a cultural being: biology played little role in his make-up. He was biologically singular but culturally plural. All humans belonged to a single race but inhabited diverse cultural and social worlds. In the postwar world, the empire of race gave way to the empire of culture. Just as race once determined every aspect of human behaviour, so now culture did the same. Unesco Man possessed a plastic mind, which could take many forms, and produce many behaviours and attitudes, depending on his particular cultural environment.

The founders of Unesco, and the creators of Unesco Man, saw themselves as standing in the tradition of the Enlightenment. They wanted not just to challenge barbarism but also to shape a new world and to create a new vision of humanity. Barbarism, they believed, derived from ignorance and prejudice. To ensure a future without another world war or a new Holocaust required cultural and moral progress. Only through education could such progress be ensured. But what began as a battle against barbarism in the name of the Enlightenment soon became a war on the Enlightenment itself. As the French philosopher, Alain Finkielkraut, has so memorably put it, 'Testifying at the trial against barbarism', Unesco came to 'identify the Enlightenment with the defence and not with the prosecution.' Racial science had treated certain peoples as superior, others as inferior. Unesco defined antiracism, therefore, as treating all peoples and all cultures with equal respect, seeing none as backward, primitive or irrational. The roots of barbarism, many believed, lay in Western arrogance and the roots of Western arrogance lay in an unquestioning belief in the superiority of Enlightenment rationalism and universalism. Unesco, Finkielkraut suggests, came to believe that, 'We would only conquer ignorance ... if we stopped trying to extend our culture to the rest of the world and accepted the idea that universalism was dead. In other words, we, the so-called civilised ones should come down from our imaginary heights and recognise with humble clarity that we were only another kind of native.'

This chapter and the next will tell the story of how the fight against barbarism turned into a war against the Enlightenment – and the consequence of this for the struggle against racism. In the next chapter, I will look at how science came to be the big bad wolf for antiracists. Before that, this chapter will tell the tale of how race was dethroned and culture came to pick up its crown.

ONE WORLD WITH MANY RACES OR ONE RACE IN MANY WORLDS?

Perhaps the most celebrated collision between scientific rationality and antiracist sensibility came in a Tennessee courtroom in 1925, when a teacher, John Scopes, was prosecuted for propagating Darwin's theory of evolution in the classroom. Leading the prosecution was America's most famous anti-Darwinist, William Jennings Bryan, whose campaigning had persuaded Tennessee to pass a law outlawing the teaching of Darwin's theory. The trial was immortalised by Hollywood in *Inherit the Wind*, which portrayed Bryan (or Brady as he is called on screen) as an ignorant, Bible-thumping, reactionary buffoon. In fact Bryan was far from ignorant and anything but a reactionary. What shaped his opposition to Darwinism was not his religious literalism (although Bryan was a Christian, he was no fundamentalist) but his search for social justice. Bryan was a left-wing Democrat of national renown, who three times ran as the Democratic presidential candidate (and three times lost). His faith and democratic instincts led to a profound suspicion of the scientific elite and of modernism. He rebelled at the suggestion that reason should be the measure of all things and held science responsible for a weakening of moral standards.

Bryan was particularly hostile to what he saw as the runaway capitalism of the turn of the century and was appalled by the wretched conditions endured by workers, conditions that were often justified by an appeal to the Darwinian struggle for existence. 'Darwinian theory', Bryan wrote, 'represents man as reaching his present perfection by the operation of the law of hate – the merciless law by which the strong crowd out and kill off the weak.' In his closing speech at the Scopes trial, he suggested that 'by paralysing the hope of reform', Darwinism 'discourages those who labor for the improvement of man's conditions.' Its 'only program for man is scientific breeding, a system under which a few supposedly superior intellects, self-appointed, would direct the mating and movements of the mass of mankind.' For Bryan, there was no way of furthering social justice without challenging Darwinism and promoting a Biblical account of human origins. There were echoes here of Wallace's argument that the mind was shaped not by natural selection but by a 'life force', an argument to which he too was led by his distaste for the racial consequences of social Darwinism.

Of course, most opponents of evolutionary theory were far from progressive. The newly-founded Ku Klux Klan was just one of many white supremacist organisations that stood four-square with God against Darwin. And not every opponent of racial science wished to roll back the gains of science and secularism. Clarence Darrow, the defence attorney in the Scopes trial, played by Spencer Tracy in *Inherit the Wind*, was, like Bryan, a radical Democrat but one for whom there could be no radicalism without Enlightenment. Nevertheless, for many individuals like Bryan, so closely identified were race and science that opposition to racial theory could only lead them to a renunciation of scientific rationality.

There is more to this story, however, than a sorry tale of antiracists being forced by circumstances to turn their backs on the modern world. The traffic moved in both directions. True, the marriage of race and science encouraged some progressives to lash out against modernity and the Enlightenment, but equally a growing disenchantment with Enlightenment ideas helped give shape to the nascent critique of racial theory. Nowhere was this more apparent than in the new anthropology that emerged, around the turn of the century, to challenge the basic tenets of racial science. At the heart of this new science were two fundamental ideas: first, that culture, not biology, was the principal force that shaped human affairs and, second, that humanity comprised a multitude of cultures that could not be ranked on an evolutionary scale but each of which had to be understood on its own terms. The new anthropology was shaped by Enlightenment views of equality; it was also shaped by a view of culture that had its roots in Romanticism and the late eighteenth-century backlash against the Enlightenment.

The Romantic idea of culture was, as we have seen, best fleshed out by Herder. Herder's notion of the *volksgeist* became transformed into the concept of racial type. Ironically, the very same notion also gave succour to the idea of culture championed by the critics of racial science at the end of the nineteenth century. Herder's defence of a plurality of cultures against the Enlightenment notion of a universal civilisation came to underlie the new anthropology.

Perhaps no figure played a greater role in easing this shift from the Enlightenment vision of civilisation to the anthropological concept of culture than the German American Franz Boas. It would be difficult to over-estimate Boas's impact, not simply on anthropology but also on our everyday perceptions of race, culture and difference.

Contemporary ideas of pluralism and multiculturalism, of respect for other cultures and of the importance of tradition and history are all significant themes in Boas's work. His legacy, however, remains ambiguous. Boas and his students, such as Edward Sapir, Ruth Benedict and Margaret Mead, who dominated twentieth-century anthropology in America, played a prominent part in the replacement of racial theories of human differences with cultural theories and in so doing helped undermine the power of scientific racism. Yet the concept of culture they helped develop to a large extent rearticulated the themes of racial theory in a different guise. Influenced both by the German Romantic tradition and by a liberal egalitarian view, the problem facing Boas, as the historian George Stocking observes, was how to define the Romantic notion of 'the genius of the people' in terms other than racial heredity. His answer, ultimately, was the anthropological concept of culture.

Born in Germany, Boas emigrated to America in 1887. As he jumped countries, so he swapped disciplines. Originally trained as a physicist, he now took up anthropology. As a physicist, Boas had made a field trip to the Arctic to study colour perception among the Inuit. He related in a letter the impact of that trip:

> I often ask myself what advantages our 'good society' possesses over that of the 'savages'. The more I see of their customs the more I realise we have no right to look down on them ... We have no right to blame them for their forms and superstitions which may seem ridiculous to us. We 'highly educated people' are much worse, relatively speaking ... As a thinking person, for me the most important result of this trip lies in the strengthening of my point of view that the idea of a 'cultured' person is merely relative.

The letter shows how much Boas's egalitarianism was shaped by his disillusionment with the values of our 'good society'. This disillusionment lay at the root of his ambivalence towards the legacy of the

Enlightenment, and in particular towards the ideas of equality, rationality and progress. The revolutionary egalitarianism that developed in the Enlightenment was positive and forward-looking. From Condorcet to Marx, such egalitarians held that social progress could overcome artificial divisions and differences and reveal our essential commonality. Boas's belief in equality arose, on the contrary, from a sense that such progress was neither fully realisable nor necessarily welcome. For Boas, no society was better, and none worse, than any other. What European or American intellectuals deemed the good life was simply one way among many of achieving social satisfaction and not inherently the best, especially for non-Europeans. Progress did not always improve a society. All too often, it made different societies more alike, which was not necessarily for the better. For Boas, human beings were equal not because social, cultural and economic differences could be overcome and all humans aspire to a common civilisation but because diverse cultures were each as good as the other. There could be no such thing as a common civilisation, only a common respect for a variety of different cultures.

'The great progress of modern thought', the French writer Ernest Renan suggested in 1891, 'has been the substitution ... of the category of the relative for the conception of the absolute.' Fellow Frenchman, Gustav LeBon, similarly believed that 'the substitution of relative ideas for abstract notions' was 'the greatest conquest of science.' Another contemporary, Hyppolite Taine, mocked the Enlightenment belief that 'men of every race and century were all but identical: the Greek, the barbarian, the Hindoo, the man of the Renaissance, and the man of the eighteenth century as if they had been turned out of a common mould, and all in conformity to a certain abstract conception, which served for the human race.' Echoing the jibe of Joseph de Maistre almost a century earlier that 'I have seen Frenchmen, Italians, Russians, and so on ... but I must say, as for *man*, I have never come across him anywhere', Taine believed that Enlightenment *philosophes*

'knew man, but not men': 'They did not know that the moral constitution of a people or an age is as particular or as distinct as the physical
structure of a family of plants or an order of animals.'

There was little of this with which Boas would have disagreed.
He too believed that the substitution of a relativist view of culture for
the abstractly universal notions of the eighteenth century was a giant
leap for humankind. He too acknowledged that we could not think of
all humans as if they were turned out of a common mould. Yet the significance that Boas drew from all this was very different from that
drawn by Renan, LeBon, Taine and de Maistre. Renan was a philologist, whose aim was to carve up humanity into a number of superior
and inferior 'linguistic races'. LeBon was a psychologist and a fervent
advocate of racial science, as was Taine. De Maistre had been a Catholic
reactionary and a supporter of the *ancien regime*. Relativism could
clearly take very different forms. Racial theory and Boas's cultural pluralism both displayed hostility to Enlightenment universalism but in
different ways. The philosopher, Ernest Gellner, has pointed out that
there are two sets of questions that arise from the debate between universalism and relativism: 'Is there but one kind of man, or are there
many? Is there but one world, or are there many?' While the first questions the biological unity of humankind, the second questions the very
idea of a single truth or objective understanding of the world.

Racial scientists believed that there was one world, inhabited by
different types of humanity. The social Darwinist, Herbert Spencer,
expressed this idea well when he explained how his views differed from
those of Enlightenment philosophers. 'In early life', he suggested, 'we
have been taught that human nature is everywhere the same ... This
error we must replace by the truth that the laws of thought are everywhere the same.' For Spencer, the same, objective social laws operated
in every society and culture but different peoples responded to these
objective laws in different ways, the nature of the response being
determined by the racial make-up of any given people.

Cultural relativists like Boas argued, on the other hand, that there was one type of humanity but it inhabited different realms. They denied that there was a common, objective, way of understanding the world and suggested instead that there were many ways of conceiving and evaluating the world, each of which was as valid as any other. Since the social world is constructed by the people who inhabit that society, not given in nature, so every world is specific to the people who dwell in it and incommensurate with the social realms in which other people dwell.

Nineteenth-century racial theorists, for all their disdain of universalist ideas, nevertheless maintained a belief in the idea of reason as a weapon of social transformation and of social progress as the companion of a teleological history. Given this belief in inevitable social progress, the growing gulf between 'civilised man' and the 'primitives' that was evident both within and without European society led many to see such differences in natural, and hence in racial, terms. Racial scientists presented a hierarchical view of humanity, seeing different groups of peoples as arrested at different point along the evolutionary scale and believing that progress and reason were the prerogative only of certain races.

The new anthropology of culture, on the other hand, reflected a disenchantment with the notion of social evolution, a disbelief in the doctrine of inevitable social progress and a disillusionment with the values of one's own culture. It was the emergence of such trends in the early part of the twentieth century, in particular in the wake of the First World War, that gave rise to relativist theories of culture. In the context of a general pessimism about social progress, the idea of difference was transformed from the notion of 'many men in a single world' to a 'single type of man inhabiting many worlds'. If social development had not overcome the vast gulfs that separated different peoples, many argued, perhaps that was because such differences reflected the fact that distinct peoples inhabited distinct social worlds, each of which was as valid and as real as the other.

CULTURE GOES FORTH AND MULTIPLIES

Franz Boas did not simply help mould a new concept of culture (albeit one that had already been given form by the Romantics); he also helped produce a new generation of anthropologists who extended and entrenched the cultural revolution. By the early decades of the twentieth century, the notion of culture had been transformed and, in the process, so had the notions both of human nature and of human differences.

Enlightenment thinkers had seen human beings as conscious, creative subjects, constantly making and remaking the world around them. In the hands of nineteenth-century social evolutionists this argument had become a rationale for race. Some societies were more advanced than others because some peoples were naturally more creative than others. Cultural anthropologists tackled the racist logic of the social evolutionists by downgrading the creative aspects of humanity. Human beings were, in their eyes, essentially uninventive. Human creativity was expressed not in independent invention but in the manipulation and reinterpretation of elements given to them by their cultural tradition or borrowed from other cultural traditions.

For Enlightenment *philosophes*, and especially for the radicals, the application of reason to social problems helped dissolve human differences and ensured that even those considered 'primitive' could enter the highest reaches of civilisation. This was the transformative content of Enlightenment universalism. For twentieth-century anthropologists, however, customs, rituals and habits were of vital importance in the maintenance of societies. Culture was synonymous not so much with conscious activity as with unconscious tradition. History and tradition moulded an individual's behaviour to such an extent that, in the words of Boas, 'we cannot remodel, without serious emotional resistance, any of the fundamental lines of thought and action that are determined by early education, and which form the subconscious basis of all our activities.' Learned 'less by instruction than imitation', cultural mores 'constitute the whole series of well-established habits according to which the necessary actions of everyday life are transformed.' According to Boas's student, Ruth Benedict, people 'are shaped to the form of their culture because of the malleability of their original endowment.' Hence 'the great mass of individuals takes quite readily the form that is presented to them.' Humans, in other words, are uninventive, easily-manipulated creatures whose very plasticity (the aspect of humanity that once expressed their ability to be creative and independent) allows their behaviour to be moulded along cultural lines. As another anthropologist, Leslie White, put it, the individual far from being 'the initiator and determinant of the culture process' is but 'a tiny and relatively insignificant part ... of a vast sociocultural system that embraces innumerable individuals at any one time and extends back to their remote past as well.' Humans do not make cultures, cultures make humans. An individual cannot escape the force of destiny imposed by his culture and history. 'The idea of culture', observes George Stocking, 'which once connoted all that freed men from the blind weight of tradition, was now identified with that very burden, and that burden was seen as functional to the continuing daily existence of individuals in any culture and at every level of civilisation.' Culture, like race, governed our very being.

This new vision of culture, and of human nature, swept all before it. By the second half of the twentieth century, culture had emerged triumphant and with it came a new sense of what it meant to be human, a sense that was embodied in Unesco Man. But it was a peculiar kind of triumph. Unesco Man did not emerge victorious after a hand-to-hand combat with the *Übermensch* of racial theory, or any kind of combat at all. The replacement of racial theories by cultural theories was not a case of a set of well-substantiated theories being unambiguously disproved and overturned by new and conclusive evidence. Rather, one set of ill-formed assumptions about human nature and human differences gave way and allowed another set of barely better-formed assumptions to hold sway.

A complex series of social and political factors emerged in the early part of the twentieth century that weakened the power of racial theories and eventually destroyed it entirely. The rising power of Japan, dramatically illustrated by its military defeat of Russia in 1905 (a defeat that all regarded as a white power being humiliated by a non-white one), helped undermine the idea of an inherent white superiority. The growing revolt in the colonies and the rise of what came to be called Third World nationalism seemed to symbolise the weakening hold of Europe and America over the rest of the world. Growing rivalries between the imperialist powers, and in particular the horrors of the First World War, led to the break up of the so-called 'white consensus'. Scientific advances helped interrogate many of the assumptions of racial theory, while the opening up of academia to what had up till then been marginal influences – Jewish and women scholars, for instance – created a more tolerant climate that was less conducive to racial argument. What finally catalysed the destruction of scientific racism, however, was the implementation of racial theories in Nazi Germany.

When the Nazis seized power in 1933, they proceeded to put into practice many of the theories of scientific racism. The eugenics movement, both in Britain and the USA, initially greeted Hitler's project with interest and even enthusiasm but as the full horror of Nazi practices, from mass sterilisation to the concentration camps, became clear, so the clamour of opposition to racial thinking grew. Following the experience of Nazism, the Holocaust and the Final Solution, biological theories of human differences became discredited. But if racial science was buried in the postwar world, racial thinking was not. While the biological arguments for racial superiority were thrown into disrepute and overt expressions of racism were discredited, many of the assumptions of racial thinking were maintained intact – in particular the belief that humanity can be divided into discrete groups, that each group should be considered on its own terms and that differences, not commonalities, shaped human interaction. These assumptions were cast, however, not in biological terms but in the language of cultural pluralism. The new anthropological concept of culture, George Stocking has noted, 'provided a functionally equivalent substitute for the older idea of "race temperament"':

> It explained all the same phenomena, but it did so in strictly non-biological terms... All that was necessary to make the adjustment ... was the substitution of a word. For 'race' read 'culture' or 'civilisation', for 'racial heredity' read 'cultural heritage', and the change had taken place.

Cultural anthropology knocked down the evolutionary ladder of Victorian racial theory but it did not dispense with it entirely; it simply turned it on its side. Anthropologists now saw humanity as horizontally, rather than vertically, segmented. Human beings were not arranged at different points on an ever-rising vertical axis, as the social evolutionists had believed, but at different points along a stationary, horizontal, axis. Humanity was composed of a multitude of peoples, each inhabiting its own symbolic and social world. Dispossessed of faith in evolutionary progress, the new breed of anthropologists envisioned society, and social differences, in a relatively static fashion. But envision it in terms of difference they did. The empire of culture, unlike the empire of race, was not hierarchically ordered but difference still sat on the throne.

FROM RACIAL TYPE TO CULTURAL IDENTITY

The anthropologist Margaret Mead once observed that in the 1930s, when she, like many of Boas's students, was busy remaking the idea of culture, the notion of cultural diversity was to be found only in the 'vocabulary of a small and technical group of professional anthropologists.' Today, everyone and everything seems to have its own culture. From anorexia to zydeco, the American philosopher Kwame Anthony Appiah has observed, there is little that we don't talk about as the product of some group's culture. In this age of globalisation, many people fret about Western culture taking over the world. But the greatest Western export is not Disney or McDonald's or Tom Cruise. It is the very idea of culture. Every island in the Pacific, every tribe in the Amazon, has its own culture that it wants to defend against the depredations of Western cultural imperialism. You do not even have to be human to possess a culture. Primatologists tell us that many different groups of chimpanzees have their own unique culture. No doubt some chimp will soon complain that their traditions are disappearing under the steamroller of human cultural imperialism.

We're All Multiculturalists Now observes the American academic, and former critic of pluralism, Nathan Glazer, in the title of a book. Ironically, though, culture has captured the popular imagination just as anthropologists themselves have started worrying about the very concept. After all, what exactly is a culture? What marks its boundaries? In what way is a sixteen-year-old British-born boy of Pakistani origin living in Bradford of the same culture as a fifty-year-old man living in Lahore? Does a sixteen-year-old white boy from Bradford have more in common culturally with his fifty-year-old father than with that sixteen-year-old 'Asian'? Such questions have led most anthropologists today to reject the idea of cultures as fixed, bounded entities. Some reject the very idea of culture as meaningless. 'Religious beliefs, rituals, knowledge, moral values, the arts, rhetorical genres, and so on', the eminent British anthropologist Adam Kuper suggests, 'should be separated out from each other rather than bound together into a single bundle labelled culture'. 'To understand culture', he concludes, 'we must first deconstruct it.'

Whatever the doubts of anthropologists, politicians and political philosophers press on regardless. The idea of culture, and especially of multiculturalism, has proved politically too seductive. Over the past two decades, nations such as Australia, Canada and South Africa have created legal frameworks to institutionalise their existence as multicultural societies. Other countries, such as Britain, make no formal recognition of their multicultural status but have nevertheless pursued pluralist policies in a pragmatic fashion. Even France, whose republican tradition might seem to be the nemesis of multiculturalism, has flirted with pluralist policies. In 1986, the *Collège de France* presented the President with a report entitled *Proposals for the Education of the Future*. The first of ten principles to which modern schools should subscribe was 'The unity of science and the plurality of cultures':

> A carefully fabricated system of education must be able to integrate the universalism inherent in scientific thought with the relativism of the social sciences, that is with disciplines attentive to the significance of cultural differences among people and to the ways people live, think and feel.

Contemporary multiculturalism marries the Romantic idea of culture, which we have discussed, to an equally Romantic idea of identity. 'There is a certain way of being human that is *my* way', wrote the Canadian philosopher Charles Taylor in his much-discussed essay on *The Politics of Recognition*. 'I am called upon to live my life in this way ... Being true to myself means being true to my own originality'. This sense of being 'true to myself' Taylor calls 'the ideal of "authenticity"'. The ideal of the authentic self finds its origins in the Romantic notion of the inner voice that expresses a person's true nature. The concept was developed in the 1950s, by psychologists such as Erik Erikson and sociologists like Alvin Gouldner, into the modern notion of identity. Identity, they pointed out, is not just a private matter but emerges in dialogue with others.

Increasingly, identity came to be seen not as something the self creates but as something through which the self is created. Identity is, in the sociologist Stuart Hall's words, 'formed and transformed continuously in relation to the ways in which we are represented or addressed in the cultural systems which surround us.' The inner self finds its home in the outer world by participating in a collective; but not just any collective. The world comprises countless groups – philosophers, truck drivers, football supporters, drinkers, train-spotters, conservatives, communists and so on. According to the modern idea of identity, each person's sense of who they truly are is intimately linked to only a few special categories – collectives defined by sex, sexuality, religion, race and, in particular, culture. A Unesco-organised 'World Conference on Cultural Policies' concluded that 'cultural identity ... was at the core of individual and collective personality, the vital principle that underlay the most authentic decisions, behaviour and actions'.

The collectives that appear significant to the contemporary sense of identity comprise very different kinds of groups and the members of each are bound together by very different characteristics. Nevertheless, what collectives such as sex, sexuality, religion, race and culture have in common is that each is defined by a set of attributes that, whether rooted in biology, faith or history, is fixed in a certain sense and compels people to act in particular ways. Identity is that which is given, whether by nature, God or one's ancestors. 'I am called upon to live my life in this way'. Who or what does the calling? Apparently culture itself. Unlike politically-defined collectives, these collectives are, in the philosopher John Gray's words, 'ascriptive, not elective ... a matter of fate, not choice.' The collectives that are important to the contemporary notion of identity are, in other words, the modern equivalents of what Herder defined as *volks*. For individual identity to be authentic, so too must collective identity. 'Just like individuals', Charles Taylor writes, 'a *Volk* should be true to itself, that is its own culture.' To be true to itself, a culture must faithfully pursue the traditions that mark out that culture as unique and rebuff the advances of modernity, pragmatism and other cultures.

This view of culture and identity has transformed the way that many people understand the relationship between equality and difference. For the Enlightenment *philosophes*, equality required that the state should treat all citizens in the same fashion without regard to their race, religion or culture. This was at the heart of their arguments against the *ancien regime* and has been an important strand of liberal and radical thought ever since. Contemporary multiculturalists argue to the contrary that people should be treated not equally despite their differences, but differently because of them. 'Justice between groups', as the political philosopher Will Kymlicka has put it, 'requires that members of different groups are accorded different rights'.

An individual's cultural background frames their identity and helps define who they are. If we want to treat individuals with dignity and respect, many multiculturalists argue, we must also treat with dignity and respect the groups that furnish them with their sense of personal being. 'The liberal is in theory committed to equal respect for persons', the philosopher Bhikhu Parekh argues. 'Since human beings are culturally embedded, respect for them entails respect for their cultures and ways of life.' The British sociologist, Tariq Modood, takes this line of argument to make a distinction between what he calls the 'equality of individualism' and 'equality encompassing public ethnicity: equality as not having to hide or apologise for one's origins, family or community, but requiring others to show respect for them, and adapt public attitudes and arrangements so that the heritage they represent is encouraged rather than contemptuously expect them to wither away.' We cannot, in other words, treat individuals equally unless groups are also treated equally. Since, in the words of the American scholar, Iris Young, 'groups cannot be socially equal unless their specific experience, culture and social contributions are publicly affirmed and recognized', so society must protect and nurture cultures, to ensure their flourishing and indeed their survival.

One expression of such equal treatment is the growing tendency in some Western nations for religious law – such as the Jewish *halakha* and the Islamic *sharia* – to take precedence over national secular law in civil, and occasionally criminal, cases. Another expression can be found in Australia, where the courts increasingly accept that Aborigines should have the right to be treated according to their own customs rather than be judged by 'whitefella law'. According to Colin McDonald, a Darwin barrister and an expert in customary law, 'Human rights are essentially a creation of the last hundred years. These people have been carrying out their law for thousands of years.' Some multiculturalists go further, requiring the state to ensure the survival of cultures not just in the present but in perpetuity. Charles Taylor, for instance, suggests that the Canadian and Quebec governments should take steps to ensure the survival of the French language in Quebec 'through indefinite future generations'.

The demand that because a cultural practice has existed for a long time, so it should be preserved, is a modern version of the naturalistic fallacy, the belief that *ought* derives from *is*. For nineteenth-century social Darwinists, morality – how we ought to behave – derived from the facts of nature: how humans are. This became an argument to justify capitalist exploitation, colonial oppression, racial savagery and even genocide. Today, virtually everyone recognises the falsity of this argument. Yet, when talking of culture rather than of nature, many multiculturalists continue to insist that *is* defines *ought*.

There is, in any case, something deeply inauthentic about the contemporary demand for authenticity. The kinds of cultures that the Enlightenment *philosophes* wanted to consign to history were, in an important sense, different from the kinds of cultures that today's multiculturalists wish to preserve. In the pre-modern world there was no sense of cultural integrity or authenticity. There were no alternatives to the ways of life that people followed. Cultures were traditional but in an unselfconscious fashion. Those who lived in such cultures were not aware of their difference, let alone that they should value it or claim it as a right. A French peasant attended Church and an American Indian warrior painted his face not because they thought 'This is my culture, I must preserve it' but for pragmatic reasons. As the political philosopher Brian Barry suggests, in the absence of some compelling reason for doing things differently, people went on doing them in the same way as they had in the past. Cultural inertia preserved traditional ways because it was the easiest way to organise collective life.

Multiculturalists, on the other hand, exhibit a self-conscious desire to preserve cultures. Such 'self-consciousness traditionalism', as Brian Barry calls it, is a peculiarly modern, post-Enlightenment, phenomenon. In the modern view, traditions are to be preserved not for pragmatic reasons but because such preservation is a social, political and moral good. Maintaining the integrity of a culture binds societies together, lessens social dislocation and allows the individuals who belong to that culture to flourish. Such individuals can thrive only if they stay true to their culture – in other words, only if both the individual and the culture remain authentic.

Modern multiculturalism seeks self-consciously to yoke people to their identity for their own good, the good of that culture and the good of society. A clear example is the attempt of the *Québécois* authorities to protect French culture. The Quebec government has passed laws which forbid French speakers and immigrants from sending their children to English-language schools, compel businesses with more than fifty employees to be run in French and ban commercial signs in English. If your ancestors were French you too must, by government fiat, speak French, whatever your personal wishes may be. Charles Taylor regards this as acceptable because the flourishing and survival of French culture is a good. 'It is not just a matter of having the French language available for those who might choose it', he argues. Quebec is 'making sure that there is a community of people here in the future that will want to avail itself of the opportunity to use the French language.' Its policies 'actively seek to *create* members of the community ... assuring that future generations continue to identify as French-speakers.'

An identity has become a bit like a private club. Once you join up, you have to abide by the rules. But unlike the Groucho or the Garrick it's a private club you *must* join. Being black or gay, the philosopher Kwame Anthony Appiah suggests, requires one to follow certain 'life-scripts' because 'Demanding respect for people as blacks and gays can go along with notably rigid strictures as to how one is to be an African American or a person with same-sex desires.' There will be 'proper modes of being black and gay: there will be demands that are made; expectations to be met; battle lines to be drawn.' It is at this point, Appiah suggests, that 'someone who takes autonomy seriously may worry whether we have replaced one kind of tyranny with another.' An identity is supposed to be an expression of an individual's authentic self but it can too often seem like the denial of individual agency in the name of cultural authenticity.

'It is in the interest of every person to be fully integrated in a cultural group', the sociologist Joseph Raz has written. But what is to be fully integrated? If a Muslim woman rejects *sharia* law, is she demonstrating her lack of integration? What about a Jew who doesn't believe in the legitimacy of the Jewish State? Or a French *Québécois* who speaks only English? Would Galileo have challenged the authority of the Church if he had been 'fully integrated' into his culture? Or Thomas Paine have supported the French Revolution? Or Salman Rushdie written *The Satanic Verses*? Cultures only change and societies only move forwards because many people, in Anthony Appiah's words, 'actively resist being fully integrated into a group'. To them 'integration can sound like regulation, even restraint'. Far from giving a voice to the voiceless, the politics of difference appears to undermine individual autonomy, reduce liberty and enforce conformity. You will speak French, you will act gay, don't rock the cultural boat. The alternatives, Alain Finkielkraut suggests, are simple: 'Either people have rights or they have uniforms; either they can legitimately free themselves from oppression ... or else their culture has the last word.'

Part of the problem is a constant slippage in multiculturalism talk between the idea of humans as culture-bearing creatures and the idea that humans have to bear a *particular* culture. Clearly, no human can live outside of culture. But then no human does. 'It's not easy to imagine a person, or people, bereft of culture', observes Anthony Appiah. 'The problem with grand claims for the necessity of culture', he adds, 'is that we can't readily imagine an alternative. It's like *form*: you can't not have it.' Culture, in other words, is like oxygen: no living human can do without it, but no living human does.

To say that no human can live outside of culture is not to say that they have to live inside a *particular* one. Nor is it to say that particular cultures must be fixed or eternal. To view humans as culture-bearing is to view them as social beings and hence as transformative beings. It suggests that humans have the capacity for change, for progress and for the creation of universal moral and political forms through reason and dialogue. To view humans as having to bear specific cultures is, on the contrary, to deny such a capacity for transformation. It suggests that every human being is so shaped by a particular culture that to change or undermine that culture would be to undermine the very dignity of that individual. It suggests that the biological fact of, say, Jewish or Bangladeshi ancestry somehow makes a human being incapable of living well except as a participant in Jewish or Bangladeshi culture. This would only make sense if Jews or Bangladeshis were biologically distinct – in other words if cultural identity was really about racial difference.

The relationship between cultural identity and racial difference becomes even clearer if we look at the argument that cultures must be protected and preserved. If a 'culture is decaying', the sociologists Avishai Margalit and Joseph Raz argue, then 'the options and opportunities open to its members will shrink, become less attractive, and their pursuit less likely to be successful.' So society must step in prevent such decay. Will Kymlicka similarly argues that since cultures are essential to peoples' lives, so where 'the survival of a culture is not guaranteed, and, where it is threatened with debasement or decay, we must act to protect it.' For Charles Taylor, once 'we're concerned with identity', nothing 'is more legitimate than one's aspiration that it is never lost'. Hence a culture needs to be protected not just in the here and now but through 'indefinite future generations'.

A century ago, intellectuals worried about the degeneration of the race. Today we fear cultural decay. Is the notion of cultural decay any more coherent than that of racial degeneration? Cultures certainly change and develop. But what does it mean for a culture to decay? Or for an identity to be lost? Will Kymlicka draws a distinction between the 'existence of a culture' and 'its "character" at any given moment'. The character of culture can change but such changes are acceptable only if the existence of that culture is not threatened. But how can a culture exist if that existence is not embodied in its character? By 'character' Kymlicka seems to mean the actuality of a culture: what people do, how they live their lives, the rules, regulations and institutions that frame their existence. In making the distinction between character and existence, Kymlicka seems to be suggesting that Jewish, Navajo or French culture is not defined by what Jewish, Navajo or French people are actually doing, for if Jewish culture is simply that which Jewish people do or French culture is simply that which French people do, then cultures could never decay or perish — they would always exist in the activities of people.

If a culture is not defined by what its members are doing, what does define it? The only answer can be that it is defined by what its members *should* be doing. The African American writer, Richard

Wright, described one of his finest creations, Bigger Thomas, the hero of *Native Son*, as a man 'bereft of a culture'. The Negro, Wright suggested, 'possessed a rich and complex culture when he was brought to these alien shores' but that culture was 'taken from him'. Bigger Thomas's ancestors had been enslaved. In the process of enslavement they had been torn from their ancestral homes and forcibly deprived of the practices and institutions that they understood as their culture. Hence Bigger Thomas, and every black American, behaved very differently from his ancestors. Slavery was an abomination and clearly had a catastrophic impact on black Americans. But however inhuman the treatment of slaves, and however deep its impact on black American life, why should this amount to a descendant of slaves being 'bereft of a culture' or having a culture 'taken from him'? This can only be if we believe that Bigger Thomas *should* be behaving in certain ways that he isn't, the ways that his ancestors used to behave. If we believe that, what defines what you should be doing is the fact that your ancestors were doing it. Culture becomes defined by biological descent; and biological descent is a polite way of saying 'race'. As the cultural critic Walter Benn Michaels puts it, 'In order for a culture to be lost ... it must be separable from one's actual behaviour, and in order for it to be separable from one's actual behaviour it must be anchorable in race.'

The logic of the preservationist argument is that every culture has a pristine form, its original state. It decays when it is no longer in that form. Like racial scientists, with their idea of racial type, some modern multiculturalists appear to hold a belief in cultural type. For racial scientists, as we saw in Chapter 5, a 'type' was a group of human beings linked by a set of fundamental characteristics unique to it. Each type was separated from others by a sharp discontinuity; there was rarely any doubt as to which type an individual belonged. Each type remained constant through time. There were severe limits to how much any member of a type could drift away from the fundamental ground plan by which the type was constituted. These are the very

characteristics that constitute a culture in much of today's multiculturalism talk. Many multiculturalists, like racial scientists, have come
to think of human types as fixed, unchanging entities, each defined by
its special essence.

In a debate on immigration and integration, the political
philosopher Sir Bernard Crick, chair of the official Crick committee on
British citizenship, wrote that he 'would accept ... gladly' the description of multiculturalism as a society 'composed of a small number of
organic cultures dancing around each other'. Multiculturalism, in
other words, is driven by a concept of 'cultural type'. For all the talk
about culture as fluid and changing, multiculturalism invariably leads
people to think of human cultures in fixed terms. Indeed, it is difficult
to imagine how multicultural policy could conceive of cultures in any
other way. How could rights be accorded to cultures, or cultures be
recognised or preserved, if they did not possess rigid boundaries?

THE TRIUMPH OF HERDER

The irony is that we've all become multiculturalists at the very time
the world is becoming less, not more, plural. The politics of difference
suggests that societies, particularly Western societies, used to be
homogenous but have become plural, thanks largely to immigration.
It is a questionable claim. 'When I was a child', the Ghanaian-born
American philosopher, Anthony Appiah, recalls, 'we lived in a household where you could hear at least three mother tongues spoken each
day. Ghana, with a population close to that of New York State, has several dozen languages in active use and no one language that is spoken
at home – or even fluently understood – by a majority of the population.' So why, he asks, in America 'which seems so much less diverse
than most other societies are we so preoccupied with diversity and
inclined to conceive of it as cultural?'

The proportion of foreign-born Americans is far lower now than it was at the beginning of the twentieth century. Intermarriage between immigrant groups is ever-increasing. Between 1960 and 1980, the number of inter-racial couples rose by 535 per cent. Japanese Americans marry 'out' at the astonishing rate of sixty-five per cent, while seventy per cent of Native Americans marry non-Native Americans. Even among African Americans 'outmarriage' is rising; in 1986, outside of the South, ten per cent of married black men were married to white women, up from 3.9 per cent in 1968. Fewer and fewer Americans live in neighbourhoods with people who share their 'national' origins. More than ninety-seven per cent of Americans speak English. Even among Hispanics, the one ethnic group defined by language, the proportion of non-English speakers is a quarter of what it was in 1890. As for the children of first generation Hispanic migrants, only half speak Spanish at all.

Compare this to the America of the 1920s. Then, new immigrants did not simply speak their own language, they also read their own newspapers, ate their own food and lived their own lives. In 1923, the Polish community alone published sixty-seven weekly newspapers, eighteen monthlies and nineteen dailies, the largest of which had a circulation of more than a hundred thousand. Today, not just language but the shopping mall, the sports field, the Hollywood film and the TV sitcom all serve to bind differences and create a set of experiences and cultural practices that is more common than at any time in the past. Indeed, before today's immigrants set foot on US soil they are probably more American than previous generations of Americans. Even immigrants from non-European countries are, as the sociologist Dennis Wrong suggests, 'probably less unfamiliar with the major features of the society than were, say, South Italian or Slavic peasants in the late nineteenth or early twentieth centuries.'

Much the same is true of Europe. Victorian Britain, as we saw in the previous chapter, viewed the working class and rural poor as the racial Other. The social and cultural differences between a Victorian gentleman and a farmhand or machinist were probably greater than those between a native white Briton and a second generation African-Caribbean or Asian today. Indeed, a sixty-something white Briton and a twenty-something white Briton would probably find each other more culturally alien than they would an Asian or an African Caribbean of their own generation. In France, there were proportionately more immigrants in the 1930s than there are today. Even though most of those migrants came from just across the border – from Italy, Spain and Portugal – they were considered culturally distinct and often unassimilable. On the other hand, North Africans, who today are seen as alien as Southern Europeans were a century ago, have intimately shaped French youth culture and have in turn been shaped by French mores.

Why is it that on both sides of the Atlantic we have become obsessed by cultural differences at the very time that real cultural differences have less and less meaning in our lives? If the empire of culture first established itself by filling the hole left by the demise of race, its recent expansion has been made possible by the even bigger hole left by the demise of politics. Ever since the French Revolution, there has been a widespread belief that through the application of reason, human activities and organisation can lead us to the good life. This belief has been enshrined in two very different forms of the progressive ideal: the liberalism rooted in the works of John Locke and John Stuart Mill and in the American *Declaration of Independence* and the French *Declaration of the Rights of Man,* and the revolutionary currents that flowed first out of the Radical Enlightenment and subsequently from Marxism. Both believed in humanism, the idea that human beings could rationally transform society through the agency of their own efforts. Both also embraced universalist principles; liberals and radicals alike accepted that there were values, practices and institutions that were the best for all humans. There were, of course, fierce disagreements about how society should be transformed and what those values, practices and institutions should be. Nevertheless, both liberals and Marxists held fast to Enlightenment ideas of commonality as the basis of social transformation and both argued that social divisions could be overcome through progress. By the end of the nineteenth century, however, many liberals had come to despair of any such transformation and were drifting over to the long-held conservative belief that inequalities were both necessary and inevitable. By the mid-point of the twentieth century, the experience of Nazism and the defeat of working-class movements had led many radicals also to abandon their faith in the ideas of commonality and progress.

Postwar radicals asked themselves why it was that Germany, a nation with deep philosophical roots in the Enlightenment project, and a strong and vibrant working-class movement, should succumb so quickly and so completely to Nazism. The answer seemed to be that it was the character of Enlightenment rationalism itself and the nature of democratic politics that had given rise to such barbarism. As Theodor Adorno and Max Horkheimer, members of the 'Frankfurt School' of radical German scholars, put it in their seminal work *Dialectic of Enlightenment*, 'Enlightenment is totalitarian'. Adorno and Horkheimer did not reject the Enlightenment in its entirety but they saw it as not only lighting the way to emancipation but also as enabling the darkness of the Holocaust. The idea that there was a direct line from the Enlightenment to the death camps became a central tenet of postwar thought. 'All the tragedies we have lived through', the anthropologist Claude Lévi-Strauss argued, 'first with colonialism, then with fascism, finally the concentration camps, all this has taken shape not in opposition to or in contradiction with so-called humanism in the form in which we have been practising it for several centuries but, I would say, almost its natural continuation.'

Postwar radicals became not only disenchanted with the ideas of rationalism and humanism but disillusioned too with the possibilities of social transformation. Even those who clung to Marxism despaired of the working class as an agency of change and despaired, indeed, of democracy itself. As the historian Stuart Hughes observes in *The Sea Change*, a wonderfully lucid study of postwar intellectual thought, there was within the radical intelligentsia a widespread 'disappointment in the course of recent history, in the strategy of the political parties that laid claim to the inheritance of Marx and, most particularly, in the proletariat itself. The class that Engels had celebrated as the "heirs of classical philosophy" had failed to perform in the style expected of it.'

Both these themes – wariness about Enlightenment rationalism and disenchantment with traditional class politics – were at the heart of the 'New Left' that emerged in the 1960s. The New Left was a loose association of disparate groups and individuals that was self-consciously opposed to the 'old left' of the Communist Parties and trades unions. Where the old left looked to the working class as the agency of revolutionary change, the New Left found new, surrogate proletariats in the so-called New Social Movements – Third World liberation struggles, civil rights organisations, feminist groups, campaigns for gay rights and the peace movement. Where the old left talked of class and sought to raise class consciousness, the New Left talked of culture and sought to strengthen cultural identity. This new idea of culture borrowed heavily from the old idea of culture fashioned in the Romantic counter-Enlightenment. Every group, whether Cuban peasants, black Americans or women, came to be seen as possessing a specific culture, rooted in its particular history and experiences. That culture gave shape to an individual's identity. In modern capitalist society, it was all too easy to assume false identities, seduced as people were by progress and consumerism. Both individual and collective identity had to be authentic, to possess what the black power activist Julius Lester called a people's 'soul'.

Romanticism was born in the late eighteenth century, partly out of the fear of the radical change and instability unleashed by the Enlightenment, and in particular by the French Revolution, and partly also out of the desire for the safe anchor of ancient traditions and established authority. In the late twentieth century, it was the fading of the possibilities of social transformation that led many radicals, albeit unwittingly, back to a Romantic view of the world. The debate between the 'old left' and the New Left was ostensibly about which group or groups should constitute the agency of change. In reality, as the cultural critic James Heartfield has pointed out, the so-called 'agency debate' expressed the beginnings of disenchantment with the very idea of agency and indeed of social transformation.

The New Left's debt to Romanticism came initially through the idea of self-organisation, a concept that emerged from the struggle for black rights in the USA. In the 1960s, black America was squeezed between an intensely racist society on one hand and, on the other, a left largely indifferent to its plight. The language of commonality hid the truth of racism. 'I am from America', Malcolm X said. 'But I am not an American.' He was, he said, 'one of the victims of America, one of the victims of Americanism, one of the victims of democracy'. It is a sentiment that echoed the despair of postwar radicals. Enlightenment humanism, Jean-Paul Sartre wrote in a famous preface to Frantz Fanon's revolutionary manifesto *The Wretched of the Earth*, 'is nothing but an ideology of lies, a perfect justification for pillage; its honeyed words, its affectations of sensibility were only alibis for our aggression.'

Many activists argued that African Americans must take matters into their own hands. They ceded from integrated civil rights organisations and set up separate black groups. It was the birth of Black Power, a phrase coined by Stokely Carmichael in 1966. Black self-organisation soon gave way to the idea of black identity. Blacks had to organise separately, not as a political strategy, but as a cultural necessity. 'In Africa they speak of Negritude', wrote Julius Lester. 'It is the recognition of those things uniquely ours which separate ourselves from the white man.'

Soon not just blacks but everyone had an identity that was uniquely theirs and separated them not only from the white man but from every other kind of man, too, and indeed from Man in general. Using the template established by Black Power activists, Native Americans, Puerto Ricans, Chicanos, Chinese Americans, not to mention myriad white ethnics, set up their separate cultural organisations. Women and gays became surrogate ethnics, each with their own particular cultures, identities and ways of thinking. 'The demand is not for inclusion within the fold of "universal humankind" on the basis of shared human attributes; nor is it for respect "in spite of one's differences"', wrote the feminist and sociologist, Sonia Kruks. 'Rather, what is demanded is respect for oneself *as* different.' At the heart of the new politics of identity was the claim that one's political beliefs and ways of thinking should be derived from the fact of one's birth, sex or ethnic origins, a claim that, historically, radicals would have regarded as highly reactionary and that lay at the heart of racial ideology. Yet by the end of the 1960s, it was not the expression of identity but the language of commonality that, as American cultural critic Todd Gitlin observes, 'came to be perceived by the new movements as a colonialist smothering – an ideology to rationalise white dominance.'

Social and political developments over the next two decades helped entrench such ideas. The collapse of both social democratic and Stalinist parties, the demise of Third World national liberation movements, the transformation of many Third World countries into tyrannies and dictatorships and, finally, the end of the Cold War – all added to the belief that social transformation was a chimera and that, in the words of Margaret Thatcher, 'There is no alternative' to capitalism or to liberal democracy. By the last decades of the century, the fire of ideological battle was all but extinguished. For the first time since the

French Revolution, politics became less about competing visions of the kind of society people wanted than a debate about how best to run the society they already inhabited. All that was left was the sense of difference that, as Todd Gitlin observes, had become 'a whole way of experiencing the world'.

As the meaning of politics narrowed, so people began to view themselves and their social affiliations in a different way. Social solidarity became increasingly defined not in political terms – as collective action in pursuit of certain political ideals – but in terms of ethnicity or culture. The question people asked themselves was not so much 'What kind of society do I want to live in?' as 'Who are we?'. The first question looked forward for answers and defined them in terms of the commonality of values necessary for establishing a progressive society; the second generally looked back and sought answers – and defined identity – in terms of history and heritage. While the first question celebrated human agency and asked how humans can shape their own future, the second embodied a desiccated view of agency, seeing humans, in the anthropologist Leslie White's words, not as 'the initiator and determinant of the culture process' but as 'a tiny and relatively insignificant part of a vast socio-cultural system'. Identity, as the philosopher John Gray put it, is 'a matter of fate, not choice.'

As hope of social transformation ebbed away, the spectre of the past acquired greater power than the visions of the future and the politics of ideology gave way to the politics of identity. Stripped of a radical idiom, Russell Jacoby observes, robbed of a Utopian hope, radicals retreated 'to celebrate diversity'. With few ideas on how a future should be shaped, they embraced all ideas. Multiculturalism, Jacoby concludes 'has become the opium of disillusioned intellectuals, the ideology of an era without ideology.'

The irony of multiculturalism is that both sides of the race debate have their own dialect of difference. The right has appropriated the language of diversity to promote its message of racial exclusion.

Liberals often turn to the idiom of exclusion to articulate a pluralist idea of culture.

'Every society, every nation is unique', claimed Enoch Powell, the most vocal opponent of black immigration in postwar Britain. 'It has its own past, its own story, its own memories, its own languages or ways of speaking, its own – dare I use the word – culture.' This is why, he argued, immigrants, who belong to different cultures and different traditions, could never fully be British. In France, similar ideas have gained currency. 'It is because we respect ourselves and others', Pierre Pascal, a leading right-wing thinker contends, 'that we refuse to see our country transformed into a multi-racial society in which each group loses their specificity'. For more than two decades, French reactionaries have astutely exploited the right to maintain cultural differences by asserting the right of the French to maintain their cultural identity. Muslims, they maintain, belong to a different culture and tradition and hence do not belong in France. 'It is a tragic mistake to want to have communities representing different civilisations live together in the same country', argues the former Gaulist minister Michel Poniatowski. 'Confrontations are inevitable. The conflicts are not about race but about systems of belief and cultures.' 'I love North Africans', Jean-Marie Le Pen, leader of the far-right *Front National*, has declared, 'but their place is in the Mahgreb'. Racism has been transformed into just another cultural identity.

If the right has embraced the language of diversity, liberals have adopted the idiom of racial identity. The political philosopher Will Kymlicka is anything but a xenophobe. Yet his pluralism leads him to adopt the language of exclusion. 'It is right and proper', Kymlicka believes, 'that the character of a culture change as a result of the choices of its members.' But 'while it is one thing to learn from the larger world', it is quite another 'to be swamped by it'. What would this mean? That a culture has the right to keep out members of another culture? That a culture has the right to prevent its members from speaking another language, singing non-native songs or reading non-native books?

Kymlicka's warning about 'swamping' should make us sit up and take notice. The right has long exploited fears of cultural swamping to promote the idea that Western nations should pull up the drawbridge against immigrants whose cultural differences make them unsuitable. It is an argument that Kymlicka undoubtedly abhors. Yet once it becomes a matter of political principle that cultures should not be swamped by outsiders, then it is difficult to know how one could possibly resist such anti-immigration arguments. And once membership of cultural types is defined by the possession of certain characteristics, and rights and privileges granted by virtue of possessing those characteristics, it is but a short step to deny membership of a culture to people who do not possess those characteristics and hence to deny them certain rights and privileges.

Herder, Alain Finkielkraut observes, has become the cheerleader for both sides of the political spectrum. 'No longer silenced by post-World War II taboos, he reigns supreme, inspiring at the same time ... unyielding celebrations of ethnic identity and expressions of respect for foreigners, aggressive outbursts by xenophobes and generous pronouncements by xenophiles.' The two sides have 'conflicting credos but the same vision of the world'. Both see 'cultures as all-encompassing entities, distinctly different, one from the other.' Multiculturalists, like racial theorists, fetishise difference. Both seek to 'confine individuals to their group of origin'. Both undermine 'any possibility of a natural or cultural community among peoples.' We believe we have discredited the concept of race but, Finkielkraut asks, 'have we really made any progress?'

8

WHO OWNS KNOWLEDGE?

W ill Thomas was waiting for the start of the annual hydroplane race on the Columbia River, near the town of Kennewick, in Washington State, USA. Larking around with his friend Dave Deacy, he decided to amuse himself by wading through the water. A few yards in, his foot hit something round. 'Hey, we have a human head', he joked. That was exactly what it was: a brownish skull, covered in mud. It was 29 July 1996 – and the beginning of an extraordinary story of skulls and bones, history and politics, race and science.

   Thomas handed the skull over to the police, who in turn handed it to Jim Chatters, a forensic pathologist who runs an archaeological consulting firm in Kennewick that, among other things, helps the local coroner identify the human skeletons and assorted body parts that occasionally turn up. Chatters's immediate response was that the skull – with its narrow cheekbones and protruding upper jaw – was from a man of European descent and probably around 150 years old. But when he examined the rest of the skeleton that had been dredged up from the river, he discovered a spear point lodged in the right hip. The projectile had penetrated deep into bone that had subsequently healed over. Doing a CAT scan on the spear point, Chatters was dumbfounded to see a distinctive leaf-shape; deep inside the man's hip was a 'Cascade Point' of the kind that had been used by local hunters some five to nine thousand years ago. 'I've got a white guy with stone point in him', an astonished Chatters told the *New York Times*.

But how could he have? The only people in the region that long ago would have been the ancestors of today's Native Americans. As every history book tells us, the first European to set foot in the New World was Christopher Columbus, in 1492. The first white men this far west would probably have been Lewis Merriwether and William Clark – the men lauded by President Clinton as he helped launch the first draft of the human genome. And they did not arrive until the beginning of the nineteenth century. How could Jim Chatters have a white guy with a five-thousand-year-old spear point in him?

To clear up the confusion, Chatters sent off a small fragment of bone to be carbon-dated at the University of California. The lab confirmed that the skeleton was between 9200 and 9600 years old – one of the oldest ever found in North America. Confused and shaken, Chatters emailed several archaeologists across the country, asking for advice: 'Subject: Need Help ASAP'. 'I knew then', he later recalled, 'it would get very hot and heavy, which it did within ten minutes.'

'Kennewick Man', as the skeleton became known, created immediate controversy. Despite the historical improbability, Chatters was convinced that the remains were of European origin. At 5' 9", Kennewick Man was taller than one would expect a Native American of that era to be. The skull did not show the flattening common among ancient Indians, caused by using cradleboards to carry infants. Nor were the teeth worn; most teeth from Indian remains are ground down because of the amount of fibre and grit in their diet. A few weeks after Kennewick Man was discovered, Chatters happened to be watching *Star Trek: The Next Generation*. 'There was Patrick Stewart [the English actor who plays Captain Jean-Luc Picard]', Chatters recalled, 'and I said "My God, there he is, Kennewick Man!".' A later facial reconstruction of Kennewick Man indeed possessed an uncanny resemblance to the chisel-faced space explorer.

Native Americans, however, did not take kindly to the idea that one of their ancestors might have looked like the captain of the Starship *Enterprise*. And Kennewick Man was one of their ancestors, they insisted, not some wandering European. 'Our oral history goes back 10,000 years', said Armand Minthorn, a leader of the Umatilla tribe. 'We know how time began and how Indian people were created. They can say whatever they want, the scientists. They are being disrespectful.'

Not only in the eyes of Native Americas, but also in the eyes of American law, Kennewick Man was an Indian. The Native American Graves Repatriation Act (or NAGPRA), a law passed in 1990, describes as 'Native American' any remains more than five hundred years old; in other words, anyone in the New World before Columbus arrived. Under the law, any such remains must be handed over to the local Indian tribe for reburial. Five tribes from the Washington region – Yakama, Umatilla, Nez Perce, Colville and Wanapum – demanded that the bones of Kennewick Man be returned to them. They insisted, too, that there should be no scientific study of the bones. Any such study, they argued, would desecrate the body of one of their ancestors.

The part of the Columbia River in which Will Thomas had discovered the skull belonged to the Army Corps of Engineers. In September 1996, two months after the discovery of Kennewick Man, the Corps decided that the bones should be returned to the Umatilla for reburial at an unknown location. Almost immediately, eight anthropologists, including the most distinguished scientists in their fields, filed a lawsuit to halt the Corps' actions, pleading that scientists should have a chance to study the bones. Kennewick Man, they pointed out, could provide invaluable scientific data that might transform the understanding of early American history. NAGPRA, they insisted, was not meant to protect nine-thousand-year-old skeletons. They accused the Army Corps of arbitrary decision-making and undermining the First Amendment, which guarantees freedom of speech and safeguards the right to gather and receive information. If the skeleton was reburied, not only scientists but also the American public would be deprived of potentially irreplaceable information about its own past. The anthropologists claimed that their constitutional rights had been violated in another way too: they were being refused access to the bones solely because they were not of the same ethnicity as the Indians.

Native American leaders, in turn, dismissed the anthropologists' demand to examine Kennewick Man scientifically. 'It's like looking at us like a bunch of rats and mice', retorted Jerry Meninick, vice-chairman of the tribal council of the Yakama Indian Nation. 'We feel offended to be classed in such a situation.' Another Indian spokesman, Marla Big Boy, Oglala Lakota Attorney General for the Colville Confederated Tribes of eastern Washington, suggested that the Kennewick Man case was simply the latest expression of scientific racism.

So began an extraordinary battle. In 1997, the court ordered the Department of the Interior to establish whether Kennewick Man was indeed physically and culturally affiliated to modern-day Indians but without using any kind of invasive technique, such as DNA testing. The first report – compiled by the anthropologists Joseph Powell and Jerome Rose – compared bone and cranial measurements of Kennewick Man to those of other populations. 'The Kennewick individual is unique relative to recent American Indians', the report concluded, 'and finds its closest association with groups of Polynesia and the Ainu of Japan ... not with American Indians or with Europeans.'

The Department of the Interior then set out to establish a 'shared cultural identity' between Kennewick Man and modern Native Americans. This second report found no definitive archaeological, historical, ethnographic or linguistic evidence of such links. Nevertheless, in September 2000, the Interior Secretary, Bruce Babbitt, declared that there was a cultural affiliation, based on the oral history of Native Americans. Native American stories tell of a people who have been in the area for many thousands of years. Babbitt admitted that 'ambiguities in the data made this a close call' but, he said, 'I was persuaded by the geographic data and oral histories of the five tribes that collectively assert they are the descendants of people who have been in the region of the Upper Columbia Plateau for a very long time.'

In August 2002, however, Judge John Jelderks overturned Babbitt's decision and ordered the US government to let scientists study Kennewick Man. Almost immediately, the five Indian tribes and the US government lodged an appeal. Eighteen months later, in February 2004, the appeals court decided in favour of the scientists. It took another year for the government to accept the scientists' protocols for studying the skeleton. Finally, on 6 July 2005, almost nine years to the day since Will Thomas found the skull, a team of researchers gathered at the Burke Museum of Natural History and Culture in Seattle for a ten-day initial 'measurement and observation trip'.

The story is still not finished. In October 2007, a Senate committee proposed a two-word amendment to NAGPRA that would return Kennewick Man to the Indians. The Senate bill sought to add the words 'or was' to the legal definition of Native American, so that 'Native American' would refer to a member of a tribe or culture that 'is or was' indigenous to the United States. Contemporary Native Americans would therefore have legal control over any ancient remains found on American soil, whatever their age and however tenuous their relationship to modern Indians.

The following month, Representative Doc Hastings of Washington State countered the Senate move by introducing a new bill that insisted that NAGPRA should apply only to 'human remains or other cultural items that have a special, significant and substantial relationship to presently existing Native Americans' and that such a relationship could not be based on geography alone. The fate of both these legal changes is still undecided.

Over the years, what had begun as a local dispute as to who should have legal possession of a nine-thousand-year-old pile of bones had become something much larger. The debate about Kennewick Man gets to the heart of many of the issues that run through this book. What is race? How do we define cultural identity? Who owns knowledge? Who defines history? What is the role of science in contemporary society? In particular, it reveals the fraught relationship, not only between race and science but also between antiracism and science and the way that, for many people, antiracism has come to be defined in opposition to scientific rationality.

In this chapter and the next I want to use the Kennewick Man controversy as a prism through which to understand the relationship between race, antiracism and science and to show how the emergence of identity politics has distorted that relationship. In Chapter 9, I will examine more closely the scientific attempt to discover the origins of Kennewick Man and ask whether this is a valid quest or a reheated form of old-fashioned racial science, as the critics allege. But first, in this chapter, I want to explore the arguments of those critics – ones who believe that Kennewick Man belongs to the Indian tribes and should not be touched by scientists – to see what their opposition to the scientific study of the skeleton tells us about the contemporary relationship between the criticism of race and the criticism of science. To put this debate into context I will begin by looking at how and why our perceptions of science have transformed over the past century.

THE RETREAT FROM REASON

Meera Nanda is an Indian-born microbiologist, who maintains an endearingly old-fashioned view of the nature of science. Traditionally, the left championed science, because science embodied its traditional belief in universalism and progress. For Nanda it still does. 'Having grown up in a provincial town in northern India', she writes, 'I considered my education in science a source of personal enlightenment':

> Natural science, especially molecular biology, had given me a whole different perspective on the underlying cosmology of the religious and cultural traditions I was raised in. Science gave me a good reason to say 'No!' to many of my inherited beliefs about God, nature, women, duties and rights, purity and pollution, social status and my relationship with my fellow citizens ... I was convinced that modern science had a role to play in religious reformation and cultural revolution in Indian society. Without knowing it then, I was speaking the language of the Enlightenment.

Nanda was so convinced of the role of science in helping foment social change that she wanted not simply to practise science but to proselytise about it too. She travelled to the USA to study philosophy of science. But once inside the portals of academic 'science studies' – the term now used collectively to describe enquiries into the history, philosophy and sociology of science – she found herself seemingly in a parallel universe:

> Enlightenment was seen as the agent of colonialism, and modern science as a discourse of patriarchy and other dominant Western interests. Salvation was to be found in debunking the universalist pretensions of science and encouraging alternative ways of knowing that would end the hubris of the West. Someone like me could only be pitied – which I often was – as a 'colonised mind', dazzled by the superficial charms of the West.

The cynicism about 'Western' science that Nanda discovered within the seminar rooms and lecture halls of American universities reflects wider insecurities about human nature and social progress. This is an age of cynicism and scepticism, particularly about human capacities.

There is a widespread sense that every impression that humans make upon the world is for the worse. The attempt to master nature seems to have led to global warming and species depletion. The attempt to master society has given us Auschwitz and ethnic cleansing. 'For the first time since 1750', Michael Ignatieff has said of the post-Holocaust world, 'millions of people experience history not running forwards, from savagery to civilisation, but backwards to barbarism'.

In the first half of the twentieth century, the contrast between the spectacular advance of science and the moral turpitude of a Western world in thrall to fascism and mass unemployment led many people to place science on a pedestal. Science, it seemed, was untouched by the mire of society. After the Second World War, however, perceptions of science began to shift. Partly as a result of the Bomb people began to view science not as a solution to social misery but, increasingly, as its cause. The close relationship between scientific and military projects, particularly in the service of the Cold War, only strengthened such beliefs. Equally troubling was the relationship between science and big business, a relationship that became more prominent after the end of the Cold War and especially with the rise of the biotech industry in the 1990s.

Whereas once science stood as a symbol of human advancement, by the end of the twentieth century it was increasingly viewed as a metaphor for human debasement. It was not only that there was greater disillusionment with science. The character of that disillusionment transformed too. Critics challenged not only the use (or abuse) of science but also its very method. The concepts of rationality and objectivity that had once expressed the triumph of knowledge over ignorance were now as often seen as markers of social enslavement.

Traditionally, radicals had drawn a distinction between scientific knowledge and the uses to which such knowledge was put. Racial science was an abomination but it was also an abomination of science, not an indictment of it. Today, this distinction between knowledge and its use has largely been eroded. If the 'sciences really are objective fields of knowledge', the cultural critic Andrew Ross asks, 'why have so many (seismography, oceanography and microelectronics, to name a few) evolved directly from military R&D as part of the spinoff system that is habitually cited to justify the benefits to society of the vast military budget?' The relationship between science and the military, in other words, does not simply reveal how scientific knowledge can be abused but also challenges the idea that scientific knowledge is objective.

In the last chapter, we saw how the Romantic view of culture, not as common and universal but as plural and incommensurate, had, by the middle of the twentieth century, come to be encamped both on the intellectual high ground and the political middle ground. However, if the Enlightenment view of culture (or civilisation) had started corroding after the late eighteenth century, the Enlightenment view of science had remained relatively intact. The positivist nineteenth century worshipped science and progress no less than had the eighteenth century. By the early twentieth century, positivism had crumbled and progress was no longer seen as an unalloyed good but few questioned the belief that science provided an objective understanding of the world that was universally valid.

In the decades following the Second World War, however, science went the way of culture; or rather, science came increasingly to be seen as just another cultural product. 'All knowledge systems', as the philosopher Sandra Harding has put it, 'including those of modern science, are local ones'. With the rise of so-called 'postcolonial' and 'postmodern' theories, science came increasingly to be viewed not as universal and objective but as a reflection of the local prejudices of European cultures. 'The Western laboratory scientist', Andrew Ross argues, 'observes the institutional rules, follows the local procedures, and accedes to the general "value-free" belief system as logically as the

Chinese barefoot doctor or the rainforest shaman functions within their own cultural environments.' What we take as scientific truth, in other words, varies from place to place, culture to culture.

In the traditional view of science, the world and the objects, processes and properties it contains exist independently of humans and our beliefs about that world and its contents. The aim of science is to give reliable, albeit imperfect and tentative, descriptions and explanations of these objects, processes and properties. Such descriptions and explanations are valid for all societies. The criteria by which we evaluate scientific claims are universal, irrespective of cultural differences. Postmodern theories challenge all these claim. They view scientific knowledge as largely determined by historical and cultural context and only comprehensible within that context. Scientific knowledge does not derive from nature but is socially constructed. 'The natural world', as the sociologist Harry Collins has put it, 'has a small or non-existent role in the construction of scientific knowledge'. The standards by which information is evaluated are relative to a culture's assumptions about nature and about the relationship between nature and humanity. For Barry Barnes and David Bloor, 'there is no sense attached to the idea that some standards and beliefs are really rational as distinct from merely locally accepted as such.'

For many postmodern thinkers, it would, in the words of Sandra Harding, be a 'tragedy ... should the human species arrive at one and only one valid scientific and technological tradition.' For Harding, 'The modern European epistemological dream of a perfectly coherent account of all nature's regularities, one that perfectly corresponds to nature's order, is beginning to take on the character of a nightmare.' Rather than view scientific knowledge as universal, we should look upon it as 'multicultural', with every piece of knowledge being relative to the needs and aspirations of particular cultures. From the viewpoint of the relativist, the difference between the laboratory scientist, the barefoot doctor and the rainforest shaman is not one of knowledge or of rationality but of power. Western science has taken over the world, Sandra Harding suggests, 'not because of the greater purported rationality of Westerners or the purported commitment of their sciences to the pursuit of disinterested truths' but 'primarily because of the military, economic and political power of European cultures'. Since the successes of these sciences 'required the military and political defeat of non-European peoples', so we are 'entitled to scepticism that the history of these sciences is unmitigatedly the history of *human* progress: progress for some has been at the expense of disempowerment, impoverishment and sometimes genocide for many others.' Science has succeeded not because it is true, rational or effective but because standing behind it is the military and economic might of Western nations. Science, Harding argues, 'is politics by other means'.

Over the past three decades, postmodern theory has made the link between the physical subjugation of the Third World through colonialism and the intellectual subordination of non-Western ideas, history and values. Just as Western politicians and generals annexe foreign lands, postmodern theorists argue, so Western scientists and intellectuals impose their knowledge on the rest of the world. According to the historian Robert Young, Western thought 'articulates a philosophical structure which uncannily stimulates the project of nineteenth-century imperialism'. Western knowledge 'mimics ... the geographic and economic absorption of the non-European world by the West.' The Indian writer, Partha Chatterjee, believes that Western imperialists assault non-Western peoples not just 'by military might or industrial strength, but by thought itself'. Another postcolonial theorist, Gayatri Spivak, has described this as 'epistemic violence'.

The consequence of such intellectual imperialism is, say the critics, the dehumanisation of non-Western peoples. According to the Native American scholar and activist, Vine Deloria Jr:

Regardless of what Indians have said concerning their origins, their migrations, their experiences with birds, animals, lands, water, mountains and other peoples, the scientists have maintained a stranglehold on the definitions of what respectable and reliable human experiences are. The Indian explanation is always cast aside as a superstition, precluding Indians from having an acceptable status as human beings, and reducing them in the eyes of educated people to a prehuman level of ignorance.

The triumph of scientific rationality has ensured that 'the stereotype of American Indians as childlike, superstitious creatures still remains in the popular American mind – a subhuman species that really has no feelings, values or inherent worth.'

In the past, reactionaries argued that reason was confined to certain human groups, while progressives believed that all humans had the capacity to reason. Today, many claim that to believe that reason is universal is itself reactionary and demand the right, in the name of antiracism, for every culture to think differently. The sociologists, Helen Watson-Verran and David Turnbull, writing in the prestigious *Handbook of Science and Technology Studies*, argue that no longer should 'Western "rationality" and "scientificity" be used as the benchmark by which other sciences be evaluated.' Rather, 'the ways of understanding the natural world that have been produced by different cultures and at different times should be compared as knowledge systems on an equal footing.' So, for Vine Deloria, 'The non-Western tribal equivalent of science is the oral tradition, the teachings that have been passed down from one generation to the next over uncounted centuries.' Until 'Indian tribes, and by extension other tribal peoples, were submerged by the invasion of Western colonizing peoples, the oral tradition represented not simply information on ancient events but precise knowledge of birds, animals, plants, geologic features, and religious experiences of a particular group of people.' Such knowledge was the 'distilled memory of the People describing the events they had experienced and the lands they had lived in.' The major difference between such knowledge and Western science 'lies in the premise accepted by Indians and rejected by scientists: the world in which we live is alive.' Scientists reject this as 'primitive superstition' and refuse to 'credit the existence of any activities of the natural world as having partial intelligence or sentience present.' But, argues Deloria, the Indian way is as valid as the scientific method. For instance, 'we know from meteorology that seeding clouds with certain chemicals can bring rain. This method of dealing with natural forces is wholly mechanical and can be described as the power to force nature to do our bidding.' Indians perform 'the same function by conducting ceremonies and asking the spirits for rain'. Indeed, Indian ceremonies are more effective than scientific methods. 'Science is severely limited ... since it cannot affect winds, clouds and storms except by certain kinds of alterations.' An Indian medicine man, on the other hand, can change the weather by becoming 'a friend to the [meteorological] forces'. Deloria adds that 'Acting in concert with friendly thunder and storm spirits is rather commonplace in many Indian tribes and demonstrates the more comprehensive scope of the oral tradition in comparison to both scientific knowledge and powers.'

Deloria rejects the theory of evolution and believes that Indians lived at the same time as dinosaurs, that mammoths and mastodons lived in America at the time the Pilgrims landed, that the Earth is not several billion years old as geologists claim, and that Noah's Flood is a reality. He is no cranky, marginal figure. He was, until 2002, professor of history, law and political science at the University of Colorado. He remains someone with whom many serious scholars regularly collaborate. Deloria penned, for instance, the foreword to *Skull Wars*, the anthropologist David Hurst Thomas's acclaimed study of the Kennewick Man affair. *Time* magazine has named him one of the eleven most significant religious thinkers of the twentieth century.

Deloria's academic status shows the consequences of a 'multicultural' view of science. Once the notion of objective knowledge is jettisoned, once science is seen as a local rather than a universal form of knowledge, once it is accepted that culturally-diverse ways of understanding the natural world should all be regarded as valid forms of truth, once rationality is regarded as a form of racist violence, then mysticism and Creationism come to be taken seriously. Not all forms of mysticism and Creationism, of course. Even the most pluralist of academics generally dismiss Christian Creationism and New Age mysticism as hogwash but many accept, even welcome, indigenous mysticism or Native American Creationism as adding colour to the multicultural map of knowledge and challenging the restraining, reactionary hand of Western rationalism.

The consequence of a multicultural science is not, however, a more equitable form of knowledge but a more racialised one. In Chapter 2, we saw how the emergence of race-based medicine has led to drugs, such as BiDiL, targeted specifically at particular races, in this case African Americans. There are innumerable problems with treating BiDiL as a black drug, not least the fact that many African Americans will be given the drug who may not respond to it, while many non-blacks will be denied it who might have benefited. But, at least advocates of race-based medicine do not suggest that medical knowledge is race-specific, just that certain medicines may be. Many multiculturalists, on the other hand, challenge the very idea of universal scientific knowledge. All knowledge, they argue, is culturally specific; scientific rationalism is simply a local Western viewpoint. It is a view of science that not only degrades the concepts of reason, objectivity and truth but also resurrects racial concepts of human differences. We can see this clearly in the debate over the fate of Kennewick Man.

SCIENTIFIC RATIONALITY AND CULTURAL IDENTITY

Two issues have dominated the debate about Kennewick Man. Who owns the bones? And who owns the right to use the bones to tell the story of the first inhabitants of the Americas? In other words, who owns history?

For many scientists, the idea that the bones belong to any one group is abhorrent. 'I explicitly assume that no living culture, religion, interest group or biological population has any moral or legal right to the exclusive use or regulation of ancient human skeletons since all humans are members of a single species', argues Douglas Ubelaker, a bioarchaeologist from the Smithsonian Institute. 'Ancient skeletons are the remnants of unduplicable evolutionary events which all living and future peoples have the right to know about and understand. In other words, ancient human skeletons belong to everyone.' While facts cannot by themselves tell a story, nevertheless any story about human origins that aspires to be more than myth must be anchored by the facts. 'Native American beliefs about the past and the dead certainly deserve respect, but they should not be allowed to dictate government policy on the investigation and interpretation of early American prehistory', write Robson Bonnichsen, one of the plaintiffs in the Kennewick Man court case, and Alan L. Schneider, the lawyer who represented the scientists. 'If a choice must be made among competing theories of human origins, primacy should be given to theories based on the scientific method. Only scientific theories are built on empirical evidence; only scientific theories can be adjusted or overturned.'

For many Indians and their academic supporters, on the other hand, the myths by which they live reveal why Kennewick Man belongs to them. 'If this individual is truly over 9,000 years old, that only substantiates our belief that he is Native American', claims Armand Minthorn of the Umatilla tribe. 'From our oral histories, we know that our people have been part of this land since the beginning of time. We do not believe that our people migrated here from another continent, as the scientists do.' History is something given, not something to be studied. 'Some scientists say that if this individual is not studied further, we, as Indians, will be destroying evidence of our own history', Minthorn writes. 'We already know our history. It is passed on to us through our elders and through our religious practices.' As for science, many Native Americans treat it with great suspicion. 'History proves that archaeology has a political context, which can be used to help or harm Native American interests', argues Rebecca Tsosie, director of the Indian Legal Program at Arizona State University. 'The discipline of science, like history, is not neutral.' Many archaeologists agree. 'It is simply untrue', David Hurst Thomas suggests, to assume that anthropologists provide 'an objective telling of events … Like it or not, the historical disciplines are the products of Western tradition, and even anthropologists, protest as they might, are the prisoners of their own cultural backgrounds.' Indeed, for Deb Huglin, a Californian archaeologist who works with tribes to protect and obtain remains, archaeologists are 'making up stories' to support 'propaganda'; Huglin talks of archaeology as employing 'displacement genocide tactics'.

This debate between scientists and Native American activists has, in recent years, taken place within the legal framework of the Native American Grave Protection and Repatriation Act. NAGPRA was the product of many years of lobbying by Native American activists, anthropologists and archaeologists and was intended to be an act of restitution for the wrongs done to American Indians by scientists over the years. Throughout the nineteenth century, and for much of the twentieth, anthropologists viewed American Indians, as they did most non-Western peoples, as objects to collect and rank, rather than people with beliefs, cultures and histories to understand.

As recompense for this history, the law requires federally-funded institutions to return human remains and objects found in Indian graves to their original owners. Who are the original owners? According to NAGPRA, they are the lineal descendants of the disinterred person or federally-recognised tribes that are 'culturally affiliated' to the group from which the ancestor came or which produced the artefact. NAGPRA defines 'cultural affiliation' as 'a relationship of shared group identity which can be reasonably traced historically or prehistorically between a present day Indian tribe or Native Hawaiian and an identifiable earlier group'. NAGPRA requires museums to provide culturally-affiliated tribes with a list of all Indian human remains they hold, as well as ceremonial and sacred objects and to offer to return such remains or objects to the tribes. Any new remains or objects discovered on tribal lands cannot be examined without the consent of culturally-affiliated tribes, who can demand their return.

NAGPRA, the anthropologist David Hurst Thomas suggests, redresses past wrongs by shifting the balance between science and Native American beliefs to ensure that 'no longer is the scientific position privileged'. His fellow anthropologist Geoffrey Clark, on the other hand, abhors the way in which 'NAGPRA puts ethnicity and religious belief on an equal footing with science, and thus provides a mandate for claims of affiliation by virtually any interested party'. As a result of NAGPRA, Robson Bonnichsen and Alan Schneider point out, 'Native American origin theories, which had long been relegated to the realm of personal religious beliefs, are suddenly being thrust into the domain of public policy.'

In the first decade after the law entered the statute book, over half a million sets of remains and artefacts had either been returned or were in the process of being returned. Such destruction of material damages our ability to understand our past. As the British biological anthropologist Robert Foley has put it, 'Destroy that record and we destroy large chunks of history, just as we would if we were to destroy libraries and books written in the past.' Human remains do more than simply tell us about the past. They can also aid medical research and help refine the forensic sciences. In 1999, Harvard University's Peabody Museum of Archaeology and Ethnology repatriated the remains of more than two thousand individuals to the Pecos and Jemez Pueblo tribes in New Mexico. The collection was of high value, because it was well-preserved, large enough to be statistically significant and demo-graphically representative of a single population. Over the years, the bones had been examined by dozens of researchers studying every-thing from head injuries to the development of tooth cavities. The anthropologist Christopher Ruff used the collection to publish a land-mark paper on osteoporosis. According to Ruff, the collection was 'an incredibly valuable resource', the data from which he will still be using 'for the next 30 years'. The bones, Ruff explains, provided 'a kind of preindustrial baseline to compare to modern populations, which may suffer ailments that weren't so prevalent before the indus-trial era.' It is a resource that will now be denied to future researchers.

Tristram Besterman, director of the Manchester Museum, in Britain, which has returned many skeletons in its collection, acknowl-edges that repatriation 'may well entail a loss to science' but believes it is a price worth paying because it also helps 'heal open festering wounds.' The archaeologists Jane Hubert and Cressida Fforde are sim-ilarly in 'no doubt of the immense spiritual and material significance' of human remains to indigenous groups.

Yet before NAGPRA there had been little demand from Native Americans for the repatriation of either artefacts or remains. The issue of repatriation became a major issue in the 1980s, not just in the USA but internationally. But while Native American activists, anthropolo-gists, archaeologists and museum curators all became involved in the debate, the issue barely registered among non-professionals. The anthropologist Russell Thornton, of the Smithsonian Institute, observes that when, in the 1980s, the museum first contacted tribes about repatriation few responded. Jim Chatters has written that in his experience (and his experience spans four decades) 'the tribes had been little interested in very ancient remains'. After NAGPRA, however, 'activists among the local tribes had begun to claim all precolonial human remains as ancestors'.

The anthropologist David Hurst Thomas tells the story of the attempt by the American Museum of Natural History in New York to repatriate the skeletons of four Inuits that it possessed. In the late 1980s, the Canadian journalist, Kenn Harper, launched a campaign for the repatriation of the skeletons with his book *Give Me My Father's Body*. The Museum of Natural History accepted that it was time to return the bones. It sent representatives to Qaanaaq, the Greenland village in which the descendants of the New York Inuits now live, to see how those descendants wished the bones to be repatriated. No one in the village seemed interested. After almost a year, the pastor of Qaanaaq's Lutheran Church agreed, under considerable pressure from his superiors, to accept the bones and conduct the re-interment ceremony. When the anthropologist Edward Carpenter, one of the Museum of Natural History's representatives, asked locals what they felt about the ceremony, one resident said, simply, 'embarrassment'. 'The whole service was really for us', Carpenter later observed, adding that the Inuit participated in the ceremony only as a courtesy to their guests.

As the surreal story of the Qaanaaq Inuits reveals, the repatriation movement was driven, at least initially, not by popular pressure but by the campaigning work of activists, archaeologists, anthropologists and museum curators. For activists, making a claim on ancestors and on ancestral heritage has provided a means of affirming a cultural identity, allowing them to 'lay claim to their own pasts, and reassert their culture and community identity'. The process, Jane Hubert and Cressida Fforde suggest, 'can change the cultural identity of a group and the way that members of the group see themselves', creating 'commonalities ... that did not exist in pre-colonial times but have become relevant and necessary in the face of the legacy of colonialism'. Not just in the USA but throughout the world, the repatriation debate has become a vehicle for identity formation. In Australia, for example, one advocate of repatriation suggests that it has helped fuel the 'Aboriginal "cultural revival" that has occurred throughout Australia since the 1970s.' It helps 'not only [to] articulate, strengthen and construct local Aboriginal identity but also Aboriginality as a pan-Australian commonality' because it clearly differentiates between 'those who are Aboriginal and those who are not'. She adds that 'repatriation and reburial are loci for processes which both construct and reaffirm Aboriginality, empowering its participants by enabling them to assert, define (and thus take control over) their own identity'.

The activists demanding repatriation are not those living 'traditional' lives, but mainly middle-class urbanites searching for a cultural authenticity that they believe they have lost. The source of Native American activism, Vine Deloria has written, is 'urban Indians seeking an Indian identity and heritage' who became 'the most militant of advocates for cultural renewal'. What fed the repatriation movement, the sociologist Joseph Tilden Rhea observes, was:

> ... the identity needs of a generation of urban Indians who felt alienated from American culture and who turned to their Indian heritage for a better alternative. Reaching for a new sense of the past, they developed an active antagonism towards the mainstream representation of their history. Acutely aware of the connection between identity, history and political power, urban Indians became increasingly active in the reshaping of American collective memory.

Cressida Fforde suggests that a similar process has taken place in Australia. 'Many of the Aborigines who have been the most visible in the requesting and receiving of ancestral remains from institutions in the 1980s and 1990s', Fforde points out, 'have been those who are perceived as "non-traditional" or "urban" people.' For such activists, 'The identification of collected remains as ancestors confirms the descent of modern "urban" communities from individuals from the traditional past, thus confirming their Aboriginal identity by virtue of descent.' Cultural authenticity is won, in other words, through biological descent. Urban Aboriginals do not live traditional lives; they are culturally similar to other urban Australians but their 'real' culture remains Aboriginal by virtue of their ancestry. Culture is not what you do but what you *should* be doing. Whatever urban Aboriginals may be doing in the here and now, the essence of their culture has remained intact over tens of thousands of years, a fixed, unchanging entity that inhabits the individual and shapes him: culture as *volksgeist* or culture as race.

For academics, as much as for activists, the process of repatriation has helped provide a new identity. It allows them to attempt to cleanse their disciplines of their racist past or at least to atone for it. 'The collections in our Western museums', Tristram Besterman has suggested, 'derive, at their most innocent, from grave robbing, and at their worst, from wholesale slaughter.' Every museum artefact is tainted and so, by extension, is the knowledge derived from them. In recent years, the cultural critic Tiffany Jenkins argues, 'The legitimacy of the museum as a harbour of truth and intellectual authority has been undermined'. As a result, 'museum professionals and academics are trying to distance themselves from their traditional role and find a new meaning for their work.' As Eillean Hooper-Greenhill, director of the Research Centre for Museums and Galleries at Leicester University puts it, 'Museums and galleries are caught in a maelstrom of cultural and social change' in which 'The ostensibly generalisable and timeless ideals of the Enlightenment (beauty, truth, knowledge) are being modified.' Museums are 'sites of cultural struggle and the stories that are told in museums of history, culture, science and art are no longer accepted as naturally authoritative. The museum is being reviewed, reassessed and reformulated to enable it to be more sensitive to competing narratives and to local circumstances; to be more useful to diverse groups; to fit current times more closely.'

Repatriation has become a means of providing a new identity for tarnished professions. The Enlightenment mission of collecting objects to further empirical knowledge of the world has given way to the belief that there are many ways of understanding the world, each of which is as valid as any other. The taintedness of Western knowledge, Tristram Besterman suggests, makes it 'both arrogant and immoral' to insist on the primacy of 'Western rationalism' and 'to deny the alternative realities and belief systems of indigenous communities'. In this context, Michael Pickering, repatriation director at the National Museum of Australia, argues that what is important about cultural repatriation is not just the 'physical return of items' but more significantly 'the repatriation of authority'. Hence, Tiffany Jenkins points out, 'In the guise of simply returning artefacts, museum professionals champion a shift of emphasis from their own intellectual authority based on knowledge and expertise, to the moral authority of others based on identity. In doing so they give themselves a new mission.'

Irrespective of its impact on science, the argument for the repatriation of human remains and cultural objects remains troubling, because its entanglement with identity politics resurrects racial ways of thinking about human groups. At the heart of the demand for repatriation is the idea of cultural continuity over hundreds, even thousands, of years, the belief that a contemporary group has a direct connection to 10,000 year-old bones or artefacts found in the same geographical location. It is a notion that most archaeologists and anthropologists dismiss as absurd. 'As a specialist in the prehistory of western North America', archaeologist Michael Moratto observes, 'I can assure you that no living society, native American or other, can credibly claim biologic or cultural affiliation with archaeological

remains 93 centuries old. This time span represents nearly 500 generations. During this time, peoples entered the New World, moved
extensively within it, evolved culturally, intermarried and sometimes
died out.' There is therefore no 'substantive or legal merit' in culturally linking Kennewick Man with any group of modern Indians.

Others, however, view culture in a very different fashion. In April
1998, the Army Corps of Engineers covered the riverbank where
Kennewick Man had been discovered in six hundred tons of rocks.
Most scientists viewed this as an act of vandalism that destroyed any
possibility of further research on the site. To this day, the Corps has
never satisfactorily explained its action. When it first proposed the
cover-up, scientists vigorously objected and Congress even passed a
law demanding that the site be left intact. Nevertheless, days before
the law came into effect, the Corps went ahead, some believe on the
direct orders of the White House. But if scientists were devastated,
many activists were elated. 'This is preservation of our culture',
claimed the Umatilla Indian leader Armand Minthorn, as he watched
Army helicopters drop their load on the riverbank.

Minthorn may well have been talking metaphorically but his
response provides a good expression of the view of culture as something as rigid as a rock-filled tomb. From the viewpoint of a repatria-
tionist, culture is like a sealed box that holds a people both in the
present and across time and any attempt to open that sealed box is an
unacceptable threat. 'We are discovering the "new human rights",
which include, first and foremost, cultural rights', the then UN secretary general Boutros Boutros-Ghali told the UN General Assembly at
the launch of the International Year of the World's Indigenous Peoples
in 1992. 'We might even say that there can be no human rights unless
cultural authenticity is preserved.' There it is, the A-word again.
Repatriation is one means of preserving cultural authenticity. It is,
Jane Hubert and Cressida Fforde write, 'a process towards the recre-
ation of the wholeness of the people receiving the remains of their

ancestors'. *The wholeness of the people.* It's a phrase that calls to mind not just Herder's concept of the *volksgeist* but the imperatives of racial science too and the idea of racial type.

Volkish notions of culture are coming into vogue. The idea of cultural repatriation is not confined to indigenous bones or tribal artefacts. From the Elgin Marbles to the Benin Bronzes, from busts of the Egyptian Queen Nefertiti to the Aztec Emperor Moctezuma's quetzal-feathered headdress, there is a cultural tug-of-war over a treasure-house of artefacts between the museums that house them and the foreign governments that claim true ownership. Ownership is defined in the same way as with Kennewick Man: through 'cultural affiliation'. Such claims of cultural affiliation are often as tenuous as those surrounding Kennewick Man. Take the Elgin Marbles, one of the British Museum's most prized treasures. In the early nineteenth century, the British ambassador to the Ottoman Empire, Lord Elgin, removed from the Parthenon in Athens some of its best statues and friezes and sold them to the newly-founded British Museum. Athens was then under Ottoman rule and the Parthenon a ruin, having been hit by a Venetian cannonball while being used as ammunition dump by the Turkish Army. Elgin, who removed many of the remaining artworks, with the blessing of the Ottoman government, saw his actions not as vandalism but as the preservation of historic treasures, though many, then and since, have doubted his saintly motives. Few doubt that the British Museum has a legal right to the Marbles but many question its moral right. Melina Mercouri, Greek Minister of Culture in the 1980s and 1990s and one of the most vociferous advocates for the return of the Marbles, argued that the Parthenon and its marbles embody the values of democracy and indeed the very spirit of Greece as a modern, democratic European nation and are therefore the exclusive cultural patrimony of the Greek people.

But does a farmer, factory worker or government bureaucrat in Greece today really have any greater cultural affinity to Aristotle or

Aristophanes than a British farmer, worker or bureaucrat? In fact does he or she have any real cultural affinity at all? Greece, in the modern sense, is not a continuation of an ancient polity but a nineteenth-century invention. The boundaries of modern Greece include many peoples – such as the Macedonians – who do not consider themselves Greek at all. Equally, what we call Ancient Greece was not a single national entity but a set of city-states, often at war with each other. The Parthenon was built by Athenians, not Greeks, and financed, moreover, from taxes forcibly imposed on the other states. Athens was not a democracy in the modern sense but a slave-owning society. The Parthenon was a paean not to democracy but to the God Athena. Modern Greek culture clearly draws upon that of the Ancient Greeks but, like all modern European nations, it also draws upon a multitude of other sources, from Babylon to Byzantine, from India to Islam. Not just the culture but the population, too, is mongrel. 'For a modern Greek to assume racial kinship with Pericles', the art critic David Lee has suggested,

> ... is like my Mancunian mother claiming a close relationship to Cartimandua, the queen of the Brigantes, a Pennine Iron Age tribe. She is just as likely to be descended from a Syrian, a Spaniard, a north African, an Angle or Saxon, a Dane, Norman or Norwegian, not to mention the armies of Irish navvies who shovelled out the Ship Canal in the nineteenth century. The idea of a trans-historically permanent idea of Greece and Greekness fails to recognise a long European history of inter-mixing nomadic tribes, slavery and successive colonising invasions.

While the cultural affiliation between the ancient Marbles and modern Greeks is tenuous, showing the Marbles in the British Museum may well allow us better to understand their place in the wider network of cultural affiliations. 'The world-wide context provided by the British Museum, and by other museums that share its range, allows more associations, more resonances, and above all more questions than do geographically or culturally more specific contexts', argues the Museum's director, Neil MacGregor. The Museum allows 'visitors to address through the filter of history, both ancient and more recent, questions of contemporary politics and international relations, to assess and consider their place in the world and to see the different parts of the world as indissolubly linked'. In the case of the Elgin Marbles, MacGregor believes, 'What becomes evident in Bloomsbury is that the Sculptures are ... part of a story that is not only national. Indeed it is not only European. In artistic terms the sculptures are clearly part of a process that embraces Egypt and Mesopotamia, Turkey, India, Rome and the whole of Europe.'

For MacGregor, illuminating these cultural relationships is not simply of aesthetic or historical importance but also of supreme political significance. 'Among the greatest threats to our liberty now', MacGregor suggests, 'must surely be the reductive identity that politicians and media often seek to pin on diverse and complicated cultures and societies.' In response to such threats, 'Collections like the British Museum and the research they generate' help provide 'a resource against those powerful myths about the past – national, ethnic, religious – which are used justify actions in the present'. For MacGregor it is important for the Museum in the twenty-first century to maintain the eighteenth-century faith of its founders, 'the Enlightenment conviction that knowledge and understanding were indispensable ingredients of civil society, and the best remedies against the forces that threatened it – intolerance and bigotry – the dreaded "enthusiasm" of religious certainties that led to conflict, oppression and civil war.'

Cynics might argue that MacGregor is simply trying to add a gloss to the British Museum's morally-suspect possession of the Elgin Marbles. But if it is morally suspect, it is not because the Greeks have a greater cultural affinity to the Marbles. The argument between Macgregor and his critics goes to the heart of the contemporary debate about cultural differences. For MacGregor, 'myths about the past' are threatening because they allow 'oversimplified notions of identity [to be] manufactured and imposed upon cultures and communities'. The British Museum's collection 'is the common inheritance of everyone on the planet'. For postmodern thinkers, myths are important precisely because they help manufacture cultural identities and challenge the Enlightenment myth of universal truths. Cultural objects are the property not of all humanity but of particular peoples, each of whose relationship to its cultural products constitutes a form of ownership. Indeed, there is an increasing tendency to claim ownership not just of tangible artefacts but of intangible ideas too.

A United Nations report on the protection of cultural and intellectual property argues that 'each indigenous community must retain permanent control over all elements of its own heritage', heritage being defined as 'all of those things which international law regards as the creative production of human thought and craftsmanship, such as songs, stories, scientific knowledge and artworks.' Unesco has envisioned the creation of 'state folklore protection boards' that would 'register works and authorize their use'. Such protection boards might intervene if other peoples produce imitations or if native art was used in 'culturally inappropriate contexts'. In 2003, Unesco adopted the *International Convention of the Intangible Cultural Heritage* that requires governments to prepare an inventory of intangible culture and thence to protect it. What particularly worries Unesco is the 'inability of states, in a globalised world, to control the cross-border flow of ideas, images and resources that affect cultural development.' By 'highlighting the culture of economically powerful nations', Unesco argues, globalisation 'has created new forms of inequality' and helped foster 'cultural conflict rather than cultural pluralism'. Unesco's long-term aim, the anthropologist Michael Brown suggests, is to help nations 'restrict the exportation of local knowledge and the importation of cultural items (such as music and film) perceived to pose a threat to national values and tradition.'

Today's cultural bureaucrats have waded much further into the swamp of authenticity than even Herder ever envisaged. Herder insisted that a culture belonged to a people in a moral and spiritual, but never in a legal, sense. He believed that a people should hold on to its culture, and only to its culture, but not that others should be formally prohibited from expanding their horizons. The ultra-volkishness of the UN and Unesco raises interesting questions. Must, for instance, the British government approve every production of *King Lear*? Should only Jamaicans be able to play reggae? Will Italian inspectors have to check every pizza to ensure its cultural appropriateness?

If all this sounds vaguely Monty Pythonish, it has nevertheless encouraged many indigenous groups to try to copyright their cultures. In America, both the Hopi and the Apache have demanded control over the cultural property of, and information about, their respective tribes, including 'all images, texts, ceremonies, music, songs, stories, symbols, beliefs, customs, ideas and other physical and spiritual objects and concepts'. In Australia, Aborigines took legal action to try to prevent the national airline Qantas from using a kangaroo as its logo on the grounds that the animal is Aboriginal intellectual property. They failed, but such demands are already having an impact on the availability of public knowledge. Harvard University's Peabody Museum deliberately allowed a historic set of photographs to disintegrate because the Navajo tribe objected to non-tribal members viewing the rituals they depicted. In many museums, the right to view certain objects is now restricted by race, sex, culture or status. At the National Museum of Australia in Canberra, only designated tribal members have access to 'secret sacred' Aboriginal objects. Neither the museum's director nor its curator is aware of the contents of the secret-sacred storage. The newly-built National Museum of the American Indian in Washington segregates and restricts access to 'sensitive' collections and has an area reserved for tribal use. New Zealand's National Museum, Te Papa Tongarewa, operates in a similar way.

The code of ethics issued by Britain's Museums Association suggests that 'cultural descendants have a greater connection and ownership of historical artefacts' and urges curators to 'consider restricting access to certain specified items, particularly those of ceremonial or religious importance, where unrestricted access may cause offence or distress to actual or cultural descendants'. At the Hancock Museum in Newcastle, parts of the collection have been placed in segregated boxes, for men's eyes only. A female researcher who makes a special request to examine the material will be 'actively discouraged'. Ratan Vaswani, ethics adviser to the Museums Association, endorses such segregation, arguing that while 'restricting access to certain objects certainly sits uncomfortably with our liberal values ... the effect of such restrictions is unlikely to be sexist or racist in the same way as discrimination in, say, recruitment for a job'. Perhaps not, but, as Tiffany Jenkins points out, the implications of such segregation are still deeply unpalatable because it cuts against the grain of the belief that knowledge and understanding are universal and should not be limited by biology and blood.

The demand for cultural protection appears to be a progressive move to protect the rights of indigenous and other marginalised groups. In fact, it is creating a form of intellectual apartheid, in which biology becomes the gatekeeper to knowledge. Access to knowledge is distributed according to one's biological ancestry. Cultural repatriation only makes sense if we accept the notion of cultural ownership and cultural ownership only makes sense if we accept a link between blood and culture: in other words, if we accept a racial view of the world.

9

ANCIENT RACE WARS AND
MODERN RACE SCIENCE

I've got a white man with a spear point in him', Jim Chatters told the *New York Times*. From the moment Chatters defined Kennewick Man as white, the question of race and identity became central to the debate about the skeleton's origins and ownership. Many Native Americans bridled at the idea that scientists, rather than they, should decide Kennewick Man's identity and whether or not he was their kin. For many white Americans, science was rewriting history in their favour. 'Europeans Invade America: 20 000 BC' ran the headline in *Discover* magazine. 'When Columbus came to the New World in 1492 and set in motion the chain of events that led to the decimation of Native Americans, was he unknowingly getting revenge for what was done to his ancestors thousands of years ago?', asked the *Santa Fe New Mexican*. Suddenly, Kennewick Man became the focus of an ancient American race war and many wanted to see him as both white and a victim.

'If a Caucasoid Kennewick Man and his tribe roamed the Cascade rain-shadow dry interior of Washington State 9,000 years ago', the conservative magazine *Frontpage* observed,

> ... we must then ask a painful question: what happened to them? Why did they vanish while Native American tribes took over the land that

once was theirs? Did white-skinned early Americans lack the skill or luck to survive? Or were they killed off by darker-skinned invaders in an act we today would define as racism and genocide (especially if its victims were not of European ancestry)?

It concluded that while 'On today's university campuses, the fashion is to depict Euro-Americans as evil and Native Americans and most Hispanics as the virtuous survivors of white colonial exploitation, rape, and genocide', Kennewick Man 'might prove the opposite – that the true Native Americans were white, victims of murderous genocide by the ancestors of today's Indians who seized their land. The European invasion of the past five centuries, in this potential revisionist history, merely reclaimed land stolen 9,000 years earlier from their murdered kin.'

For many antiracists, on the other hand, Chatters' description of Kennewick Man resurrected an age-old racial science. According to the anthropologist Chris Kortright, Kennewick Man maintains the practice by which 'Intellectuals and academics have built names and careers for themselves' by proposing theories that 'reinforce the ideologies of colonisation and racial hierarchy'. In a history of American anthropology, the writer Jack Hitt suggests that 'Racial preferences color America's oldest skulls and bones', including the scientific study of Kennewick Man.

Why did Jim Chatters think that Kennewick Man was white? And what does his belief tell us about science, and in particular about the relationship between science and race? The campaign for the repatriation of Kennewick Man helps resurrect, as we have seen, old ideas of race in a new form. Does the scientific study of the skeleton equally do so?

THE RETURN OF THE CALLIPER MAN

Kennewick Man's skull convinced Chatters of his race. Native Americans typically have broad faces and round heads; Kennewick

Man was different. Jim Chatters describes his feeling as he first inspected the skull found on the river bank:

> Removing it from the bag, I was immediately struck by its long narrow shape and the marked constriction of the forehead behind a well-developed brow-ridge. The bridge of the nose was very high and prominent. My first thought was that this skull belonged to somebody of European descent.

The use of skull characteristics to determine racial identity is an old technique and one with a shameful past. Nineteenth-century racial scientists, such as Samuel Morton and Paul Broca, travelled with callipers and scales, created libraries of thousands of skulls and used their measurements to establish a hierarchy of races. There was, as George Armelagos and Dennis van Gerven observe, 'a love affair between race science and the skull'. Craniometry helped distinguish between Aryans and non-Aryans, explain the superiority of the white race and identify the criminal type. Little wonder that, following the Second World War, as the edifice of racial science crumbled, most anthropologists dismissed craniometry as mumbo-jumbo science. In a key paper on 'The New Physical Anthropology', published in 1951, Sherwood Washburn, perhaps the most important biological anthropologist of his generation, proposed that the study of the human skeleton should turn away from trying to categorise racial types to understanding the dynamic impact of evolutionary and cultural processes on the human form.

In recent years, anthropologists have started polishing up their callipers again. Over the past two decades, a number of researchers have developed new computer programs that make use of a sophisticated statistical technique, multivariate analysis, to compare unknown skulls with those of people from different regions of the world and different periods of history. Perhaps the best known is CRANID, created by the Australian anthropologist Richard Wright.

Another is FORDISC, a program written by two American anthropologists, Richard Jantz and Stephen Ousley. Proponents of such programs argue that instead of being limited to comparisons of one or two
variables of dubious quality, as nineteenth-century craniometrists
were, researchers can now use up to ninety measurements to look for
patterns in the detailed topography of skulls, including length, width
and projection of the nasal bones, the form of the chin, the shape of the
skull and brow and the way the bones have fused together.

In the nineteenth century, craniometry was the property of racial
scientists seeking to rank the peoples of the world. There are certainly
some today, such as the psychologist Phillipe Rushton (whose work we
will discuss in the next chapter), who look on a skull as one imagines
Samuel Morton or Paul Broca might have done. Even more mainstream physical anthropologists often speak a language that appears as
archaic as many of the remains they investigate. 'I am more accurate in
assessing race from skeletal remains', the anthropologist George Gill
has written, 'than from looking at living people standing before me.'
Such sentiments have led to criticism of today's skull science as simply
nineteenth-century racial prejudice dressed up in twenty-first-
century technology. The new 'racial diagnosticians', writes the anthropologist George Armelagos, 'armed with new techniques and technology, map the terrain of cranial morphology much as their forebears did
over a century ago.'

The majority of scientists wielding the callipers today are, however, more likely to be members of Amnesty International or Médecins
Sans Frontières than the Brotherhood of Scientific Racists. Software
such as CRANID and FORDISC 2.0 is now widely used by anthropologists tracking the origins of remains they have unearthed, by
police forces trying to identify a corpse and by human rights workers
attempting to put names and faces to bodies in a mass grave. Jim
Chatters argues that the comparison between today's craniometry and
nineteenth-century racial science is 'specious'. It is true that both use

skull measurements but for entirely different purposes: one to identify the dead, the other to justify racial thinking. Criticism of today's craniometry, Chatters writes, 'is like condemning heart surgery because knives are often used to commit murder'. Many former sceptics have become converts. Rob Kruszynski, of London's Natural History Museum, describes the day a policeman walked through the door with a skull in a cardboard box. It had been unearthed in a Cardiff garden. Police suspected murder and wanted to know the victim's identity. Working with his colleagues Chris Stringer and Theya Molleson, Kruszynski took thirty-three measurements from the skull and fed them into CRANID. The program revealed that the skull probably belonged to a Caucasian female of mixed British and non-British descent. The police made a facial reconstruction from the data and within days the victim was identified as Karen Price, a teenage runaway of Welsh, Greek-Cypriot, Spanish and American ancestry. Kruszynski, who had been sceptical of CRANID's utility in forensic cases, became convinced of its effectiveness. Research by forensic scientist Jenny Lumb suggests that CRANID can correctly locate a skull's continent of origin four times out of five.

Others, however, are less impressed by the new techniques. Several studies of FORDISC 2.0 have shown that, when applied to skulls from known African populations, some fifty per cent were placed in non-African categories. In other studies, the software misidentified a large proportion of skulls from Cuba, India and China. The program, George Armelagos observes, 'forced a solution on *a priori* racial criteria (as all racial schemes do) to delimit patterns of human variation. What we see with the African test is the result of an astounding mismatch between actual cranial variation and the variation modelled by racial constructs.'

Human variation is continuous and seamless. Software such as FORDISC has a limited number of racial categories into which to carve up that variation. Each category is defined by a particular set of skull measurements; if the measurements of an actual skull do not conform to those of any particular racial pigeon-hole, that skull is nevertheless forced into whatever category the software decides is the most suitable, even though it may have no real biological relationship to the other skulls with which it is grouped. A second problem arises from the fact that the boundaries of the racial categories have been established through the study of skulls and skeletons contained in reference collections. These collections contain thousands of specimens amassed during the twentieth century and earlier. They may have come from archaeological digs, hospital post mortems or even grave robbing. Their race might have been determined by the archaeologist or grave robber who dug them up, by the individual's own testimony before death or from a death certificate or other legal document. All these methods can be deeply flawed. Archaeologists often determined racial categories according to their particular prejudices. In the 1920s, the Harvard graduate, Alfred Kidder, excavated Pecos Pueblo, a few miles south east of Santa Fe, New Mexico. Several thousand skulls were eventually dug up and Kidder asked America's foremost anthropologist, Earnest Hooton, to confirm their racial identity.

Hooton saw considerable variety among the skulls and eventually sorted them into eight racial types. These included 'nondescript specimens of a generalised Southwestern Indian appearance', 'Long-faced Europeans', a 'pseudo-Alpine' type with 'a very broad, short face and rounded contours', a 'short, slender dolicocephalic' type that bore a resemblance to 'the brunet or brown-skinned group often called the Mediterranean race', a 'pseudo-Australoid' type which 'may be an ancient form of brunet white man' and a 'pseudo-Negroid' which he was 'of the opinion that it is in truth Negroid.' Hooton saw Pueblo Pecos as the original American melting pot and developed fanciful theories about how the various groups had arrived there, including stories of marauding Scandinavians and of a fantastic journey of a group of Negroids from Northwest Africa who travelled across Asia and entered the Americas via the Bering Straits. Trapped in a scientific *zeitgeist* in which the world was divided into a fixed number of racial types, it never occurred to Hooton that the Native American populations of the Pueblo Pecos might simply have been morphologically diverse.

Hooton was a pioneer of the use of statistical methods in determining racial categories and his Statistical Laboratory at Harvard, equipped with what were then state-of-the-art IBM punch card machines and computers, performed the 'most sophisticated "data crunching" operation that anthropologists had seen until the 1950s' using early versions of CRANID and FORDISC 2.0. However, if the database on which the analysis is performed is contaminated by prejudice, then so will the conclusion be.

The social prejudices of American society infected the categorisation of skulls in other ways too. As we saw in Chapter 2, the distinction between black and white or Negroid and Caucasian is governed by the 'one drop rule': one drop of African blood and you are deemed irrevocably black. Many a skull of an individual with predominantly European ancestry would have been categorised as 'African American' or 'Negroid'. As a result, many anthropologists today dismiss the baseline racial labels in reference collections as little more than 'folk stereotypes'. Since reference skulls were labelled wrongly in the first place, they argue, so any comparisons between unknown skulls and reference skulls will not yield useful information.

Who is right in this debate? Is today's craniometry a science reborn or nineteenth-century prejudice resurrected? How good is it in racially categorising skulls? Are the results of skull science good enough to demonstrate the reality of race? These questions are very similar to those we considered in Chapter 2 when we looked at the impact of genetic variation on medicine and asked whether or not medicine should be colour-blind. The answer to the question 'Who is right?', now as then, is 'both and neither'.

'If races don't exist, how come forensic anthropologists are so

good at identifying them?' the forensic anthropologist (and disbe-
liever in race) Norman Sauer pointedly asked, in the title of an academic paper. How come, indeed? As a forensic scientist, Sauer daily
distinguishes between skeletons according to race yet he rejects the
idea that race has biological meaning. Is his view of race a political
stance at odds with the evidence he can see with his scientific eyes?
Not at all, Sauer rejoins. 'The successful assignment of race to a skeletal specimen is not a vindication of the race concept', he observes, 'but
rather a prediction that an individual while alive was assigned to a particular socially constructed "racial" category.' In Chapter 2, we saw
how geneticists use socially-defined groups as surrogates for natural
populations. Many of the ways in which we customarily group
people socially – by race, ethnicity, nationality, religious affiliation,
geographic locality and so on – are not biologically arbitrary. Members
of such groups often show greater biological relatedness than two ran-
domly chosen individuals. Categories such as 'African American',
'people of Asian descent' and 'Ashkenazi Jew' can be important in
medical research not because they are natural races but because they
are social representations of certain aspects of genetic variation. We
can use genetics to distinguish between socially-defined populations.
The same is true of skull science. Because we can define in statistical
terms the differences between the measurements of a Caucasian,
African and Native American skull, we can distinguish between them
to a limited degree. To use skulls in this fashion is not necessarily to
resurrect nineteenth-century prejudices but neither is it to demonstrate the reality of race.

The real problem arises when anthropologists attempt to extend
modern racial categories into the past. This suggests that physical
form is fixed in time, rehabilitating the idea of racial 'type'.
Kennewick Man possessed certain features – such as narrow cheekbones, protruding upper jaw and a well developed brow-ridge – that
are often categorised as 'Caucasoid' but these features refer to a

socially-defined population now, not one that might have existed nine thousand years ago. There is no reason to assume that because Kennewick Man possessed these features he came from a population ancestral to today's Caucasians, still less that he was 'white'. Part of the problem is that race is defined in terms both of morphology (an individual's physical form or appearance) and ancestry but the two are not necessarily connected. John may suffer from sickle cell anaemia because he is James's grandson or because he, like James, comes from a population that has in the past suffered from malaria and which has adapted to it through the process of natural selection. The same is true of skull shape.

Some anthropologists have suggested that the label 'Caucasoid' is a useful one for Kennewick Man because, while he may not have been European, he might indeed have belonged to another Caucasoid population. Many have suggested that there are similarities between Kennewick Man and the Ainu, the vestige of a hunting gathering fishing people who occupied the northernmost islands of the Western Pacific, including parts of Japan and the Siberian islands of Kurile and Sakhalin. They are believed to be the descendants of a people, the Jomon, who first occupied the Japanese archipelago some 15,000 years ago, before the arrival, around 10,000 years later, of the Yajoi, as the Japanese rice-farming culture is known. While the Ainu have virtually disappeared as a distinct group because of acculturation and intermarriage with their Japanese and Siberian neighbours, they are nevertheless thought to have had a distinct appearance. The Yajoi have a typical 'East Asian' look, described by anthropologists as having flat faces, epicanthic folds, yellow-brown skin, brown eyes, thin, straight black hair and virtually hairless bodies. The Ainu had 'short faces, high-bridged prominent noses, no epicanthic folds, light skins, sometimes gray eyes, dense, wavy to frizzy hair on their heads and unusually hairy bodies'. They were considered by physical anthropologists of the late nineteenth and early twentieth centuries to be a

Caucasoid people and there has been endless (and fruitless) speculation about historical ties between Europeans and the Ainu. Some anthropologists continue to think in this vein.

To test such speculation, Jim Chatters ran a multivariate analysis on Kennewick Man's skull, comparing it to skulls of modern populations. Kennewick Man turned out to be closest not to the Ainu but to certain Polynesian groups. Polynesians are thought to be descendants of a population that originated from the southern coast of China – not too distant from the Japanese homeland of the Ainu. They set out in large outrigger canoes, probably around six thousand years ago, carrying dogs, chickens, pigs, coconuts and taro. They progressively colonised various islands, from the already-inhabited lands of Indonesia and Melanesia to the uninhabited volcanic atolls of the Pacific. Loring Brace has conducted cranio-facial studies of Asians and Pacific Islanders and found that the Ainu, their Jomon ancestors and the Polynesians form a single group that he calls the Jomon-Pacific cluster. Together they appear to be remnants of a population that occupied coastal eastern Asia in the late Stone Age, before the advent of rice farming and the subsequent rapid spread of north-eastern Asian peoples.

Perhaps it is not surprising, then, that Kennewick Man might resemble both the Ainu and Polynesians. Except that he doesn't. While Kennewick Man is statistically closest to Polynesians when it comes to skull measurements, he is actually not very close even to them. Modern Polynesians are morphologically more akin to modern Europeans than to Kennewick Man. Chatters discovered that Kennewick Man is quite unlike *any* modern people.

Kennewick Man is not the only ancient skeleton that has been found in America. Some thirty-nine skeletons more that nine thousand years old have now been discovered. Most are very fragmentary – not much more scattered bits of bones. Sixteen skeletons, however, are at least half-complete and of these eleven include complete or near-complete skulls. Jim Chatters and Richard Jantz (the co-author of FORDISC) compared the skulls of six of these with those of modern populations. Four appeared closest to Polynesians, one to Europeans and one to Africans. But, once more, such closeness is illusory. All the skulls lay outside the framework of modern humans. In a two-dimensional graphical representation of cranial measurements of ancient and modern skulls, modern populations form a series of tightly-bunched, overlapping groups slightly to the left of centre of the graph. Ancient Americans skulls are widely scattered throughout the bottom right quadrant. 'The skulls of recent members of our species', Chatters observes, 'are more like one another than they are like those of Ancient Americans'. Analyses by other anthropologists bear this out. Kennewick Man, and his ancient brethren, are not like Native Americans but nor are they particularly akin to any other modern people. Meanwhile, craniometric studies on ancient South American skulls show that they are distinct from both modern and ancient Americans.

Kennewick Man was not white, nor European, nor even Caucasian. He was just very different from modern Native Americans and indeed from all modern peoples. How can we account for this difference? There are two possible explanations. Kennewick Man may have belonged to one population and the ancestors of today's Native Americans to another, very different-looking one, which migrated at a different time and from a different place. Or the population to which Kennewick Man belonged may have originally looked like a bunch of 'Jean-Luc Picards' but evolved over time into very different looking people with Native American features. The first explanation says that there were several migrations into the Americas and the Native Americans were simply the last; the second insists that there was only one migration but the first Americans changed their looks, with natural selection acting as the cosmetic surgeon. The jury is still out as to which theory is right – though the data from anthropology, archaeology, genetics and linguistics all seem to favour the idea of multiple migrations. Whichever theory is right, there is no reason to believe that Kennewick Man was white.

SCIENCE AND STORIES

Kennewick Man was no wandering European. He was not a white man of any description. He was simply different from all modern peoples. What does the belief that he was white say about the scientific study of human history?

Scientific stories about the peopling of the Americas have long been shaped by politics, prejudice and straightforward racism. When Europeans first arrived in the New World they conjured up wonderful tales of Indian origins. For the sixteenth-century Dominican priest, historian and archaeologist Diego Duran, Indians were the Lost Tribe of Israel. Ignatius Donnelly, the Irish American writer, lawyer and politician, suggested that they had originated in the fabled lost continent of Atlantis. Others thought that Indians were descended from a wandering group of Europeans, North Africans or Asians: Egyptians, Vikings, Phoenicians, Basques, Greeks, Mongols, Romans, Persians and Japanese were all deemed suitable candidates.

In the early nineteenth century, as Meriwether Lewis and William Clark tramped across America on their epic journey west-wards, they came across a number of huge earthen mounds and hill forts. Subsequent expeditions reported earthworks shaped like birds, bears and snakes. Inside were ancient graves, often overflowing with strange and magnificent artwork. Few white Americans believed that Indians were capable of building such impressive constructions. So the myth of the Moundbuilders grew: the mounds were the work of the first Americans, an ancient and now-vanished white civilisation that had been exterminated by the Indians.

In the middle of the nineteenth century, the discovery in Europe of several archaeological sites in which ancient stone tools were found together with the fossilised bones of extinct animals, helped overturn the Biblical idea of human origins and led to the acceptance of the notions not just of human antiquity but also of human prehistory and of a 'Stone Age' when humankind had not yet advanced enough to use metal but had to make tools from flint and bone. In America, however, the most influential figures in anthropology – in particular William Henry Holmes, head curator of anthropology at the Smithsonian Institute and his student Aleš Hrdlička, who was to became the nation's leading racial scientist of the early twentieth century – refused to countenance the idea that Native Americans could be an ancient people and denounced any and all discoveries of 'Stone Age' tools as fakes. Critics of Holmes and Hrdlička, both at the time and since, have suggested that they acted as a kind of 'paleopolice', the Wyatt Earp and Doc Holliday of American archaeology, driving out of town anyone with different views.

The discovery, in the 1920s and the 1930s, of human tools among the fossilised remains of extinct animals in two New Mexican towns, Folsom and Clovis, finally led scientists to accept the idea that the Americas too had passed through a Stone Age. The culture that produced these ancient tools came to be called 'Clovis' and over the next half a century, archaeologists discovered a number of Clovis sites across America, dating from 11,500 to 10,900 years ago. The so-called 'Clovis First' argument – which suggested that the Clovis were the first Americans – came to dominate American archaeology. It claimed that these first Americans came from Asia around 12,000 years ago, across Beringia, an ancient landmass which connected Siberia to Alaska but which has since been covered by the oceans.

Then, Clovis-style fluted points were discovered in South America, as far south as Tierra del Fuego and as ancient as 11,000 years old. This meant that, if the Clovis First theory was right, the first

Americans must have travelled from northern Alaska to the southern-most tip of South America in a few hundred years, a speed of colonisa-tion far quicker than that found anywhere else in the world. In response to this conundrum, the archaeologist Paul Martin developed in the 1960s what became called the 'Overkill' theory. One of the peculiarities of the Americas is that there are so few big mammals. Once, cheetahs, mammoths, mastodons, lions, camels, giant beavers and sabre-tooth tigers had roamed the continent. Why had they van-ished? Martin suggested that the invading Clovis had wiped them out. A handful of Eurasian hunters – perhaps as few as twenty-five males – had, Martin suggested, entered the Americas across Beringia around 12,000 years ago and swept through the continent at breath-taking pace, slaughtering virtually everything that moved across their path.

Martin's thesis caused a sensation. It appeared to reconcile the Clovis First theory with the evidence from South American excava-tions. Its political implications only added to its notoriety. Conservatives loved the idea that Native Americans were not the Noble Savages of myth but a seemingly ignoble people with a bent for mass killing. The National Rifle Association was thrilled that big game hunting was rooted deep in American history. The idea that humans were responsible for destroying much of the American fauna struck a chord with the nascent environmental movement. Native Americans, on the other hand, detested their portrayal as bloodthirsty killers, viewing it as yet another assault on the moral values of their people. For many South American scholars, 'a rapid-fire blitzkrieg by Clovis hunters' seemed, in archaeologist James Adovasio's words, 'a bit too much like a familiar story in Latin America: Yankee imperialism.'

In the end, it was not the political implications but the scientific evidence that did for Martin's theory. Clovis tools were in use for just over half a millennium, between 11,500 and 10,900 years ago. The great North American beasts disappeared, however, over a much longer period. No cheetah remains have been found less than 17,000 years old; the last mammoth disappeared about 10,500 years ago; lions lasted for another 1,000 years and the sabre-tooth tiger only became extinct around 9,500 years ago. For whatever reason these creatures vanished, it is unlikely to have been because of Clovis über-hunters.

Almost as soon as the 'Clovis First' thesis became established, some began suggesting that the first Americans had arrived on the continent even earlier. From the late 1930s onwards, archaeologists announced the discovery of hundreds of sites supposedly demonstrating human presence before the Clovis. Almost all were dismissed as frauds. Frustrated pre-Clovis enthusiasts pointed the finger at a new posse of archaeological sheriffs, the intellectual descendants of Holmes and Hrdlička, who patrolled the Clovis frontier, gunning down any evidence that the Americas might have been home to an earlier people.

After nearly half a century of searching, archaeologists finally found definitive evidence that the Americas were populated before the Clovis. In the 1970s, the archaeologist Tom Dillehay, then teaching at the Southern University of Chile, began excavating a site on the banks of Chinchihuapi Creek in southern Chile that came to be known as Monte Verde. Dillehay discovered a Stone Age village and evidence of a people with a complex social structure and relatively sophisticated lifestyle. Most astonishingly, radiocarbon dating showed it to be 13,500 years old – almost two millennia before the earliest known Clovis occupation of *North* America. Dillehay spent nearly two decades excavating the site and trying to persuade a sceptical archaeological community that it was not a fraud. He has been accused, fellow archaeologist James Adavasio observes, 'of virtually every lapse an archaeologist can make; in fact he has been slandered and libelled by colleagues here in America who went so far as accusing him of faking evidence.' If he had to do it all over again, Dillehay once told Adavasio, he wouldn't; it wasn't worth the agony. Eventually, in 1997, a blue-riband panel of archaeologists, including many vocal sceptics, inspected the site. All agreed that the site was, as Tom Dillehay claimed, some 13,500 years old and that people had inhabited the New World even before the Clovis.

Many see the debate about Kennewick Man as the latest stage in this long history of scientific origin stories that have been shaped as much by politics and prejudice as by evidence. The key theme in the scientific study of deep American history, many argue, is the attempt to deny Native Americans their history and heritage and to fashion instead a 'white' vision of the Americas. 'Since the colonisation of the Americas', the anthropologist Chris Kortright claims, 'there has been a desire to historically connect the "Old World" with the "New World". Intellectuals and academics have built their names and careers for themselves by connecting the two worlds; at the same time these individuals reinforce the ideologies of colonisation and racial hierarchy.' The debate about Kennewick Man, he believes, shows that 'this practice is still strong'. Not only do some scientists view Kennewick Man as white but some have also claimed that Clovis was really a European culture. The archaeologists, Dennis Stanford and Bruce Bradley, have suggested that the earliest Americans came not out of Siberia but Iberia. They point out that Clovis tools are very similar to those of the Solutrean culture that occupied south-western France and the Iberian peninsula between 25,000 and 19,700 years ago. The oldest and most numerous Clovis sites are to be found in the south-eastern states of America – the ones closest to southern Europe. And during the last Ice Age – roughly the time when the Clovis first appeared in the New World – sea levels were much lower and ice-free parts of Europe were within 1400 miles of the coastline of North America. 'It wouldn't take too much for an intelligent person to learn how to handle the ocean and perhaps even get to North America', Stanford suggests. But, he cautions, 'this is really an off the wall kind of idea right now but it's one I don't think we should overlook.'

For Vine Deloria, any such speculation is politically suspect. 'By making us immigrants to North America', he argues, scientists 'are able to deny the fact that we were the full, complete and total owners of this continent. They are able to see us simply as earlier interlopers and therefore throw back at us the accusation that we had simply found North America a little earlier than they had.' Deloria objects not just to the theory that the first Americans came from Europe but to any theory that appears to deny Native Americans their 'ownership' of the continent . He rejects not just the Iberian connection but the Siberian connection too. The Bering Land Bridge theory is as unacceptable as the Solutrean connection theory because it too turns Native Americans into immigrants. Science, Deloria believes, 'should drop the pretense of having absolute authority with regard to human origins and begin looking for some other kind of explanation that would include the tradition and memories of non-Western peoples'. And there is the irony. Critics such as Deloria denounce scientific origin stories as shaped more by prejudice than evidence. Yet Deloria rejects any scientific theory, based on any evidence, that is not politically correct. Far from challenging politicised science, postmodern critics such as Deloria want to make all knowledge political.

Scientific stories of human origins may be, and often have been, shaped by politics yet at their heart lies evidence. It is the actuality of the material world that constrains the shape of a scientific history. As new evidence accumulates, so new, and better, theories arise. The discoveries at Folsom and Clovis overturned the belief that the first Americans had arrived relatively recently. The Clovis First account was in turn overthrown by new discoveries in Monte Verde and elsewhere. Paul Martin's 'Overkill' thesis generated huge controversy because of its apparent political implications until it was finally killed off not by politics but by fact and reasoning. It is true that, in each case, the debates were fractious and much more was involved than just the facts – political prejudice, personal ambition and academic inertia all played their part. Yet what made these discussions of the early peopling of the Americas scientific was that they were a discussion of the facts. Facts certainly do not speak for themselves but in science the facts inevitably anchor the debate.

Religious origin stories, or those rooted in folklore, are, on the other hand, anchored not by facts but by faith. They are believed in spite of the facts, not because of them. The facts of evolution do not change the story of Genesis one whit, nor do the facts of the Asian origin of Native Americans matter to those who believe the Indian oral tradition. That is why, unlike scientific histories that change as the facts change, religious origin stories are set in stone. That is also why there is, inevitably, conflict between traditional origin stories and scientific accounts. For many, such conflict creates a moral dilemma. Jonathan Marks suggests that the Kennewick Man debate highlights 'scientists' belief they have a right – perhaps even a duty! – to delegitimise other peoples' ideas about who they are and where they came from.' This he calls 'the problem of colonial genetics in a postcolonial age'. Marks condemns the way that 'self-righteous, self-interested, self-proclaimed and slightly paranoid advocates of science' often 'rewrite origin narratives and identities of other peoples on the basis of partial, ambiguous and dubiously interpreted evidence'.

Marks is no postmodernist or irrationalist. Quite the opposite – he stands in the Enlightenment humanist tradition and at the heart of much of his work is the debunking of irrational myths that often pass for scientific theory. Yet there is, in Marks' charge sheet against the Kennewick Man scientists, an echo of the Romantic complaint about Enlightenment rationalism. His comments reveal again how progressives, who in the past would have welcomed the scientific challenge to traditional stories and histories, now wish to shore up those traditional accounts against the onward march of scientific reason. It is a view that raises some interesting questions. Should Darwinists refrain from promoting the theory of evolution because it 'delegitimises' the Christian (and indeed all religious and many non-religious) origin stories? Is it 'self-righteous' and 'self-interested' to propose that the first Americans may have come from Asia via the Bering Land Bridge? Marks suggests that Creationism should be 'acknowledged and engaged (rather than accepted or combated)'. It is difficult to know, however, how it is possible for rationalists to 'engage' with Creationism without combating it.

A different view of the relationship between science and tradition comes from Joallyn Archambault, Director of the American Indian Program at the Smithsonian Institute and a member of the Standing Rock Sioux Tribe. 'I am' she writes, 'personally familiar with Sioux religious and cultural traditions and I have great pride in my Indian heritage'. She has 'personally participated in all of the major traditional ceremonies appropriate for a Sioux woman of my age and position in life, including a vision quest and a Sun Dance.' In an affidavit to the judge considering the Kennwick Man case, she wrote that while 'I respect the traditional religious and cultural beliefs of my tribe and those of other tribes', such respect 'does not mean that we must accept all of those beliefs as invariably accurate statements of historic or scientific fact':

> To do so would be contrary to commonsense and what we know about the world from other sources of knowledge. For example origin stories ... vary widely from tribe to tribe. Depending upon the tribe, creation may be the work of Coyote, a bird, a first man, a turtle and so on. Even within the same tribe, traditional beliefs can include multiple creation stories. For example, three different creation stories were accepted in my father's tribe when I was a child ... ordinary logic tells us that not all of these different stories or versions can be true, at least in a factual sense. And we should not expect them to be. The purpose of origin stories is to provide metaphysical, rather than historic or scientific,

explanations ... Like other forms of great literature they should be interpreted symbolically rather than literally.

For Archambault, 'the Kennewick skeleton should be made available for study so we can learn as much from it as possible. The past is important because it can help to teach us who we are and how we fit into the world.' She adds that 'the anti-science and anti-intellectual arguments espoused by some Native American religious and political factions do not represent the views of all, or even the majority of, American Indians. Most American Indians are as interested about the past as other people. They want to know the truth about the past, and they should be entitled to do so.'

Knowledge, for Archambault, is a public affair and the property of all. Identity is a private matter. Traditional stories of a people's history may be important for cultural and symbolic reasons but there is no reason that science should defer to them. American Indians, she argues, 'have as much right as anyone else to be exposed to different ideas and to make up their own minds about what they believe or do not believe.' For Archambault, there is no such thing as *an* American Indian culture. Some Indians may draw on traditional stories, others on scientific knowledge, still others on both. American Indians, in other words, are no different from other people and no less diverse in their views and identities than other people.

Marks, however, appears to view knowledge as, to a significant degree, culturally bound. What does this say about science? When Marks complains about scientific accounts helping to 'delegitimise other peoples' ideas' and to 'rewrite origin narratives and identities of other peoples' he seems to be suggesting that science belongs to one culture (presumably modern Western) and those 'ideas' and 'narratives' to other cultures. It is a view of cultures as organic entities and of knowledge as organically bound to particular cultures. For Marks, it is not enough to say, as Archambault does, that science tells us factual truths and that origin stories are like works of literature. The importance of origin stories is that they help define questions of 'morality, ultimate justice, good and evil, happiness and what lies beyond death' and so shape the identity of a culture and its relationship to the rest of the world. Origin stories, he argues, 'are culturally integrated to a far greater degree than science'. He worries that 'science's standard operating procedure is to take some aspect of new knowledge and to substitute it for whatever alternative existed before it – generally without looking for or dealing with the broader implications or cultural and symbolic connections.' Scientific truth, in other words, may not matter as much as social cohesion and cultural survival.

This, of course, is the classic Romantic view of culture and knowledge: knowledge as culturally-bound, culture as a bounded entity, the importance of social cohesion and cultural survival and the significance of identity to the survival of a culture and a people. These sentiments, as we have seen, lie at the heart of the modern pluralist view of culture and knowledge and, by creating a fixation with identity, have helped resurrect ideas of racial difference in a new form. It is a fixation with identity that has shaped the debate on Kennewick Man. On the one side, opponents of the scientific study of Kennewick Man suggest that the demands of science must defer to the needs of cultural identity. On the other, many have hailed the scientific study of Kennewick Man as revealing his true (white) identity. Kennewick Man is no more a white man than he is a Native American, but the belief that he is has been fuelled less by old-fashioned racism than by the new-fangled politics of identity – the same as that which drives critics of the scientific study of Kennewick to claim him as Native American.

10

THE END OF UTOPIA AND THE RETURN OF RACE

Jacob X might sound like the name of a wannabe Jewish porn star. In fact, it was the pseudonym of a French Army surgeon, whose most famous work *The Untrodden Fields of Anthropology* was a fine example of what has come to be called 'anthroporn'. Obviously viewing himself as an Alfred Kinsey of the colonial world (albeit half a century before Kinsey published his ground-breaking studies of America's sex life), Jacob X set out, in the name of science, to handle testicles, measure labia and record a thousand exotic sexual peccadilloes. Among his research findings was that black men have smaller testicles than white men and that their 'erection is never hard like that of the European, the Chinese and the Hindoo. It is always rather soft and feels to the hand like a strong elastic tube of black india-rubber'. 'The experimental method', the writer Marek Kohn dryly observes, 'is not detailed.'

Almost a century after his book was published, Jacob X finally received the kind of recognition he had craved all his life: his research was cited in an academic work. Unfortunately, the academic in question was J. Phillipe Rushton, a British-born psychologist, based in Canada, who has spent much of life collecting data on racial differences in the size of skulls and penises and out of these differences building a truly vertiginous cosmology of race. According to Rushton, the world can be divided into three main races: Orientals, Blacks and Whites. Orientals he describes as East Asians or Mongoloids, Whites as Europeans or Caucasoids and Blacks as Africans or Negroids. Everybody else either does not interest Rushton or has become a surrogate member of one of the three principal races.

The three races are, in Rushton's cosmology, arranged on an evolutionary ladder with Orientals at the top, Blacks at the bottom and Whites in the middle. Orientals, he suggests, have the largest brains and the greatest intelligence. They are the least promiscuous, aggressive and criminally-minded of the races, the hardest workers and the best parents. They have the lowest rates of sexually transmitted diseases, the longest life expectancy, the greatest degree of emotional control and, or so Rushton informs us, the least amount of body odour. Blacks are at the opposite end on all of these scales and Whites in the middle (though, naturally, closer to Orientals than to Blacks). These data come from a veritable smorgasbord of sources from World Health Organization information on condom sizes (the WHO apparently recommends 49mm condoms for distribution in Asia, 52mm for North America and Europe and 53mm ones for Africa), to surveys Rushton has conducted in shopping malls asking men about the size of their penis and the strength of their ejaculation (the erect Oriental penis is supposedly 4–5½ inches in length compared to 5½–6 inches for Whites and 6¼–8 inches for Blacks), to helmet sizes used by the US Army and hitherto hidden scientific gems such as *The Untrodden Fields of Anthropology*.

According to Rushton, the differences between the three races can be explained in terms of what evolutionary biologists call the 'r/K' or 'life history' theory. First developed in the 1960s, by the ecologists R.H. MacArthur and E.O. Wilson (later of sociobiology fame), the theory attempts to explain how organisms respond to changing environmental conditions by changing their reproductive strategies. In difficult circumstances (such as a population colonising a new terrain), individuals try to reproduce quickly but spend little time looking after their offspring. This is the 'r' strategy. In more favourable circumstances, organisms move to a 'K' strategy – they produce fewer offspring but take better care of those that they have.

In the original theory, the distinction between r and K was an expression of differences not in intelligence but in environmental conditions. The same population could follow a different strategy depending on the circumstances. Rushton, however, translates the r/K difference into a marker for low and high intelligence, the K-strategists possessing 'a more complex nervous system and a bigger brain' than r-organisms, and then exploits this as a way of establishing a ladder of evolutionary progress within both nature in general and humanity in particular. Oysters, Rushton writes, 'have a nervous system so simple that they lack a true brain.' To offset this 'they produce 500 million eggs a year'. In contrast, 'chimpanzees have large brains but give birth to one baby about every four years.' Because there is a consistent relationship between high intelligence and low reproductive rates, all organisms can be ranked on an evolutionary scale; from oyster we go through fish, frog, rabbit and cat before arriving at chimpanzee. With Rushton, Marek Kohn observes, 'the Great Chain of Being is back in the idiom of population biology.' The Great Chain extends to humankind, too. Blacks follow an r-strategy, being highly sexually active but not particularly clever, while Orientals are a K people; they are in Rushton's words ' "dads" rather than "cads" '. Whites, as ever, fall somewhere in between and, as ever, are closer to Orientals than they are to Blacks.

These different strategies are not pragmatic responses to particular circumstances but evolved dispositions hard-wired into the brain. According to Rushton, Blacks developed an r-strategy because Africa is an unstable, unforgiving environment with 'unpredictable droughts and deadly diseases'. The best strategy is to have 'more children ... and less parental care'. Since 'less culture is passed from parent to child ... this tends to reduce the intellectual demands needed to function in the culture'. In Europe and Asia, the climate was colder and the problems were different: 'gathering and storing food, providing shelter, making clothes and raising children through the long winters.' These tasks 'were more mentally demanding' and 'called for larger brains and slower growth rates'.

Distilled down, Rushton's thesis comes to this: big penis, small brain, pretty stupid; small penis, big brain, very clever. Everything else, from the ability to win Olympic Gold medals to the capacity for civilisation, flows from this. For Rushton, the size of Linford Christie's lunchbox accounts for famine in Africa, while Oriental men's apparent distaste for sex explains the size of the Japanese economy.

The argument is as incoherent as it is preposterous. Why should the harsh climate of Siberia, central Asia and Northern Europe create a more stable and predictable environment than living in the warmth of the African sun? Why should the process of 'gathering and storing food, providing shelter, making clothes and raising children' be more mentally demanding in Europe and Asia than in drought- and disease-ridden Africa? Because, Rushton suggests, 'in Africa, food and warmth were available all year round'. He seems not to recognise that this picture of a benign, predictable Africa is the opposite of his initial assumption of a disease- and drought-ridden continent. Nor does Rushton seem to recognise that birth rate is historically changeable. In 1980, the birth rate for black Americans stood at 22.1 births per 1000 population, considerably higher than the figure for whites at 14.9. In 1800, however, the white birth rate had stood at an astonishing 55 per 1000 population – nearly three times the current black rate (there are no figures for the black birth rate in 1800). The white birth rate did not fall below 22.1 until 1970. Viewed historically, Rushton's racial distinctions disappear.

It is tempting to call Rushton a dinosaur, following in the footsteps of the likes of Samuel Morton. In fact, he is more like one of those exotic pre-Cambrian creatures found in the Burgess Shale in British Columbia and described by Stephen Jay Gould in his book *Wonderful Life*: creatures with names like *Hallucigenia*, *Wiwaxia* and *Anomalocaris*, which seem too primeval to classify with modern organisms. The work of racial scientists like Morton was often scientifically flawed and morally reprehensible. Yet many, including Morton himself, were serious investigators who set out to unearth real empirical data. Rushton, however, trundles down the well-worn roads of racial anthropology, scavenging for titbits to feed his eccentric arguments. Morton, and other nineteenth-century racial scientists, worked in a era in which a racial view of the world appeared rational and coherent. Rushton lives at a time when even most race realists disavow the kinds of nineteenth-century concepts to which he still clings.

Unsurprisingly, Rushton's work has come under sustained and hostile fire. His concept of race, his notion of intelligence, his belief in the link between race, intelligence and brain size, his method of aggregating data, his abuse of the r/K theory – all have been shredded by his critics. Rushton dismisses such criticism as coming from the usual suspects – Marxists driven by political correctness, like Stephen Jay Gould. Much of the criticism, however, comes from some highly unusual quarters. The anthropologist C. Loring Brace – long a critic of Gould – describes Rushton's *oeuvre* as 'an amalgamation of bad biology and inexcusable anthropology. It is not science but advocacy and advocacy of racialism.' The sociobiologist, David Barash, dismisses Rushton's 'pious hope' that 'by combining numerous little turds of variously tainted data, one can obtain a valuable result; but in fact the outcome is merely a larger than average pile of shit.' This is not the kind of language that one usually sees in academic journals. Nor is Barash the kind of critic one might expect to find. A hard-nosed sociobiologist, who has faced considerable abuse for his academic theories, he is certainly no lily-livered Marxist.

Rushton's work, and the criticism it draws, reveals how marginalised such racial science has become. Of course, Rushton is not the only proponent of the idea that intelligence is racially distributed. Richard Lynn, professor emeritus of psychology at the University of Ulster, has, for even longer than Rushton, peddled a tripartite division in race and intelligence. 'My major discovery', Lynn has written 'is that the Oriental peoples of East Asia have higher average intelligence by about 5 IQ points than Europeans and peoples of European origin in the United States and elsewhere.' Lynn also believes that 'the average IQ of blacks in sub-Saharan Africa is approximately 70', a figure that would brand the majority of Africans as mentally retarded. According to Lynn, the average IQ of African Americans is higher than that of native Africans because 'they have about 25 per cent of Caucasian genes and a better environment.'

A survey of psychologists in the mid-1980s showed that more than half believed in the concept of '*g*', a controversial unit of intelligence especially exploited by those who seek hereditary distinctions. 'In *g*', Marek Kohn suggests, 'psychologists have found a universal factor to replace typological race'. With *g* in the armoury, 'Hierarchy is no longer wordy ruminations on national character but read off from a numerical scale.' The survey also showed that half of those expressing an opinion believed that IQ differences between blacks and whites were, at least partly, innate. Both the concept of *g* and the belief in innate racial differences in intelligence have been central to two of the most talked-about accounts of the relationship between race and intelligence in the postwar years. Thirty years ago, the respected educationalist, Arthur Jensen, created an intellectual firestorm with a paper in the *Harvard Educational Review* entitled 'How Much Can We Boost I.Q. and Scholastic Achievement?'. It concluded, among other things, that 'Head Start' programmes designed to boost African American IQ scores had failed and that the gap between black and white IQ scores was never likely to be bridged because it was largely the result of genetic factors.

More recently, Charles Murray and Richard Herrnstein whipped up an even larger controversy with their publication, in 1994, of *The Bell Curve*. At 845 pages long and packed with dense statistics, it was not a ready-made bestseller. Yet it sold 300,000 copies in hardback, largely on the back of the international storm it generated. Murray and Herrnstein set out to prove that American society had become highly meritocratic. Wealth, and other social outcomes, were being distributed increasingly on the basis of individual talents (especially intelligence) and decreasingly on the basis of social class. There were, they argued, strong correlations between intelligence and various types of social performance and that differences in intelligence explained stratification in American society. They also suggested that differences in intelligence explained a large part of the social and economic differences between racial and ethnic groups in America.

Despite the length and strength of the controversies that both Arthur Jensen's paper and *The Bell Curve* generated, neither work has had a major impact on the way that either academics or lay people think about the relationship between race and intelligence. If you already believed that intelligence was racially distributed, then Jensen and *The Bell Curve* would have confirmed your suspicions. If you already rejected the idea that blacks were disadvantaged because they were naturally less intelligent, then you were unlikely to have been persuaded otherwise by either work. The controversies have been generated as much by the critics as by the works themselves and reveal less the strength of racial science than the depth of the sensitivity that still exists in any discussion about racial differences in intelligence. When, in 1998, Jensen wrote his *magnum opus, The g Factor: The Science of Mental Abilities*, no major publisher would touch it; it was eventually published by a small mail-order imprint, Praegar, which specialises in promoting outcast academics. Charles Murray – like most race realists never one to pass up an opportunity to play the victim – continues to believe that it remains a 'taboo' to talk of racial differences in intelligence.

Actually, in certain circumstances it seems perfectly acceptable to talk of such ideas. In 2006, the anthropologists Henry Harpending and Jason Hardy and the physicist Gregory Cochrane published a paper entitled 'A Natural History of Ashkenazi Intelligence', which argued that Jews are more intelligent because their history of money-lending and other financial occupations had favoured genes associated with cleverness. It was greeted not with vitriol but with quizzical interest. Murray himself wrote an essay on 'Jewish Genius', for the American magazine *Commentary*, which speculated on the genetic reasons for the fact a group that make up 0.02 per cent of the world's population had nevertheless contributed fourteen per cent of Nobel Laureates in the first half of the twentieth century, twenty-nine per cent in the second half and thirty-two per cent so far in the twenty-first century. Again, the piece attracted little opprobrium. The moral, Marek Kohn suggests, is that if you want to link race and intelligence, do so by talking of the benefits rather than the disadvantages of racial belonging.

In the main though, those who explore racial differences in intelligence tend to be treated with suspicion by their academic peers. One reason, Kohn argues, is that most biologists today 'share the views about racial equality that prevail throughout society as a whole'. This makes them particularly sensitive to the 'embarrassing capacity' of writers like Rushton, Lynn, Jensen and Murray, 'to demonstrate just how readily modern evolutionary ideas lend themselves to racialisation'. Should there be a 'change in the *Zeitgeist*', Kohn warns, 'modern Darwinism appears to present few theoretical barriers' to the return of racial science.

Interestingly, something a bit different seems to be happening. The postwar *zeitgeist* has, in many ways, held firm. Indeed, the political and intellectual classes are probably more sensitive today to the charge of racism than they were half a century ago. Yet over the past few years we have become much less inhibited in using the language of biology to talk about race. From science and medicine to genealogy and pop culture, discussion of racial differences has become acceptable. Even that impeccably liberal newspaper of record, the *New York Times*, sometimes reads as a champion of race realism, with a series of articles by its science correspondent Nicholas Wade endorsing the biological reality of race. Race, in other words, has returned to our vocabulary with neither the dismantling of the postwar *zeitgeist* nor the return of old-fashioned racial science. In this chapter, I want to explore how this has happened and to look at the relationship between biological ideas of race and political notions of identity. Far from new biological theories resurrecting old ideas of race, the very idea of race has changed as biology has become the handmaiden of the politics of identity.

RACE AND HUMAN NATURE

'What biology has done with race', Marek Kohn memorably suggested in his seminal book *The Race Gallery*,

> ... bears a certain resemblance to what physics has done with particles. It has extracted the contradictions and ambiguities hidden within the solid, discrete certainties of traditional race theory and founded the populational concept upon them. Examined at the equivalent of the quantum level, races are revealed as fluid, elusive and paradoxical, if not illusory.

Traditionally, populations were viewed as fixed, eternal entities. For Linnaeus, as for Aristotle, the essence of a species was present in each member of that species and it is that which made it a member of that species and separated it from others. This idea came to underlie the notion of type that was to be so central to racial science. Darwin decisively challenged the Aristotelian concept of species. For Darwin, classification was not based on the possession of common characteristics but was 'genealogical'. The 'hidden bond which naturalists have been unconsciously seeking', he wrote, is 'not some unknown plan of creation' or 'the mere putting together and separating [of] objects more or less alike' but a 'community of descent'.

Far from undermining the concept of race, however, the immediate impact of Darwinism was to strengthen it, as racial scientists adapted Darwin's theory to suit their preconceived ideas, successfully marrying the dynamic Darwinian concept of evolutionary change to the static Aristotelian view of fixed types. It was not until the second half of the twentieth century that the quantum revolution swept through biology and the Aristotelian concept of type decisively gave way to a Darwinian notion of population. Biologists continued to classify species according to Linnaeus's system but, with a few exceptions, they rejected the idea that species could be defined in terms of their physical (or genetic) similarities. Instead they began to treat species as historical entities, populations created through descent by modification. This shift from a typological to a populational view has transformed the debate, undermining the concept of races as fixed, bounded groups with set characteristics. The demise of racial science was largely the consequence not of scientific advances but of political developments – in particular the experience of Nazism. Nevertheless, the emergence of population biology provided in the postwar years a scientific grounding for antiracist arguments and forced even the majority of race realists to rethink their view of racial differences.

If the triumph of population biology was one major postwar development in biology, a second was the return of human nature. If postwar biology came to see populations as fluid and elusive, it came to view human nature as universal and fixed. First through sociobiology in the 1970s, and subsequently through evolutionary psychology (descended by modification from sociobiology) in the 1990s, human nature has returned to the heart of biology. Darwinian theory, having been exiled for much of the postwar period from discussions of the human condition and forced simply to appraise animal behaviour, has, over the past three decades, broken free of its shackles and returned to devour human behaviour too. The evolutionary psychologist Geoff Miller has called it a 'paradigm shift': where once the idea of human nature was treated with suspicion and ridicule, today there is barely a human activity for which someone does not have an evolutionary account. Discussions of human behaviour, political policy and social organisation all invoke human nature.

For most contemporary Darwinists, human nature describes a set of evolved behavioural dispositions that all humans possess. As the psychologist Steven Pinker has put it, 'the mind is a system of organs of computation designed by natural selection to solve the kind of problems our ancestors faced in their foraging way of life, in particular, understanding and outmanoeuvring objects, animals, plants and other people'. Evolution, in other words, honed the minds of our Stone Age ancestors, selecting for cognitive abilities and behavioural dispositions that helped them survive better in the Pleistocene environment. As descendants of those Stone Age hunter-gatherers we possess the same abilities and dispositions. And that is what we call human nature. So, evolutionary psychologists argue, all humans are disposed to show preference for kin over non-kin; all humans smile when happy and cry when sad; all humans respond to music. And so on. The only exception to the universality of human nature – and it is a very big exception – is the universal difference between the sexes.

The emergence of such theories of human nature in the 1970s, and particularly the publication in 1975 of E.O. Wilson's *Sociobiology*, created a firestorm of protest, generating a controversy that still has not fully died down. It is perhaps telling that the fiercest political row involving biology in the postwar years has not been about race but about human nature. In part, this reflects the strength of the postwar consensus on race. While critics of sociobiology and evolutionary psychology have often tarred their opponents as racists, even Nazis, few Darwinists have dissented from the general belief in racial equality and many continue to believe in the non-existence of races. According to Leda Cosmides and John Tooby, two of the founders of evolutionary psychology, 'Race exists in the minds of human beings. But geneticists have failed to discover objective patterns in the world that could easily explain the racial categories that seem so perceptually obvious to adults.' Race, in other words, is an illusion, found in human minds but not in the world outside.

It is true that a handful of sociobiologists have looked to the new Darwinism to buttress an old-style racial science. Rushton is one such figure. Kevin MacDonald is another. A professor of psychology at California State University, MacDonald is the author of a trilogy on Jews, published in the 1990s. Jews, he suggests, are not so much the Chosen People, as a people that chose itself, or rather, a people that bred itself. Judaism, for MacDonald, is best understood not as a religion but as an experiment in eugenics. The success of Jews, he argues, is the result of an ethnocentric 'group evolutionary strategy' that has involved the creation of a closed society with strict rules against marrying out to ensure racial purity through 'the segregation of the Jewish gene pool from surrounding gentile societies'. Such segregation has allowed Jews to launch 'eugenic efforts directed at reproducing high intelligence, high investment parenting and commitment to group, rather than individual, goals.' For thousands of years, Jews deliberately cut themselves off from the rest of the world to breed a master race. And they succeeded – their highly-developed genes have, MacDonald claims, allowed the Jews to dominate other ethnic groups, accumulate enormous wealth and achieve a political and intellectual prominence out of all proportion to their numbers. Anti-Semitism, for MacDonald, is simply the natural response of non-Jewish groups to the Jewish eugenics programme – an attempt to destroy the Jews before the Jews destroyed them.

MacDonald has played an important role in the Human Behaviour and Evolution Society (HBES) – the professional body for evolutionary psychologists in America – for which he has been secretary, archivist, newsletter editor and executive board member. His work, however, was fairly obscure, even to evolutionary psychologists and would probably have stayed that way but for the fact that, in 2000, he testified in a libel case brought by the Holocaust denier, David Irving, against the American historian, Deborah Lipstadt. MacDonald's appearance in a London witness box brought him and his books to the attention of the media and led to a withering attack by the journalist Judith Shulevitz in the online magazine *Slate*. Shulevitz excoriated both MacDonald's ideas and the community of evolutionary psychologists (and the HBES in particular) for tolerating them. 'It is the job of a scholarly association', she wrote, 'not just to foster discussion but also to police the boundaries of its discipline.'

Most evolutionary psychologists are loath to organise such police patrols because they see it as succumbing to the forces of political correctness. Given the widespread attempts to censor sociobiologists and evolutionary psychologists in the 1970s and 1980s, they rightly view any curtailment of academic freedom with great suspicion. Yet most also treat MacDonald with embarrassment. Like Rushton, he is a reminder both of Darwinism's dark past and of the possibility of a darker future. MacDonald presents a particular problem, because some of his themes resonate more widely among evolutionary psychologists. For instance, belief in the universality of ethnocentrism, a foundation stone for MacDonald's arguments, also helps anchor, as we shall see, contemporary Darwinian theories of human nature. This only makes MacDonald's anti-Semitism all the more embarrassing. As a result, figures like MacDonald tend to be tolerated but marginalised and ignored – until, that is, outside critics enter the fray. In response to Shulevitz's attack, John Tooby, president of the HBES, suggested that MacDonald was a 'fringe' academic who occupied 'the nether-world of marginal scholarship'.

Whatever the predilections of the likes of Kevin MacDonald, even hard-line sociobiologists have in general toed the postwar party line on race. There is no species of intellectual that evolutionary psychologists despise more than the 'social constructionist'. When it comes to race, however, most evolutionary psychologists are happy to accept that it is a social construction. Hence, the debate about sociobiology has centred not on race but on human nature – and on the discipline's treatment of alleged racists within its ranks.

The fierceness of the debate about human nature also reflects the peculiar character of the postwar consensus on race. Nineteenth-century racial science had viewed humans as entirely moulded by the laws of nature and the differences between human groups as the consequence of distinct evolutionary paths. In response, postwar thinkers tended to reject not just racial essentialism but any form of essentialism, including the very idea of human nature. Every kind of biological explanation of human activity or behaviour came to be seen as suspect.

Sociobiologists may have kept to the party line on race but they challenged the taboo on biological explanations. For many of their critics, this revealed the true nature of the discipline. In the words of a letter to the *New York Review of Books*, signed by, among others, Stephen Jay Gould and Richard Lewontin, sociobiology was 'the latest attempt to reinvigorate ... theories [that] provided an important basis for the enactment of sterilization laws and restrictive immigration laws by the United States between 1910 and 1930 and also for the eugenics policies which led to the establishment of gas chambers in Nazi Germany'. In response, sociobiologists have insisted that it is possible to talk of human nature and to promote biological explanations of human activity without summoning up the ghosts of racial science. 'Claims about a complexly organised, universal human nature, by their very character cannot participate in racist explanations', claim Leda Cosmides and John Tooby. Indeed, they argue, if natural selection had not created a universal human nature, 'individuals would be free to vary in important ways and to any degree from other humans' and 'the psychic unity of humankind would simply be a fiction'. In other words, antiracism would be an empty shell without a biological theory of human nature.

This debate between sociobiologists and their radical critics reflects a broader struggle for the soul of antiracism, between universalists and particularists. Antiracism has come to mean hostility to Enlightenment universalism and disquiet about scientific rationality. The idea of human nature is an expression of both. It embodies the idea of human universals and the quest for such universals is pursued through highly-mechanistic means. Inevitably, therefore, antiracists came to challenge the very concept of human nature. Sociobiologists, in their desire to rehabilitate human nature, held fast to universalist beliefs. But theirs was a highly-impoverished view of what constituted a universal. In the nineteenth century, and for much of the twentieth, important strands of both radical and liberal thought accepted that through human agency, social divisions could be overcome, backward practices erased and a more universal society established. Universalism was understood in a social as well as a biological sense. In the postwar years, however, universals came to be seen, by both sociobiologists and their critics, as phenomena rooted in biology. Both sides also accepted that human activity – or culture – gave rise to a multitude of variations in human behaviour and beliefs. In an influential paper on 'The Scope of Anthropology', Claude Lévi-Strauss argued that 'universal forms of thought and morality' pertain solely to 'biology'. From the other side of the fence, the primatologist, Frans de Waal, has suggested that culture 'explains why two groups of the same species may behave differently.'

Whatever their other differences, both sides in this debate have come to accept that human unity is manifested solely at a biological level, while culture expresses human differences. What separates the warring parties is largely a clash about the relative weights that should be attached to one's biological nature and cultural upbringing in shaping beliefs and behaviours. For sociobiologists, humans are defined primarily by their nature. Given the pliability of human nature, relativists retort, the universal aspects of the psyche are largely unimportant.

What is lost in this dichotomy between biological universals and cultural differences is the sense of human *agency*; that is, the existence of humans as rational, social beings with the power to transform themselves and their societies through reasoned dialogue and activity. All animals have an evolutionary past. Only humans make history. The existence of humans as a uniquely history-making species has moulded the relationship between universals and particulars in human society, and between human nature and human differences. Humans are able both to create social distinctions (and to view them as natural or fixed) and to ignore natural differences (as irrelevant to social intercourse).

For many sociobiologists, however, the universal character of human nature sets severe limits on the possibilities of human agency and social change. 'Boundaries limit the human prospect', E.O. Wilson has observed. 'We are biological and our souls cannot fly free.' Darwinism, Steven Pinker suggests, supports the conservative, Burkean belief that social change should be slow and limited and that 'religion, the family, social customs, sexual mores and political institutions' are the necessary foundations of social cohesion. There is, ironically, more than an echo here of the relativist argument that social progress should be limited in the name of preserving traditions.

It is ironic, too, is that in the name of challenging cultural relativism, the evolutionary idea of human nature may have transformed such relativism into a natural feature of the human condition. Human nature may be universal but so too, many Darwinists argue, is cultural diversity. The evolutionary biologists Mark Pagel and the anthropologist Ruth Mace asked why it was that around 1,000 different languages, about fifteen per cent of the total on Earth, are spoken in Papua New Guinea whereas only ninety are spoken in China. Their answer was that human cultures distribute themselves around the world in a pattern similar to animal species. The density of species is highest in equatorial regions and declines steadily toward the poles. Human cultures, Pagel and Mace argue, behave just like animal species. 'Humans have a proclivity for drawing a ring around themselves and saying, "This is my territory and I'm going to exclude others from occupying it"', Pagel observes. 'That leads to different cultures arising through the usual processes of diversification and drifting apart when they're isolated from each other.' There is, Pagel adds, a 'natural tendency for cultures to be quite cohesive and exclusive'.

On either side of the sociobiology debate, both what we have in common and what differentiates us have come to be viewed as fixed. And, as the idea of human nature has become rehabilitated, so both our commonalities and our differences have come to be seen increasingly as rooted in nature.

FROM THE BIOLOGY OF RACE TO THE EVOLUTION OF RACISM

Back in the 1970s, one of the charges against sociobiology was that it 'made group conflict seem inevitable'. By the 1990s, group conflict did seem, to many people, to be inevitable. In a fragmented, tribal world, in which ethnic and cultural conflict appeared to be the norm, Darwinism became less a threat to liberal values than a reassuring explanation for a world that traditional political and social scientific theories found difficult to comprehend. Whereas in the nineteenth century, Darwinists insisted on the biology of race, in the twenty-first, sociobiologists speak of the evolution of racism. They seek to explain the roots not so much of racial differences as of racial feelings. And as they do so, they help transform cultural diversity – and identity politics – into natural features of the human condition.

Sociobiologists argue that there exists a natural tendency among humans to create in-groups and out-groups, to favour members of your own group and to be hostile towards members of other groups. There have been many theories as to why and how this happens but most rely on two principal mechanisms: kin selection and reciprocal altruism. Both ideas have developed over the past half-century to explain a long-standing conundrum for Darwinism: how can altruistic behaviour arise in the natural world when genes are, in Richard Dawkins's phrase, inherently 'selfish'? According to Darwin's theory, nature selects for traits beneficial to the individual. Individuals that survive and reproduce better – those that are, in Darwinian terms, more 'fit' – pass on their genes and hence some of their physical and behavioural traits to the next generation. The genes and traits of less-fit individuals are less likely to be passed on. By definition altruism – an act whereby you help another at some expense to yourself – reduces your genetic fitness while increasing another's. How could such a trait have evolved?

Kin selection rests on the insight that it makes evolutionary sense for an individual to be altruistic towards a blood relative because close relatives, unlike strangers, share many of the genes you possess. By helping a relative, even at some cost to yourself, you increase the possibility of these common genes surviving into the next generation. The closer the relative, the higher the proportion of common genes and the greater the sacrifice that makes evolutionary sense. As the biologist JBS Haldane once jokingly put it, he would lay down his life for two brothers or eight cousins.

What about altruism towards non-relatives? Such altruism might evolve in situations in which the altruistic individual can be certain that his generosity will be reciprocated. More than thirty years ago, the American biologist Robert Trivers showed that such reciprocal altruism could arise through natural selection in communities in which individual organisms possess three attributes: the opportunity to interact often with other individuals, so that they can gauge each other's characters; the capacity to keep track of how others have behaved; and the cognitive skill to help those and only those, who reciprocate your favours – in other words, to help only those who play by the rules. Many social animals, Trivers pointed out, particularly primates and most especially humans, possess these requirements.

Kin selection and reciprocal altruism describe how evolution might select for altruistic behaviour. But there is a darker side to these evolutionary mechanisms. They favour the emergence of altruistic behaviour towards members of closely-knit groups bounded by common genes or reciprocal promises but also of wariness, even hostility, towards those who do not belong. Kin selection and reciprocal altruism generate both group solidarity and group conflict, both altruism and self-sacrifice towards one's own people and selfishness and antagonism towards others. Pierre van den Berghe, a sociobiologist who was among the first to view racism as an evolved trait, calls this process 'ethnic nepotism'. An ethnic group is like a family, not just because its members share some characteristic genes derived from common descent but because, psychologically, group members perceive this common descent and feel and act like a family. There are, Berghe suggests, no clear boundaries between nuclear family, extended family, clan, tribe, ethnic group, nation and race. Racism and ethnocentrism are just extended forms of love of kin.

More recently, Frank Salter, an Australian political ethologist based at the Max Planck Institute in Germany, has stretched this argument in a controversial way. Since the wider population to which an individual belongs (which Salter calls an 'ethny') is akin to an extended family, so every individual has a 'genetic interest' in copies of his own 'distinctive genes' that are to be found not only among close relatives but within the ethny. Given that we have many more fellow ethnics than we have relatives, ethnies are repositories of far more copies of each of an individual's genes than is his family. For Salter, ethnies have a greater claim to an individual's loyalty even than his immediate family. Salter argues for 'the importance of genetic continuity as an end in itself.' From an 'evolutionary perspective', he suggests, 'genetic continuity is the ultimate interest of all life, since it has priority over other interests'. Genetic continuity appears to mean the preservation of the ethny's gene pool. A shrinking ethny, for Salter, is like a family whose members are dying off; both conditions represent a loss of genetic interests. 'Failure to show ethnic loyalty', he claims, 'is the genetic equivalent to betraying a child or a grandchild.' For Salter, ethnocentrism is adaptive, because it helps preserve genetic continuity. He has tried to buttress his argument with empirical evidence showing that people prefer their own kind and discriminate against outsiders, especially when distributing resources. Individuals, he believes, are more likely to give blood, support charities, volunteer for community work and pay high levels of taxes if they know members of their own ethnic group will benefit. 'Ethnic diversity', he concludes, 'seems to inhibit public altruism'.

Salter's most controversial arguments emerge from his use of the theory of genetic interests to make a case against immigration and mixed marriage. Both, he suggests, undermine genetic continuity and diminish genetic interest. In a particularly inflammatory passage, he argues that 'It would appear to be more adaptive for an Englishman to risk life or property resisting the immigration of two Bantu immigrants to England than taking the same risk to rescue one of his own children from drowning.' Immigration, for Salter, is not only a genetic problem but also a political predicament. Because people are more generous to their own kind than to others, immigration undermines the welfare state. 'From an evolutionary perspective', Salter argues, 'welfare systems should be easier to develop and maintain in ethnically homogenous societies than in more heterogeneous ones; mono-ethnic welfare states should be more generous than multi-ethnic ones.' Evolutionary theory, Salter believes, poses a major threat to the left because 'The liberal left supports generous welfare but also policies that add to ethnic heterogeneity, such as high levels of immigration. It does not seem to have occurred to them that they must choose between maximizing the two.' The ideal liberal state, he suggests, would not be a multicultural society – a recipe for conflict and illiberalism – but an ethnically homogenous one. In an ethnically homogenous society, there would be minimum conflict over resources, maximum extension of welfare provisions and greatest scope for the establishment of liberal institutions.

Sociobiologists seem unsure whether to place Salter in the 'netherworld of marginal scholarship' with Rushton and MacDonald or to view him as an important mainstream scholar. Many are impressed by the strength of his empirical research and the bravura of his arguments yet many also question the coherence of his theories and are embarrassed by his political claims. Take, for instance, his notion of genetic interest and his belief that since 'genetic continuity is the ultimate interest of all life', so it is to the benefit of every individual to preserve his ethny. As many critics have pointed out, life has no more 'interest' in genetic continuity than water has 'interest' in flowing downhill. Genes have interests only in a metaphorical sense but human beings have interests in the real sense of wants, needs and desires. Salter confuses the two in suggesting it is to the advantage of every individual to preserve his ethny because in doing so he preserves his distinctive genes.

Many sociobiologists also dispute the wisdom of extending the concept of kin selection much beyond the family. In the Stone Age, they argue, human groups were small and likely to have been made up largely of close relatives. In the modern world, however, in-groups may be huge (an ethnic group, a nation or a race may cover millions of people) and the relatedness between members of an in-group likely to be very small. 'Sameness' is signposted not just by family ties but by all manner of social markers, including language, culture, religion and history. Salter accepts this but suggests that, in the modern world where family relationships are often difficult to discern and societies have become ethnically mixed, language and culture have become markers for extended family ties. For Salter, racism and ethnocentrism are adaptive, because they help maintain genetic continuity. Many of his sociobiological critics argue that psychological dispositions that may have been suitable for the Stone Age are often maladaptive when translated into the modern world; hence both the virulence and destructive character of racism. As John Tooby and Leda Cosmides put it, 'Modern phenomena such as friction between people of different "races", war between nation states and so on, cannot be adaptations to modern circumstances but rather reflect the operation of Pleistocene adaptations misfiring under modern circumstances.'

What really worries sociobiologists are Salter's politics. Peter Gray, professor of psychology at Boston University, has described Salter's work as the 'Misuse of evolutionary theory to advocate for racial discrimination and segregation'. Reviewing Salter's book *On Genetic Interests* in one of the leading sociobiological journals, the *Bulletin of the International Society for Human Ethology,* Gray not only criticised it for its 'contradictions and pseudo-logic' but also lambasted Salter's 'fantasy world ... of powerful racially ("ethnically") defined nations, each of which confines itself to its own territory, each of which works with patriotic pride to promote the interests of its racially homogenous inhabitants without interfering with the rights of other nations to promote the interests of their inhabitants.' Sociobiological schizophrenia is illustrated by a laudatory review of the book by Kevin MacDonald in same issue of the *Bulletin. On Genetic Interests* is also accompanied by high praise from two of the grandees of sociobiology, E.O. Wilson and Irenaus Eibl-Eibesfeldt. Wilson described it as 'a fresh and deep contribution to the sociobiology of humans' while Eibl-Eibesfeldt, a pioneer of the study of the evolution of ethnocentrism, believed that 'the synthesis is persuasive'.

Salter's arguments have, unsurprisingly, been championed by the right and by anti-immigration polemicists. But the liberal left too is wrestling with contemporary conflicts between diversity and solidarity, immigration and the welfare state. In his influential and much talked-about essay 'Too Diverse', David Goodhart, the liberal editor of *Prospect* magazine, made a case for restricting immigration and the extent of social diversity. Goodhart wrote his essay before being aware of Salter's arguments. Yet there are echoes. 'The diversity, individualism and mobility that characterises developed economies – especially in the era of globalisation – mean that more of our lives is spent among strangers', Goodhart argues. This is a particular problem because 'in a developed country like Britain ... we not only live among stranger citizens but we must *share* with them.' In such a society we need to rethink 'a question as old as human society itself: who is my brother? With whom do I share mutual obligation?' The 'traditional, conservative, Burkean view is that our affinities ripple out from our families and localities, to the nation and not very far beyond'. Against this is pitted a liberal, universalist view 'which sees us in some sense as equally obligated to all human beings – an idea associated with the universalist aspects of Christianity and Islam, with Kantian universalism and with left-wing internationalism'. While Goodhart suggests that science 'is neutral in this dispute', he believes that it provides greatest comfort to the Burkean vision. While evolutionary psychology 'stresses ... the universality of most human traits', it also stresses 'the instinct to favour one's own ... through the notion of kin selection and reciprocal altruism.'

Goodhart presents evidence to show that 'sharing and solidarity can conflict with diversity'. This creates an 'especially acute dilemma for progressives who want plenty of both solidarity – high social cohesion and generous welfare paid out of a progressive tax system – *and* diversity – equal respect for a wide range of peoples, values and ways of life.' Goodhart concludes that 'A generous welfare state is not compatible with open borders and possibly not even with US-style mass immigration.'

The echoes that reverberate between Goodhart's and Salter's arguments are not because Goodhart has accepted Salter's unsavoury claims about the dangers of miscegenation or the need for an ethnically homogenous society. Rather they reveal the ways in which contemporary anxieties about diversity can be reformulated into different political idioms. In part, this is because diversity has today become so ambiguous, indeed incoherent, in its meaning that both sides of the debate can simultaneously be for and against it. Critics of diversity view ethnocentrism, and hence the tendency to diversity, as universal and often as adaptive. Proponents of diversity wish to limit the corrosive character of diversity in the name of cultural authenticity. Pierre van de Berghe describes Salter's *On Genetic Interests* as a riposte to the 'liberal multicultural' view that 'we should extend our fraternal embrace to humanity as a whole'. A liberal multiculturalist like Bhikhu Parekh, on the other hand, excoriates liberalism for its abstract universalism and its failure to attend to difference. On the one side, the failures of multiculturalism reveal the limits of universalism. On the other, the limits of universalism reveal the need for a multicultural sensibility. Both cannot be right; in fact neither is. Each reflects the incoherent ways in which we speak both of universalism and diversity these days.

Frank Salter worries about the consequence of diversity for social cohesion and genetic continuity, a view echoed by some sections of the liberal left, but his is also a vision of a world composed of a patchwork of racially and culturally distinct groups, each preserving its own particular, authentic, brand of genes and lifestyle. Liberal multiculturalists are hostile to Salter's argument for the creation of ethnically homogenous states, yet they too envision the world as a patchwork of peoples and cultures, each deserving respect for its uniqueness. Multiculturalists, as we have seen, link culture and biological descent. So do Salter and his supporters. Preserving one's biological heritage, they argue, is necessary to preserve one's cultural heritage. An essay on Salter's work in the far-right magazine *American Renaissance*, puts this very well:

> It is both in the cultural and broad genetic sense that a person's ethny can be said to deserve even greater loyalty than his family, whenever the ethny is threatened. If a man's family is wiped [sic] it is a great personal tragedy. However, if his whole tribe disappears, it takes with it far more copies of his genes than he could ever produce as children. It also takes with it the culture and folkways that make his ethny what it is. In this sense cultural and ethnic extinction is infinitely more terrible than one's own death or the death of one's family.

Diversity has become the bridge between the cultural and the biological and between the liberal left and the reactionary right. Because we now view diversity as a good in itself, so cultural diversity and biological diversity are seen as on a par. In an essay for the *New York Times*, the developmental biologist Armand Marie Leroi argued that one of the reasons 'race matters' is that 'it gives us reason ... to value and protect some of the world's most obscure and marginalised people'. Leroi referred to an article in the *Times of India* published shortly after the terrible tsunami of 2004 that devastated the lands around the Indian Ocean. Headlined 'Tsunami May Have Rendered Threatened Tribes Extinct', the article bemoaned the fate of the Onge, Jarawa, Great Andamanese and Sentinelese, all tribal groups living on the Andaman Islands, numbering some four hundred people in all. Since several of the islands are low-lying and in the direct path of the wave, casualties were high. 'Some beads may have just gone missing from the Emerald Necklace of India', wrote the *Times* colourfully.

Why, in a catastrophe that cost more than 150,000 lives, should the survival of a few hundred tribal people have any special claim on our attention? Partly because, Leroi argued, 'The people of the Andamans have a unique way of life'. As hunter-gatherers, they are 'a rarity in the modern world'. Linguists, too, find them interesting 'since they collectively speak three languages seemingly unrelated to any others'. And most importantly, Leroi suggested, because the islanders are racially unique. As the *Times of India* put it, they are of 'Negrito racial stocks', the 'remnants of the oldest human populations of Asia and Australia'.

It may seem old-fashioned, even Victorian, Leroi observed, to talk of 'Negrito racial stocks' but it is also biologically correct. Negrito is 'the name given by anthropologists to a people who once lived throughout Southeast Asia' and who are 'very small, very dark ... have peppercorn hair' and 'look like African pygmies who have wandered away from Congo's jungles'. In fact they are the descendants of the first group of migrants to have come out of Africa along the coastal route to Asia. Today, they are largely confined to the Malay Peninsula, a few islands in the Philippines and the Andamans. Negrito populations, Leroi warned, 'are so small, isolated and impoverished that it seems certain that they will eventually disappear.' And when they do 'the unique combination of genes that makes the Negritos so distinctive and that took tens of thousands of years to evolve, will have disappeared. A human race will have gone extinct and the human species will be the poorer for it.'

Leroi's biological argument is, as I hope will be clear by now, nonsense. Populations are not fixed and sealed. Genes flow in and out of every population. The Negrito population today is genetically different from what it would have been a thousand or ten thousand years ago. Nor is it distinct because it possesses unique genes. Apart from in rare circumstances, particular gene variants (or alleles) are not confined to any one population. What makes a population different is simply that its proportions of different alleles are unique. Thirty per cent of population A has allele X, as compared to fifty per cent of population B. Seventy per cent of population A has allele Y, as compared to forty per cent of population B. And so on. Preserving the Negritos as a race would simply mean preserving a particular combination of alleles in a particular proportion. Why this would make the world a better place, Leroi does not say.

If Negritos disappear it will not be because they have been made extinct by some sort of Holocaust. It will be because they have intermarried with members of other populations or have moved away from the land of their birth. Why should this be seen as a disaster? Only because we have developed a Romantic view of human authenticity, in which beauty is beheld as the pickling in genetic aspic of populations whose diversity can be displayed to the world in an ethnic zoo. Such a view has primarily been developed not by race realists but by antiracists and cultural relativists. Race realists are simply holding on to the coat-tails of antiracists, refashioning the idea of race in the language of diversity. This is why Frank Salter's work feels so much more acceptable than that of Rushton and MacDonald (with both of whom he has considerable intellectual affinity). Rushton's tripartite racial division of the world and his hierarchy of intelligence and moral worth appear repulsive to the post-Holocaust world. MacDonald's vision of Jewishness as an evolutionary strategy and of anti-Semitism as a rational response to Jewish success appears scarcely more acceptable. Frank Salter's work, however, touches a number of hot political buttons that connect with liberal concerns. The universality of difference; respect for other peoples but preference for one's own; race, ethnicity and culture as the roots of personal identity; the conflict between the inevitability of tribalism and the desire for cohesion; the dilemmas of liberalism in the post-ideological world – all these issues, which are at the heart of Salter's work, have also come to shape contemporary political debate. Despite the reactionary smell of many of Salter's arguments, his defence of genetic diversity and ethnic identity and his call both for the preservation of ethnic differences and for the strengthening of ethnic solidarity strike a chord in our ever more Romantic world.

In many ways, the real problem with Salter's argument lies less in those aspects that many sociobiologists find politically embarrassing than in those aspects that he shares with the wider debate on the evolution of ethnocentrism and, indeed, with the wider debate on the politics of identity – his failure to attend to history. The expression of group differences is, in Salter's eyes and in the eyes of most sociobiologists, an ever-present, unchanging phenomenon rooted in the human condition. It is a view that tends to distort the interpretation of the empirical data.

Consider, for instance, a famous study of Moscow beggars conducted by Salter and the Russian physical anthropologist Marina Butovskaya. Most of the beggars were Russian, just like the vast majority of passers-by. Some were Moldovan and a few were Roma. The researchers found that Russians preferred to give money to their fellow Russians, were less generous to the Moldovans and were downright miserly to the Roma. Evidence, Salter suggests, for the naturalness of ethnocentrism. The treatment of the different beggars illustrates how we prefer to share resources with members of the same ethnic group and reveals why, in policy terms, a generous welfare state is incompatible with high levels of immigration.

In fact, the study shows what we already knew: that Russians today tend to be nationalistic and despise the Roma. Beyond that it says nothing about *why* they are nationalistic or *why* they despise the Roma. It may be, as Salter assumes, that innate ethnocentrism leads Russians to favour Russian beggars and discriminate against Romany ones. It may also be that the age-old practice of discrimination against the Roma has led many Russians to despise them and hence to ignore their begging.

Group formation is a fluid process and often has little to do with ethnic relatedness. Take the suggestion that Americans are reluctant to fund a more generous welfare system because most of the tax revenue would come from whites and most of the benefits would go to blacks and Hispanics. What constitutes 'white' has changed dramatically over the past century. At the beginning of the twentieth century, most of those who now constitute white America – Irish, Poles, Italians and so on – were viewed as being of a darker shade of pale. Only over the past half-century have they joined the white community. Similarly, half a century ago, most white Britons probably thought of Afro-Caribbean immigrants as 'Not One of Us'. Today, most treat Afro-Caribbeans settled in Britain as fellow-countrymen but look upon East European migrants, who in Salter's terms are ethnically closer, as free-loaders and welfare scroungers.

The history of race, as we have seen in this book, reveals the mutability of the ways in which we understand 'Us' and 'Them'. Consider, for instance, the infamous 'Governor Eyre' incident of 1865. In October of that year, a local rising by Jamaican peasantry was put down by the island's governor, Edward John Eyre, with the utmost ferocity. Eyre's actions created much debate in Britain. Many of those who defended his actions did so on the grounds that black peasants were like British workers and required similar treatment. 'The negro', the writer Edwin Hood observed, 'is in Jamaica as the costermonger is in Whitechapel; he is very likely often nearly a savage with the mind of a child.' Sometimes commentators went so far as to refer to British workers as 'negroes'. The *Daily Telegraph*, on hearing reports that the pro-independence Jamaica Committee was planning a counter-rally to a banquet in Eyre's honour in Southampton, was moved to comment that 'there are a good many negroes in Southampton, who have the taste of their tribe for any disturbance that appears safe and who are probably imbued with the conviction that it is a proper thing to hoot and yell at a number of gentlemen going to a dinner party.' In fact, as the historian Douglas Lorrimer observes, 'the *Daily Telegraph's* "negroes" were ... the very English and very white Southampton mob who thronged the streets outside the banquet hall, while their more respectable working class colleagues attended the largest popular meeting in the city's history to protest against the official reception given to Governor Eyre'.

The Southampton incident reveals well the view of the mid-Victorian elite that blacks and British workers belonged to the same tribe. It also demonstrates that, even as late as the 1860s, there remained considerable working-class sympathy for the plight of blacks in the colonies. Indeed, British workers identified so strongly with black slaves, with whom they possessed a political but no racial connection, that during the American civil war, when the Union blockade of the South starved the Lancashire mills of cotton and caused hundreds of thousands of workers to become unemployed and face starvation, most nevertheless continued to support the campaign for black emancipation. On 31 December 1862, Manchester workers held a rally in the city's Free Trade Hall in support of the fight against slavery. Abraham Lincoln was moved to pen a letter to 'the working people of Manchester'. 'I know and deeply deplore the sufferings which the working people of Manchester and in all Europe are called to endure in this crisis', he wrote on 19 January 1863:

> Under the circumstances I cannot but regard your decisive utterances on the question as an instance of sublime Christian heroism which has not been surpassed in any age or in any country. It is indeed an energetic and re-inspiring assurance of the inherent truth and of the ultimate and universal triumph of justice, humanity and freedom.

The support that British workers gave to black Americans was, as Lincoln himself recognised, an act of altruism that required far greater personal sacrifice than paying taxes or giving to charity but was nevertheless determined by class rather than by ethnic interests.

I am not suggesting that there may not be an evolved tendency to form in-groups and out-groups. But group conflict is not a given. The nature and strength of such conflict is historically contingent. Today, white workers may see blacks as the racial Other; a hundred and fifty years ago, they were willing to make great personal sacrifices to identify with them as 'One of us'. Today white workers and the white elite may be regarded as sharing a common race. That is not what the white elite believed 150 years ago. Once we take the long view, the idea that we have a natural tendency to extend our altruism from our family to our race – and only to our race – becomes as suspect as Phillipe Rushton's belief that birth rates are racially fixed. The problem with such explanations is not that they look to evolution for answers but that they pay too little heed to what history can teach us.

Not only do many evolutionary accounts of the impact of diversity on altruism pay too little heed to history, they also often misread the results of contemporary research. In 2007, the American sociologist Robert Putnam published the findings of a huge research project on the impact of diversity. Putnam and his colleagues interviewed 30,000 people in forty-one communities across America. The more diverse a community, the less socially-engaged were its members; they voted less, did less community work, gave less to charity, had fewer friends and spent more time watching television. Many took this as providing yet more evidence for the argument that ethnic diversity inhibits public altruism because people favour their own kind, and that welfare systems are easier to maintain in more homogenous societies. The British sociologist, Anthony Giddens, argued that while he had some reservations about Putnam's data, nevertheless it 'does provide some backing for [David] Goodhart's view'. Putnam himself held back from publishing the data for nearly five years because of its potentially explosive political message. The implications of the data are, however, far from straightforward.

The study showed that in more diverse communities people are more distrustful not only of members of other ethnic groups but also of their own. It is not the case that people are less altruistic in diverse societies because they prefer helping those who are racially similar. Diversity, Putnam writes, 'seems to trigger *not* in-group/out-group division but *anomie* or social isolation. In colloquial language, people living in ethnically diverse settings appear to "hunker down" – that is, to pull in like a turtle.' Whatever the political meaning of Putnam's research – and the debate is only just beginning – it provides little evidence for the claim that there is necessarily a trade-off between immigration and welfare because of an evolved preference to favour one's own ethnic group. One interpretation of the data may be that diversity weakens social engagement because, as we saw in Chapter 7, the narrowing of politics has changed the nature of social affiliation. Social solidarity has become increasingly defined not in political terms – as collective action in pursuit of certain political ideals – but in terms of ethnicity, culture or faith. The question people ask themselves is not so much 'What kind of society do I want to live in?' as 'Who am I?'. It may be that, in a more diverse community, people feel less able than they were, even in the recent past, to reach out and create social bonds, not because of an evolved desire to be with one's own kind but because an historical transformation of politics has also transformed our understanding of what solidarity entails.

Whatever the conceptual problems with the sociobiological view of ethnocentrism, nevertheless it makes considerable political sense. 'The political utility of the idea of difference', Marek Kohn observes, 'suggests that there might be widespread demand in the contemporary world for scientific theories of ethnocentrism, just as there was a requirement in the colonial era for theories of racial hierarchy'. This is not to suggest that science is just a social construction, buffeted hither and thither by the winds of political fashion. Rather, it is to argue that political tendencies often shape the interpretation of scientific data.

Just as in the nineteenth century the seeming impossibility of viewing the world except through racial eyes shaped the character of racial science, so today the seeming inevitability of group conflict has created the space for theories of innate ethnocentricity. A more fragmented, Balkanised world gives credibility to the Darwinian idea that ethnocentrism is innate and universal. At the same time, biological theories of in-group and out-group formation transforms the contemporary search for identity into an inevitable aspect of the human condition.

THE END OF UTOPIA AND THE RETURN OF RACE

If population biology undermined nineteenth-century typological views of race and sociobiology helped turn the quest for identity into a natural odyssey, a third major development in postwar biology – the genetics revolution – has provided a toolkit with which to unearth that identity. We have already seen how the emergence of new genetic techniques to map genes both in the body and in the world, and to link the internal and the external, is helping to change the kinds of questions that medicine asks about human differences. It is also helping to transform the notion of identity and in the process to bridge the gap between race realism and identity politics. In an age in which 'Who am I?' has become a defining question and in which people increasingly mine the past to find meaning in the present, genetics-as-genealogy is beginning to change the meaning of race.

Race realism is developing into the search for identity. In his article for the *New York Times* on the Negritos of the Andaman Islands, Armand Leroi argued that 'Race is merely a shorthand that enables us to speak sensibly, though with no great precision, about genetic rather than cultural or political differences'. Genetics, he suggests, can help us 'sort the world's population into 10, 100, perhaps 1000 groups, each located somewhere on the map'. Europeans form a race. So do

Basques. And so do the Andaman Islanders. Any group with a distinct genetic signature is, in Leroi's view, a race. Race becomes a badge to say 'This is who I am, this is who my family is, this is where we've come from.' Defining a race as an extended family gets round many of the problems of traditional racial science but, as we saw in Chapter 1, it also squeezes dry any meaning from the concept. Race becomes an emblem of identity and a form of family history. Leroi suggests that one of the 'pleasures' of the return of racial concepts into science is 'the discovery of a new kind of genealogy'.

If race realists talk increasingly in terms of identity and genealogy, multiculturalists increasingly look to biology for answers to questions of identity. 'One of the many impacts of biotechnology concerns the issue of identity', the geneticist and activist Jose Morales has written. 'The existential question "Who am I?" will be answered by asking the question "Where did I come from?".'. This will have noteworthy consequences for the social reality of people of colour in the United States.' Among those consequences is that political and cultural notions of identity are increasingly underpinned by DNA. Over the past decade, geneticists have traced the histories of countless populations – African Americans, English, Celts, Jews, Indian untouchables. Dozens of commercial companies have sprung up to help individuals trace their family history. Many see this not as an entertaining bit of genealogy but as a fundamental act of recovering an authentic identity, 'a route to a new identity', in the words of the black British journalist, Joseph Harker, and the possibility of 'a whole new history and culture'.

One of the first such companies in Britain was the Cambridge-based *Roots for Real*. Among its first customers were Rachel Hunt and Matthew Barrett. They were married in October 2003, which, in Britain is 'Black History Month'. The couple turned to *Roots for Real* 'to bring something from their ancestral roots into the ceremony' so they could understand 'who they are and where their culture comes from'. 'Our DNA holds perhaps the most intact record of our family, our lands, language, tribes, customs and traditions', Rachel Hunt told a reporter. 'It would be so satisfying to know that our children can grow up with a strong sense of identity and heritage by being able to unravel a time we thought would be lost for ever.'

Some voices have warned against turning the search for identity into such a genetic quest. But so narrow has become even the critics' vision of selfhood that such warnings rarely persuade. In 2002, the Cultural Wellness Centre (itself a telling name for our times) in Minneapolis jointly hosted, with the University of Minnesota's Center for Bioethics, a conference entitled 'African Genetics and Genealogies: Looking Backward to Look Forward'. One of the speakers was the bioethicist, Annette Dula. 'The premise of African genealogies', she argued, 'is to reconstruct a stolen identity':

> Reconstructing identities is a problem when it comes to African Americans because of the slave trade. This morally outrageous practice killed, enslaved and destroyed families and cultures. It deliberately erased the identities of millions of people and many groups of Africans … So the premise of African genealogies is to try to undo this erasure, to try to recover and restore some of that stolen identity. Tracing genealogies … is an attempt to reclaim history, to regain culture and to gain knowledge that has been denied us.

'If the goal of African genealogies is to reclaim stolen and savaged identities', Dula concluded, 'then genetics does not seem to be the place that we should be going … Genetics alone cannot restore our identities because identities do not reside on the genes. Identity is who you are as a person. It has to do with what your values are.'

For Dula, identity is not just shaped by history but is held prisoner by it. Identity is not that which African Americans create but that which they must 'restore', because it has been 'stolen' from them by the slave trade. Culture is not what you do now but what your ancestors did then. Once we adopt such a racialised view of culture, then a genetic view of identity begins to make sense. If identity is fixed like a fly in amber, then it makes little difference whether that amber is history or biology. It is only a step from believing, with Annette Dula, that 'Tracing genealogies … is an attempt to reclaim history, to regain culture and to gain knowledge that has been denied us' to suggesting, as Rachel Hunt does, that 'Our DNA holds perhaps the most intact record of our family, our lands, language, tribes, customs and traditions' that can allow 'our children can grow up with a strong sense of identity and heritage by being able to unravel a time we thought would be lost for ever.'

What links these two views of identity is the sense that the present is determined by the past and this in turn derives from the sense that there is little that we can do in the present to shape the future. As politics has become less about competing visions of the kinds of society that people want than a debate about how best to run the society we already inhabit, so our identity – our sense of who we are – is shaped more by the historical relationships that have brought us to where we are than by the social and political relationships that might transport us to where we want to go. Multiculturalism, as Russell Jacoby has observed, is the ideology of an age robbed of Utopian hope. And increasingly the end of Utopia is itself being understood not as a political phenomenon but as a biological inevitability. In his book, *The Blank Slate*, Steven Pinker draws on the work of the American economist Thomas Sowell to suggest that there are two broad visions of what it is to be human: the Tragic and the Utopian. The Tragic Vision recognises that humans are 'inherently limited in knowledge, wisdom and virtue and all social arrangements must acknowledge those limits.' Such limits highlight the importance of tradition. 'Religion, the family, social customs, sexual mores and political institutions are a distillation of time-tested techniques that let us work around the shortcomings of human nature.' It is a vision associated with Thomas Hobbes, Adam Smith, Edmund Burke, Friedrich Hayek, Milton Friedman, Isaiah Berlin and Karl Popper.

In the Utopian Vision, by contrast, 'psychological limitations are artefacts that *come from* our social arrangements and we should not allow them to restrict our gaze from what is possible in a better world.' Traditions are regarded as 'the dead hand of the past, the attempt to rule from the grave' and hence must be subject to the scrutiny of reason. Only in this fashion have we rid ourselves of practices such as absolute monarchy, slavery and patriarchy 'that were once thought to be rooted in human nature.' It is a vision that Pinker attributes to Jean-Jacques Rousseau, Thomas Paine, John Kenneth Galbraith and Ronald Dworkin.

'The new sciences of human nature', Pinker suggests, 'vindicate some version of the Tragic Vision and undermine the Utopian outlook.' Since 'our moral sentiments, no matter how beneficent, overlie a deeper bedrock of selfishness', Pinker suggests, so 'we should not aim to *solve* social problems like crime or poverty, because in a world of competing individuals one person's gain may be another person's loss. The best we can do is to trade off one cost against another.' Or as the science writer Matt Ridley has put it, communism collapsed because Marx 'designed a social system that would only have worked if we were angels; it failed because we were beasts.'

As the end of Utopia turns into a natural event, so too does human variety. And, with the demise of Utopia, comes the return of race not as the vicious nineteenth-century vision of superiority and inferiority but rather swaddled in the gentle warmth of diversity. We have come full circle. In the late eighteenth century, fearful of the unsettling, transformative quality of Enlightenment rationalism, the Romantics fashioned culture, tradition and authenticity as shelters from the storm of progress. In the nineteenth century, Romantic pluralism hitched itself to scientific positivism to create racial science. The genocidal consequences of racial science helped refashion

Romantic cultural pluralism as an antiracist philosophy. By the end of the twentieth century, the demise of Utopian hope, together with disenchantment with Enlightenment rationalism, had led to the radical celebration of Romantic irrationalism and the transmutation of antiracism into a backward-looking, reactionary creed whose aim was to preserve difference. With the fading of the possibilities of social transformation, diversity became remade into a natural feature of the human condition. At the end of Utopia we once more find the crock of race but now smelling sweetly of difference.

AFTERWORD: BEYOND
RACE AND UNREASON

'I am inherently gloomy about the prospect of Africa ... All our social policies are based on the fact that their intelligence is the same as ours – whereas all the testing says not really.' I opened the book by looking at what the row over James Watson's comments tells us about both sides of the race debate. I want to close the book by returning to that row, in the light of the argument I have sketched out.

I hope it is clear by now why Watson's notion of race is untenable. For a scientist who has spent a lifetime studying genes and genetic differences, Watson possesses a curiously cartoonish view of race. He confuses blacks and Africans, seems to assume that Africans constitute a single population, as do Africans and African Americans, and that this population is naturally, rather than socially, constituted. As he himself suggested later, 'If I said what I was quoted as saying then I can only admit that I am bewildered by it.' The problem, though, is not simply confusion in Watson's mind. It is also that such confusion is in the DNA of contemporary scientific discussions of race.

Scientific categories need to be consistent, reliable and reproducible. Racial categories are none of these. Races are difficult to define and there are no objective rules for deciding what constitutes a race, to what race an individual belongs or indeed to how many races he or she belongs. Even Neil Risch, the contemporary geneticist whose work has done the most to gain acceptance for a race realist viewpoint, both within the academy and among the wider public, is 'not sure what race means [because] people use it in many different ways'. Risch adds that 'In our own studies, to avoid coming up with our own definition of race, we tend to use the definition others have employed, for example, the US census definition of race.'

The trouble is that census categories are as reliable a guide to human biological variation as the *Da Vinci Code* is to Christian history. During the course of the twentieth century the US census used twenty-six different schemes to characterise racial differences in the American population. Guidelines issued in 1977 defined an American Indian as 'A person having origins in any of the original peoples of North and South America, and who maintains cultural identification through tribal affiliations or community recognition'. An Asian was 'a person having origins in any of the peoples of the Far East, Southeast Asia, or the Indian subcontinent including for instance Cambodia, China, India, Japan, Korea, Malaysia, Pakistan, the Philippine islands, Thailand and Vietnam'. Someone whose ancestors were American Indian but who maintained no cultural affiliation to an Indian tribe was not considered Native American; but someone whose ancestors came from India or Korea was always Asian, whatever their cultural affinities. The census categories lumped together South Asians and East Asians as a single racial group – 'Asians'. Traditionally, however, race realists have viewed the peoples of the Indian subcontinent as Caucasian (and grouped them with 'whites') and regarded those of the Far East as belonging to a distinct race, the East Asians, Orientals or 'Mongoloids'. Risch himself defines his races in this way; in other words, he makes use of census categories when they do not offend his definition of how races should be carved up but where the two diverge, he appears to fall back on to his own taxonomy. Little wonder that group identities used in biomedical studies tend to be so flexible, unreliable and vague and that there is a marked contrast in scientific papers between the tightness of language used to discuss the loci of genes or physiological processes and the looseness of the language about racial differences. In the absence of a scientific classification of race, researchers are forced to import the Disneyfied racial categories we use in everyday life – which is precisely what Watson did in his now-notorious interview.

If the concept of race is problematic, that notion of intelligence is even more so. Intelligence has never been properly defined, no one knows what IQ tests actually measure and we have yet to identify the genes that underlie the myriad attributes that collectively give rise to intelligence. Even if we were to ignore such fundamental issues, there remain considerable empirical problems in linking race and intelligence. For a start, there has, over the past century, been a dramatic rise in IQ scores, a rise that clearly cannot be explained in genetic terms. This secular rise in IQ scores is called the 'Flynn effect' after James Flynn, the political scientist from New Zealand who discovered it. Flynn showed that increasing scores appear in every major test, in every age range and in every modern industrialised country. The increase has been continuous and roughly linear from the earliest days of testing to the present. The gain amounts to three IQ points per decade. In some cases it has been far greater. The sheer size of such gains means that, if we take IQ tests at face value, every industrial country, as the influential psychologist Ulric Neisser puts it, is either 'now a nation of shining intellects' or 'was then a nation of dolts'. Since neither appears to be a plausible explanation, Flynn himself argues that the tests do not measure intelligence but only a minor sort of abstract problem-solving ability with little practical significance. Neisser, who in 1995 headed an American Psychological Association task force that reviewed controversial issues in the study of intelligence, believes that IQ tests are more worthwhile. Nevertheless, even he accepts that the existence of the Flynn effect 'undermines the very concept of "general intelligence"' – which is the basis for most debates about race, genes and IQ.

Not only has IQ in general risen but, in America, the IQ of blacks has risen faster than the IQ of whites, so much so that the gap between the IQ scores of the two groups has dramatically narrowed in recent years. A study by William Dickens and James Flynn showed that between 1972 and 2002, blacks reduced the IQ gap by between five and six points – even though the average IQ of whites themselves increased in that same period, thanks to the Flynn effect. Dickens and Flynn considered the factors that might possibly provide a genetic explanation for the narrowing gap – such as a greater rate of intermarriage between blacks and whites – and dismissed these as largely irrelevant. The reason for the change, they insist, is environmental. 'The last two decades', Dickens and Flynn conclude, 'have seen both positive and negative developments: gains in occupational status and school funding have been accompanied by more black preschoolers in single-parent homes and lower income in those homes. We believe that further black environmental progress would engender further black IQ gains.'

This conclusion is given considerable weight by research that demonstrates how IQ scores often reflect power relations. For instance, in America, both Korean and Japanese students score above average in IQ tests, helping to fuel the idea that East Asians are an especially intelligent race. In Japan, though, Koreans, who face considerable discrimination, have a much lower IQ score. In Belgium, French speakers, who form the dominant group, do better than Flemish speakers. In Northern Ireland, Catholics fare worse than Protestants. In South Africa, blacks do badly in IQ tests – but so do Dutch-descended Afrikaners when compared to the English-speaking white elite.

Once we give up on the idea both that there is some inherent, essential, natural quality to a race and that differences in IQ between populations are necessarily genetic, then the claim that 'testing' shows that 'their intelligence is [not] the same as ours' becomes about as scientifically meaningful as the belief 'their women are not as good-looking as ours'. And the belief that such differences in intelligence explains the failure of social policy in Africa smacks more of alchemy than of science.

* * * *

If the use of race as a scientific category should lead us to raise more than a quizzical eyebrow, we should look equally askance at what the practice of antiracism has become. The science of race is irrational, albeit not in the eyes of race realists. The practice of antiracism has come self-consciously to embrace irrationalism as a political strategy. Where once radicals championed scientific rationalism and Enlightenment universalism, now they are more likely to decry both as part of a Eurocentric project. Where once the left believed in the ideas of a common humanity and universal rights, argued that everyone should be treated equally despite their racial, ethnic, religious or cultural differences and looked to social progress as a means of overcoming cultural differences, now it promotes the idea of multiculturalism and of group rights, argues that different people should be treated differently *because* of their racial, ethnic, religious and cultural differences and worries that social progress is undermining cultural authenticity.

The radical espousal of difference and authenticity, and the insistence that science and reason are peculiarly local, Western perspectives, often makes it difficult to distinguish between the racist and the antiracist. One of James Watson's fiercest critics was the Ghanaian writer and broadcaster Cameron Duodu. After condemning the media for giving space to Watson's 'malignant racism', Duodu, in an online essay for the *Guardian* newspaper, dismissed the claim that Africans are less intelligent on the grounds that for life in Africa 'you do not need a high "IQ" – such as found in tests devised by westerners'. 'Africa may look dismal today to the likes of Professor James Watson',

Duodu suggested, but only because 'the western way of life has been *imposed* on Africans.' According to Duodu, 'It is quite stupid to expect total efficiency from a people who are being torn in two directions at the same time – between an inherited, ancient culture, and a modern, imported one.'

Africans are different. Modernity is alien to them. They don't need a high IQ for the kind of lives they lead. Even Watson might have blanched at describing Africans in this fashion – and had he done so, he would undoubtedly have faced an even greater firestorm of protest. In Duodu's hands, however, 'malignant racism' was transformed into antiracist indignation. 'When Watson said that people want to believe that Africans' "intelligence is the same as ours – whereas all the testing says not really"', the philosopher Julian Baggini observed, 'he is being no more racist than his critic Duodu, who also asserted the typically different – not superior or inferior – intelligence of Africans.'

The real victims of this new irrationalism are the very groups that radicals wish to protect from the ravages of Eurocentric science: minorities in the West and the peoples of the Third World. The politics of difference has helped the most conservative sections of minority communities to reassert their authority at the expense of the most vulnerable groups and to undermine more progressive trends. In 2005, the Australasian Police Multicultural Advisory Bureau published a 'religious diversity handbook', which advised that 'In incidents such as domestic violence, police need to have an understanding of the traditions, ways of life and habits of Muslims'. The police should consult the local Muslim religious leader, who will work against 'fragmenting the family unit'. The implication, as Joumanah El Matrah of the Islamic Women's Welfare Council observed, is that 'one needs to be more tolerant of violence against Muslim women' rather than that Muslim women 'should be entitled to the same protection' as everyone else. It is not just Muslim women who suffer from having their differences respected. In 2002, in Australia's Northern Territory, Jackie

Pascoe Jamilmira, a fifty-year-old Aboriginal man was given a twenty-four-hour prison sentence for assaulting and raping a fifteen-year-old girl. He had apparently been plying the girl's family with gifts since her birth so that she would become his wife upon coming of age. According to the judge, because the girl was an Aborigine she 'didn't need protection. She knew what was expected of her. It's very surprising to me he was charged at all.' That same year in California, a young Laotian American woman was abducted from her work at Fresno State University and raped. Her assailant, a Hmong immigrant (one of the boat people who had fled Cambodia and Laos in the final stages of the Vietnam War) explained to the court that this was a customary way of choosing a bride among his tribe. The court agreed that he had to be judged largely by his own cultural standards and sentenced him to just 120 days in jail.

The celebration of difference has an even more devastating impact, the Indian writer Meera Nanda suggests, on the peoples of the Third World. While Western postmodernists can 'at least take the hegemony of modern, mostly liberal, ideas for granted', Nanda observes, 'postmodernism in modernising societies like India serves to kill the promise of modernity even before it has struck roots.' The rise of postmodernism 'has totally discredited the necessity of, and even the possibility of, questioning the inherited metaphysical systems, which for centuries have shackled human imaginations and social freedoms in those parts of the world that have not yet had their modern-day enlightenments.'

Nanda shows how the radical 'preoccupation with the preservation and cultivation of "local knowledges"' has given credibility to chauvinist and ultra-nationalist interest groups such as the Hinduvta movement, which has gained prominence in India since the late 1980s. At the heart of Hindu supremacist ideology, Nanda observes, 'lies a very postmodernist assumption, namely, each society has its own distinct norms of reasonableness, logic, rules of evidence and conception of truth and there is no non-arbitrary, culture independent way to choose among these various alternatives.' While India's postmodernist intellectuals 'hoped for a new, more humane, feminist and less reductionist science to emerge from the traditions of the oppressed and the neglected peoples in non-modern cultures, Hindu nationalists were claiming that such a humane, ecological and non-reductionist science was already present in the worldview of the Vedas and Vedanta, the dominant tradition of Hinduism.' The arguments of the postmodern left 'were being used by Hindu chauvinists, the enemies of the left, to present Hinduism itself as a paradigm of "alternative science" that will lead to the "decolonisation of the mind"'. The 'left inclined anti-Enlightenment movements', Nanda concludes, 'have been successful in silencing the modernist, Enlightenment style thought in India' and helped 'deliver the people they profess to love – non-Western masses, the presumed victims of "Western science" and modernity – to the growing forces of hatred, fascism and religious fanaticism.'

* * * *

Race is not a scientific category. The pursuit of difference is a reactionary strategy. But racial divisions are a fact of life and racism a blight on the lives of millions of people. So how should we deal with race as it is actually lived? The day before the biologist Armand Leroi published his *New York Times* article welcoming the return of race, the novelist Sean Thomas wrote an essay for the *Daily Telegraph* in London, in which he argued that we should 'start teaching people to forget about race'. 'Instead of obsessing about race', suggested Thomas, 'we could try to build a race-blind society'. In response, the American anthropologist Alan Goodman argued that both Leroi and Thomas were wrong. 'Contra Leroi', he wrote, 'I argue that race is no longer the right way to describe biological variation. Contra Thomas, I argue that race is not a mere social construct but as a lived experience has devastatingly real effects':

Even though race was invented and made to seem real by social humans, and even though race makes little sense on the genetic level, this does not mean that it is not real in other ways. Thomas makes the mistake of thinking that because race is a social construct race cannot have real effects. To the contrary, processes of racing, racializing and practicing racism have enormous and powerful consequence for human wealth and health.

It is true that to say that race is a social construction is not to say that it is unreal. Money, after all, is a social construction but few would deny that money has a real effect in the real world. The social world can be as real as the natural world. It is also true that ignoring racial differences can lead us to ignore racism. The burning cars that littered the streets of French *banlieus* in the autumn of 2005 put to the torch the belief that *liberté, egalité, fraternité* can be crafted by turning a blind eye to racial divisions that torment the nation. To challenge racism, one has first to open one's mind to the reality of a world socially fragmented into races. Yet the conclusions I draw from this are almost the reverse of Goodman's. Goodman suggests that race should have no place in biomedical research because it is not a natural category but that race should form a central part of social policy because of the social impact of racial divisions. I suggest, to the contrary, that biomedical research should make pragmatic use of the social categories into which we divide humans, including racial categories, while recognising that these are social, rather than natural, divisions. Ironically, it is precisely because racial groupings are social rather than natural categories – because they are the everyday ways in which we talk about ourselves – that they can sometimes be so useful to scientists and doctors. It makes sense for biomedical researchers both to make use of race pragmatically and to drop the pretence that it is a scientific category. Politically, however, we should challenge the use of racial categories in public life and social policy, not by being blind to racial differences but by seeking to transcend them. Racism continues to blight the lives of many people and often of whole communities but it is antiracism that, perversely, often helps keep the racial pot boiling.

In her book *Colormute*, the anthropologist Mica Pollock described her time at a Californian high school investigating how the staff, children and parents talked about racial differences. They were, she observed, continually wrestling 'with the paradoxical reality that in a world in which racial inequality already exists, both talking and not talking of people in racial terms seems alternately necessary'. 'All Americans, every day', Pollock suggested, 'are reinforcing racial distinctions and racialized thinking by using race labels, but we are also reinforcing racial inequality by refusing to use them.' The dilemma of which Pollock speaks is a recent predicament and one that is largely of antiracists' own making. Through the politics of difference we have come to celebrate the blossoming of 'racial' identities and to see them as critical to our social survival. Hence, there is no getting away from race talk. At the same time, we have come to view an 'identity' as so critical to the very survival of the individual that we have become frightened of 'disrespecting' identities by challenging or offending their values, beliefs or ways of being, or of saying anything that might dislocate their sense of belonging. 'Equal respect for persons', the philosopher Bhikhu Parekh suggests, 'entails respect for their cultures and ways of life'. Charles Taylor believes that to be denied 'recognition' – or to be 'misrecognized' – is to suffer both a distortion of one's relation to one's self and an injury to one's identity. The sociologist Tariq Modood thinks that people should be 'required' to show respect for other people's 'origins, family ... [and] community'. This demand that we should 'respect' other cultures, races and peoples and not offend their values and beliefs has made it much more difficult to talk openly about difference. The result has been both the flowering of race talk and a greater reticence to talk of differences, whether cultural or racial.

Historically, antiracists challenged both the practice of racism and the process of racialisation; that is, both the practice of discriminating against people by virtue of their race and the insistence that an individual can be defined by the race to which he or she belongs. They did not ignore racism but they recognised that fighting racism meant treating everybody equally despite their differences, not differently because of them. This was the essence of universalism.

Today's antiracists continually confuse the edict 'You can't fight racism if you ignore racial divisions' with the demand 'You can only fight racism by celebrating racial identity'. As the rise of the politics of difference has turned the assertion of group identity into a progressive demand, so racialisation is no longer viewed as a purely negative phenomenon. The consequence has been the resurrection of racial ideas and the imprisonment of people within their cultural identities. Challenging the politics of difference has become as important today as challenging racism. This does not mean ignoring the reality of race but seeking rather to transcend the politics of difference, whether promoted by racists or by antiracists.

The concept of race is irrational. The practice of antiracism has become so. We need to challenge both, in the name of humanism and of reason.

NOTES AND REFERENCES

Foreword: Race, science and James Watson

page 1: 'I am inherently gloomy': Grubbe, *Sunday Times*, 14 October 2007.

2 'There is no firm reason': Watson, *Avoid Boring People*, p. 326.

2 'Censure was swift and universal': Milmo, *Independent*, 29 October 2007; McKie and Harris, *Observer*, 21 October 2007.

2 'In America, too, the criticism was almost total': Thomas H. Maugh, 'DNA pioneer quits after race comments', *Los Angeles Times*, 26 October 2007; 'FAS condemns comments made by Dr James Watson: http://fas.org/main/content.jsp?formAction=297&contentId=572 (last visited 1 November 2007).

3 Pinker: *Harvard Crimson*, 19 January 2005.

4 Venter: *A Life Decoded*, p. 315; and cited in McKie and Harris, *Observer*, 21 October 2007.

5 Harding: *Is Science Multicultural?*, pp. x, 6, 8; *Whose Science? Whose Knowledge?*, p. 10.

Chapter 1: The people's genome

7–8 ceremony to mark completion of the Human Genome Project: transcripts of the speeches by President Clinton, Tony Blair, Francis Collins and Craig Venter are published by the White House Office of the Press Secretary at http://www.ornl.gov/sci/techresources/Human_Genome/

project/clinton2.shtml (last viewed 1 November 2007); see also Venter, *A Life Decoded*, pp. 310–19.

8 'other scientists and journalists quickly took up the refrain': Editorial, *Nature Genetics*, 2001; Schwartz, *New England Journal of Medicine*, 2001; Angier, *New York Times*, 22 August 2000.

9 Kemp: *townhall.com*, 21 February 2001.

9 Collins: The quote is from a lecture that Collins gave on 'The Human Genome Project And Beyond'; the transcript is at http://www.nhgri.nih.gov/DIR/VIP/ShortCourse01/SC_01collinsTranscript.html (last visited on 1 November 2007).

9 Risch: Risch *et al.*, *Genome Biology*, 2002.

10 'Risch is not the only party-pooper': Leroi, *New York Times*, 14 March 2005; Sarich and Miele, *Race*, p. xi; Gill, *Nova Online*.

10 'race realists': The phrase is a loaded one, suggesting that only those who believe in the concept of race are in touch with reality. Nevertheless, for the sake of simplicity I will continue to use it to describe proponents of the race concept.

11 Lewontin: *Human Diversity*, p. 117.

11 O'Neil: 'Distribution of Blood Types'.

12 Hedren: The speech can be found at http://www.nobel.se/medicine/laureates/1930/press.html (last visited 1 November 2007).

14 Lewontin: *Journal of Evolutionary Biology*, 1972; see also Lewontin, *Genetic Basis of Evolutionary Change*, 1974.

14 Rosenberg: Rosenberg *et al.*, *Science*, 2002.

15 Gould: *Natural History*, November 1984.

15 Sykes: *Seven Daughters of Eve*, p. 284.

15 Cavalli-Sforza: Cavalli-Sforza, Menozzi and Piazza, *History and Geography of Genes*, p. 19.

15 Diamond: *Discover*, November 1994.

16 Mayr: 'Typological versus Population Thinking'.

16 Brues: *People and Races*, p. 1.

17 Graves: *Emperor's New Clothes*, p. 186.

18 Entine: *World&I*, 1 September 2001.

18 Dunn and Dobzhansky: *Heredity, Race and Society*, p. 110.

18–19 **Sarich and Miele:** *Race*, p. 211.

19–20 **Rosenberg:** Rosenberg *et al.*, *Science*, 2002.

20 **Cavalli-Sforza:** Cavalli-Sforza, Menozzi and Piazza, *History and Geography of Human Genes*, p. 19.

20 **Gould:** *Natural History*, November 1984.

21 **Tishkoff:** Tishkoff *et al.*, *Science*, 2001.

23 **Sarich:** Sarich and Miele, *Race*, p. 212.

24 **Entine:** *World&I*, 1 September 2001.

25 **Coon:** *The Origin of Races*, p. 411.

25 **Sarich:** Sarich and Miele, *Race*, p. 207.

25–6 **Brues:** *People and Races*, p. 1.

26 **Cavalli-Sforza:** *Genes, Peoples and Languages*, pp. 25–26.

26 **Sarich:** Sarich and Meile, *Race*, p. 163.

27 **Risch:** Risch *et al.*, *Genome Biology*, 2002.

29 **Zack:** *Philosophy of Science and Race*, pp. 40, 38.

30 **Risch:** Risch *et al.*, *Genome Biology*, 2002.

30–1 **Wilson *et al.*:** *Nature Genetics*, 2001.

32 **Naggert:** cited in Angier, *New York Times*, 22 August 2000.

32 **Brace:** cited in Begley, *Newsweek*, 13 February 1995.

33–4 **Hocutt:** *The Independent Review*, 2002.

34 **Sailer:** 'It's All Relative'.

34 **Zack:** *Philosophy of Science and Race*, p. 69.

34 **'Northern Ireland Protestants, he argues, *are* a distinct race':** Sailer, 'It's All Relative'. Sailer has a highly sophisticated explanation for the conflict in Northern Ireland: 'One family used to own Northern Ireland until the other family took it away from them. Some members of the first family want it back.'

34 **Levin:** *Behaviour and Philosophy*, 2002.

35 **Hocutt:** *The Independent Review*, 2002.

36 **Broca:** cited in W.Z. Ripley, *The Races of Europe*, p. 111.

36 **Sollas:** *Paleolithic Races and their Modern Representatives*, p. 505.

Chapter 2: Should science be colour-blind?

38 'a new era of race-based therapeutics': Bloche, *New England Journal of Medicine*, 2004.

38 **Kahn:** *Yale Journal of Health Policy, Law and Ethics*, 2004.

39 **Criticism of the race concept:** Schwartz, *New England Journal of Medicine*, 2001; Wilson *et al.*, *Nature Genetics*, 2001; Editorial, *Nature Genetics*, 2001.

39 **'Others beg to differ':** Risch *et al.*, *Genome Biology* 2002; Burchard *et al.*, *New England Journal of Medicine*, 2003; Satel, *New York Times*, 5 May 2002.

40 **Satel:** *Policy Review*, 2001.

43 **Cohn:** Exner *et al.*, *New England Journal of Medicine*, 2001.

44–5 **Bowker and Star:** *Sorting Things Out*, pp. 10–11.

45–6 **'a much-quoted paper in the New England Journal of Medicine':** Burchard *et al.*, *New England Journal of Medicine*, 2003.

48 **'terms used for race are seldom defined':** Williams, *Health Services Research*, 1994.

48 **'a report in the journal *Science'*:** Sankar and Cho, *Science*, 2002.

49 **Details of the Schering Plough trial come from bioethicist Karama Neal:** http://openlettersforchange.blogspot.com/2006/04/follow-up-to-march-29-letter-on.html (last visited on 1 November 2007).

49 **'much research shows, however, that self-identity can be very unstable':** Hahn *et al.*, *Journal of the American Medical Association*, 1992; Harris and Sim, 'Who is Mixed Race?'.

50 **'have a history of significant gene flow among parent groups':** Smith *et al.*, *American Journal of Human Genetics*, 2001.

50 **Risch:** Risch *et al.*, *Genome Biology*, 2002.

51 **Grant:** *The Passing of the Great Race*, p. 31.

51–2 **'One academic study expressed a fear':** Lee *et al.*, *Yale Journal of Health Policy, Law and Ethics*, 2001.

52 **Juengst:** *American Journal of Human Genetics*, 1998.

52: **'Such fears have led to calls for race and ethnicity to be excluded from scientific and medical research':** Lee *et al.*, *Yale Journal of Health*

Policy, Law and Ethics, 2001; Stevens, *Journal of Health Politics, Policy and Law*, 2003; Editorial, *Nature Genetics*, 2000.

53 Racism and sickle cell anaemia: Melbourne, *In the Blood*, 1999.

53–4 Kahn: *Yale Journal of Health Policy, Law and Ethics*, 2004.

54 Stevens: *Journal of Health Politics, Policy and Law*, 2003.

57 Foster: 'Ethical Issues in Developing a Haplotype Map with Socially Defined Populations'; Foster and Sharp, *Genome Research*, 2002.

58 Satel: *Policy Review*, 2001.

58 Yancy: *American Heart Journal*, 2003.

59 Kahn: *Yale Journal of Health Policy, Law and Ethics*, 2004.

60 Unesco: *Cultural Diversity: Common Heritage, Plural Identities*, p. 3.

60 Lieberman: *Phylon*, 1968.

62 Kruks: *Retrieving Experience*, p. 85.

62–3 Dunkee: *Sequencing the Trellis*, p. 62.

63 Murray and Herrnstein: *New Republic*, 1994.

63 Harker: *Guardian*, 14 February 2003.

64 Heys: cited in Stephen McGinty, 'Meet the Family', *Scotsman*, 4 June 2003.

64 Kittles: quoted in Sailer, *UPI*, 29 April 2003.

64 Leroi: *New York Times*, 14 March 2005.

Chapter 3: There be monsters

66 Pagden: *European Encounters with the New World*, pp. 4–5.

67 Keneally: *Times*, 22 March 1994.

67 Hannaford: *Race*, p. 12.

68 Augustine: *City of God*.

69 Barckley: cited in Wiener (ed.), *Dictionary of the History of Ideas*, vol. 2 p. 435.

69 'fabulous tales about monsters': Friedman, *The Monstrous Races in Medieval Art and Thought*.

70–1 Armesto: *So You Think You're Human?*, pp. 75–6.

71 Herbert: cited in Fryer, *Staying Power*, pp. 137–8.

71 Hannaford: *Race*, pp. 147, 148.

72 **Las Casas:** Hanke, *Bartolomé Las Casas*, p. 82; see also, Hanke. *All Mankind is One;* Las Casas, *The Defence; idem, The Devastation of the Indies;* Keen, 'The Legacy of Bartolomé de Las Casas'.

73–4 **Israel:** *Radical Enlightenment*, pp. vi, 3–4.

75 **Buffon:** Lyon and Sloan (eds.), *From Natural History to the History of Nature*, p. 102.

76 **'Tulp thought that the specimen had come from Angola':** cited in Yerkes and Yerkes, *The Great Apes.*

77 **Montagu:** *Memoirs of the American Philosophical Society*, 1943.

77 **Tyson:** cited in Hodgen, *Early Anthropology in the Sixteenth and Seventeenth Centuries*, p. 419.

78 **'all living things, plants, animals, and even mankind themselves':** cited in Bendyshe, 'History of Anthropology', p. 435.

78 **'Ray ... suggested that the species should be regarded as the fundamental unit of life':** Ray, *The Wisdom of God;* Raven, *John Ray, Naturalist.*

81 **'that the attributes of apes are mixed up with those of men':** cited in Marks, *What it Means to be 98% Chimpanzee*, p. 21.

83–4 **'This has led many recent scholars to argue that modernity itself':** Mosse, *Towards the Final Solution*, p. 3; Eze (ed.), *Race and the Enlightenment*, p. 5.

84 **Goldberg:** *Racist Culture*, p. 28.

Chapter 4: Enlightened Man

87 **Zeitlin:** *Ideology and the Development of Sociological Theory*, pp. 2–3.

87–9 **Israel:** *Radical Enlightenment*, pp. vi, 11; *Enlightenment Contested*, pp. 551–552.

90 **Buffon:** *A Natural History*, pp. 107, 306, 398.

90 **Hume:** *Inquiry Concerning Human Understanding*, VIII.1.

91 **Montesquieu:** cited in Smith, *The Fontana History of the Human Sciences*, p. 289.

91–2 **Buffon:** *A Natural History*, p. 7.

93 **Tench:** *Sydney's First Four Years*, p. 281.

93–4 **David Hume:** 'Of Commerce', in *Selected Essays*, p. 166.

94 **Cunningham:** cited in McGregor, *Imagined Destinies*, p. 6.

94 **Tench:** *Sydney's First Four Years*, p. 294.

95 **conjectural histories:** Mackintosh cited in Burrow, *Evolution and Society*, p. 12; Ferguson, *The History of Civil Society*, p. 123.

95–6 **Diderot:** cited in Muthu, *Enlightenment Against Empire*, p. 53.

97 **Linnaeus:** *Prelude to the Betrothal of Plants*.

98 **Locke:** *Essay Concerning Human Understanding*, IV.iv.16: 507.

99 **Buffon:** cited in Sloan, *Isis*, 1976, p. 359.

100 **Blumenbach:** *Anthropological Treatises of Johann Friederich Blumenbach*, p. 98.

100 **Smith:** *Essay on the Causes of the Variety of Complexion and Figure in the Human Species*, p. 240n.

101 **Paine:** *Rights of Man*, p. 66.

101 **Greene:** *American Anthropologist*, 1954.

102 **Marks:** *Human Biodiversity*, pp. 52, 53, 60; *What it Means to be 98% Chimpanzee*, p. 60.

102–3 **Hocutt:** *The Independent Review*, 2002.

103 **Levin:** *Behavior and Philosophy*, 2002.

103 **Gibbon:** *Decline and Fall of the Roman Empire*, vol. IV, p. 167.

104 **Humboldt:** cited in Montagu, *Man's Most Dangerous Myth*, p. 44.

104 **Kames:** cited in Gossett, *Race*, p. 46.

105 **Hume:** 'Of National Characters', in *Selected Essays*, p. 360 n.120.

105 **Smith:** *An Essay on the Causes of the Variety of Complexion and Figure in the Human Species*, pp. 91–3.

105–6 **Jefferson:** 'Notes on Virginia' in *The Writings of Thomas Jefferson*, pp. 194–6.

106–7 **Kant:** 'On the different races of men', in Eze (ed.), *Race and the Enlightenment*, pp. 38–48; cited in Greene, *American Anthropologist*, 1954, pp. 31–41.

107 **Bernasconi:** *Concepts of Race in the Eighteenth Century*, pp. v–xi.

108 **Jefferson:** 'Notes on Virginia' in *The Writings of Thomas Jefferson*, pp. 194–6; letter to French correspondent cited in Gossett, *Race*, p. 52.

Chapter 5: The romance of type

110 History of the La Société des Observateurs de l'Homme: Chappey, *La Société des Observateurs de l'Homme.*

111–12 Degerando's Memoirs: *The Observation of Savage Peoples.*

112 Cuvier: cited in Stocking, *Race, Culture and Evolution*, pp. 29–30.

113 Huxley: 'Emancipation: Black and White', in *Lay Sermons, Addresses and Reviews.*

114 Porter: cited in Himmelfarb, *The Idea of Poverty*, p. 362.

115 Weber: *Peasants Into Frenchmen.*

115 Buchez: cited in Pick, *Faces of Degeneration*, p. 60.

117–18 Burke: cited in Kirk, *The Conservative Mind*, p. 47.

118 Bagehot: cited in Jones, *Social Darwinism and English Thought*, p. 42.

118 Pick: *Faces of Degeneration*, p. 57.

119 Martineau: cited in Burrow, *Evolution and Society*, p. 94.

119–20 Burrow: *Evolution and Society*, p. 93.

120 Maine: cited in Burrow, *Evolution and Society*, pp. 110–111.

120 Comte: *The Essential Comte*, pp. 37–8.

120 Marineau: cited in Burrow, *Evolution and Society*, p. 106.

121 Stepan: *The Idea of Race in Science*, p. 4.

123 Hume: *Inquiry Concerning Human Understanding*, VIII.1.

124 Burke: *Reflections on the Revolution in France*, p. 106.

124–6 Herder: *Reflections on the Philosophy of the History of Mankind*, p. 249, 203, 440, 219; *Herder on social and political culture*, pp. 186–187; and cited in Berlin, *Vico and Herder*, pp. 181, 165, 180, 159, 182, 186; Hampson, *The Enlightenment*, p. 240; Muthu, *Enlightenment Against Empire*, pp. 231, 255; and in Mosse, *Towards the Final Solution*, p. 37.

129 Herder: cited in Bruford, *Culture and Society in Classical Weimar*, p. 201.

130 Edwards: cited in Banton, *Racial Theories*, p. 31.

Chapter 6: To make an accomplice of nature

133 Lavater: cited in Zebrowitz, *Reading Faces*, p. 41.

134 *New York Tribune*: cited in Stanton, *Leopard's Spots*, p. 144.

134 **Agassiz:** cited in Gould, *The Mismeasure of Man*, p. 50.

134 **American Golgotha:** 'Golgotha', which means 'the place of skulls', is the term used to describe the place of Christ's crucifixion.

135 **Spurzheim:** cited in Stepan, *The Idea of Race*, p. 24.

136–7 **Gould on Morton:** Gould's recalculation of Morton's data was first published in *Science* (Gould, *Science*, 1978). A subsequent paper in *Current Anthropology* pointed out that Gould's recalculation of Morton's Caucasian average was in error (Michael, *Current Anthropology*, 1988). In fact in the first edition of *The Mismeasure of Man*, published in 1981, Gould had already acknowledged the error (he had apparently been working from a photocopy of Morton's original chart, and one of the figures was smudged). The error was embarrassing but bore out the thesis of his argument – 'the social embeddedness of science'. He had too easily accepted the lower figure for Caucasian skulls because it better fitted his social theories (*The Mismeasure of Man*, note, p. 66). However, Gould's error, embarrassing though it was, did not affect his argument about the bias in Morton's analysis. The story, however, does not end there. Ever since there has developed a kind of academic urban myth that Gould deliberately falsified his figures, did not acknowledge his error and that Morton's analysis was unbiased. Not just racial scientists such as J.P. Rushton, but antiracists, such as the anthropologist Loring Brace, a severe critic of race realism as we saw in Chapter 1, have lambasted Gould's 'dishonesty' over the Morton analysis (see Rushton, *Personality and Individual Differences*, 1996; Brace's comments can be found on the evolutionary psychology discussion group: http://groups.yahoo.com/group/evolutionary-psychology/message/19101).

137 **Morton:** *Crania Americana*, p. 1.

137 **Frederickson:** *The Black Image in the White Mind*, p. 43.

138 **Nott and Gliddon:** *Types of Mankind*, pp. 399–400; *Indigenous Races*, pp. 399–400.

139 **Stepan:** *The Idea of Race in Science*, p. 4.

140 **Thomas:** *Skull Wars*, p. 42.

140 *Richmond Inquirer* and **Bachman:** cited in Gossett, *Race*, pp. 66, 63; and in Stanton, *The Leopard's Spots*, p. 194.

141 **'Either the brute is a king':** cited in Cannadine, *Ornamentalism*, p. 8.

141–2 **Lorrimer:** *Colour, Class and the Victorians*, pp. 67–8.

142 **'Nurse can't understand it all':** cited in Cannadine, *Ornamentalism*, pp. 59, 123, 124.

142–3 *Saturday Review*: 16 January 1864.

143–4 **Mill:** cited in Briggs, *Past and Present*, 1956.

144 **Spurzheim:** *Phrenological Journal*, 1829–1830.

144 **LeBon:** *The Psychology of Peoples*, pp. 29, 43.

144 **Galton:** cited in Chase, *The Legacy of Malthus*, p. 14.

146 **Beddoe:** *The Anthropological History of Europe*, p. 53.

146–7 **Wallace:** *Journal of the Anthropological Society*, 1864, p. clvii–clxxxvii; 'The Development of Human Races Under the Law of Natural Selection', in *Natural Selection and Tropical Nature*, pp.167–85.

147–8 **Wallace rethinking race and natural selection:** *The Quarterly Review*, 1869, pp. 185–205; 'The Limits of Natural Selection as Applied to Man' in *Natural Selection and Tropical Nature*, pp. 211–2.

148 **'I hope you have not murdered':** cited in Marchant, *Alfred Russel Wallace*, vol. 1, p. 240.

148 **Darwin on race:** *Descent of Man*, vol. 1 pp. 214–250; vol. 2, pp. 316–384.

149 **'When two races of men meet':** Darwin, *Notebooks*, Fourth Notebook, p. 166.

150 **Condorcet:** *Sketch for a Historical Picture of the Progress of the Human Mind*, p. 83.

150 **Stepan:** *The Idea of Race in Science*, p. 5.

152 **'Camper "determined that blacks were the missing link" ':** Calixte and Trocha, *Origins of the Aryan Myth*.

152 **Camper:** cited in Poliakov, *The Aryan Myth*, p. 162.

152 **Blumenbach:** cited in Walker, *Physiognomy Founded on Physiology*, p. 59.

Chapter 7: The burden of culture

154 **Eisenman:** Interview on Channel 4 News, 18 April 2005.

155 **Bauman:** *Modernity and Ambivalence*, p. 272.

156 **Marcuse:** *Eros and Civilisation*, p. 23.

156 **Bell:** *Sociological Journeys*, p. 149.

157   Unesco   constitution: http://portal.unesco.org/en/ev.php-URL_
ID=15244&URL_DO=DO_TOPIC&URL_SECTION=201.html (last vis-
ited 1 November 2007); for full documentation of the conference that led to
the   establishment   of   Unesco,   see   http://unesdoc.unesco.org/images/
0011/001176/117626e.pdf

157–8 Unesco statement on race: http://unesdoc.unesco.org/images/
0012/001282/128291eo.pdf

158–9 Finkielkraut: *Defeat of the Mind*, p. 57.

160 Bryan: cited in Larson, *Summer of the Gods*, p. 39.

162 Stocking: *Race, Culture and Evolution*, p. 214.

162 Boas: cited in Stocking, *Race, Culture and Evolution*, p. 148.

163 Renan: *The Future of Science*, p. 169.

163 LeBon: *The Psychology of Peoples*, pp. 216–17.

163 Taine: *History of English Literature*, vol. 1, p. 8.

163 de Maistre: *Considerations on France*, p. 47.

164 Gellner: *Relativism and the Social Sciences*, p. 83.

164 Spencer: cited in Stocking, *Race, Culture and Evolution*, p. 117.

166–7 Boas: *Journal of American Folklore*, 1904.

167 Benedict: *Patterns of Culture*, pp. 254–5.

167 White: *The Science of Culture*, p. 181.

169 Stocking: *Race, Evolution and Culture*, p. 227.

169 Stocking: *Race, Evolution and Culture*, p. 265–6.

169–70 Mead: 'A New Preface', to the 1959 edition to Ruth Benedict's
Patterns of Culture.

170 Kuper: *Culture*, p. 245.

171 College de France report: cited in Finkielkraut, *Defeat of the Mind*,
p. 96.

171 Taylor: 'Politics of Recognition', pp. 30–1, 28.

172 Hall: 'The question of cultural identity', p. 277.

172 Unesco: World Conference on Cultural Policies, *Final Report*, p. 22.

172 Gray: *Two Faces of Liberalism*, p. 121.

172–3 Taylor: 'Politics of Recognition', p. 28.

173 Kymlicka: *Multicultural Citizenship*, p. 47.

173 Parekh: *Times Literary Supplement*, 25 February 1994.

173 Modood: 'Introduction', to Modood and Werbner (eds.), *The Politics of Multiculturalism in the New Europe*, p. 20.

173 Young: *Justice and the Politics of Difference*, p. 174.

174 MacDonald: Quoted in David Fickling, 'Bridging whitefella law and clan justice', *Guardian*, 30 December 2002.

174 Taylor: 'The Politics of Recognition', n. 16, pp. 40–41.

175 Barry: *Culture and Equality*, p. 259.

175–6 Taylor: 'The Politics of Recognition', pp. 58–9.

176 Appiah: *Ethics of Identity*, p. 110.

176 Raz: *Ethics in the Public Domain*, p. 177.

177 Appiah: *Ethics of Identity*, p. 125.

177 Finkielkraut: *Defeat of the Mind*, p. 104.

177 Appiah: *Ethics of Identity*, p. 124.

178 Margalit and Raz: *Journal of Philosophy*, 1990.

178 Kymlicka on where 'the survival of a culture is not guaranteed': *Multicultural Citizenship*, p. 83.

178 Taylor: 'Politics of Recognition', pp. 40–1, n. 16.

178 Kymlicka on the distinction between the 'existence of a culture' and 'its "character" ': *Multicultural Citizenship*, p. 104.

179 Wright: *Atlantic Monthly*, June 1940.

179 Michaels: *Our America*, p. 123.

180 Crick: *JCWI Bulletin*, Winter 2004/2005.

180 Appiah: *Ethics of Identity*, p. 117.

181 Polish community: Hollinger, *Postethnic America*, p. 152.

181 Wrong: *Critical Review*, 1997.

183 Adorno and Horkheimer: *Dialectic of Enlightenment*, p. 6.

183 Lévi-Strauss: cited in Todorov, *On Human Diversity*, p. 67.

184 Hughes: *The Sea Change*, pp. 135–6.

185 Heartfield: *The 'Death of the Subject' Explained*, pp. 146–53.

185 Malcolm X: From a speech given at the University of Ghana, 13 May 1964; transcript at http://www.hartford-hwp.com/archives/45a/460.html (last visited 1 November 2007).

185 Sartre: Preface to Fanon, *Wretched of the Earth*, p. 22.

186 Lester: cited in Lasch-Quinn, *Society*, 39, 2002.

186 **Kruks:** *Retrieving Experience*, p. 85.

186 **Gitlin:** *Twilight of Common Dreams*, p. 100.

187 **Gitlin:** *Twilight of Common Dreams*, p. 100.

187 **Gray:** *Two Faces of Liberalism*, p. 121.

187 **Jacoby:** *End of Utopia*, pp. 32–3.

188 **Powell:** *Sunday Express*, 24 April 1983.

188 **'In France, too, similar ideas have gained currency':** Pierre Pascal, 'Les Vrais Racistes', *Militant*, 16, Jan. 1984; Le Pen cited in Taguieff, *Telos*, 1990.

188 **Kymlicka:** *Multicultural Citizenship*, p. 104.

189 **Finkielkraut:** *Defeat of the Mind*, pp. 91–2, 79.

Chapter 8: Who owns knowledge?

191 **Chatters:** cited in *New York Times*, 30 September 1996.

191 **'My God, there he is, Kennewick Man!':** *New Yorker*, 16 June 1997.

192 **Minthorn:** *New York Times*, 30 September 1996.

192 **'Eight anthropologists... filed a lawsuit':** The eight plaintiffs were Robson Bonnichsen, director of the Center for the Study of First Americans at Oregon State University; Douglas Owsley, divisional head for physical anthropology at the Smithsonian Institution, Washington DC; Dennis Stanford, chairman of the Smithsonian's anthropology department; D Gentry Steele, Professor of Anthropology at Texas A&M University; C Loring Brace, Curator of the Museum of Anthropology at the University of Michigan; George Gill, Professor of Anthropology at the University of Wyoming; C Vance Hanes, Jr, Professor of Archaeology at the University of Arizona; Richard Jantz, Professor of Anthropology at the University of Tennessee, Knoxville.

193 **Meninick:** cited in *TriCity Herald*, 18 October 1996.

193 **Marla Big Boy:** cited in 'Colville Tribe on Kennewick', *AAA Newsletter*, May 1999.

193 **Report by Powell and Rose:** *Report on the Osteological Assessment of the 'Kennewick Man' skeleton* (1999).

193   Cultural   affiliation   report: http://www.nps.gov/archeology/
kennewick/index.htm#cultaff (last visited 1 November 2007).

194 Babbitt response: 'Interior Department Determines "Kennewick
Man" Remains to Go to Five Indian Tribes', Press release from the Office
of the Interior, 25 September 2001, http://www.nps.gov/archeology/
kennewick/doi9_25_00.htm (last visited 1 November 2007); see also Letter
from the Secretary of the Interior to Laura Caldera, Secretary of the Army,
21 September 2001, at http://www.nps.gov/archeology/kennewick/babb_
letter.htm

196 Nanda: *Prophets Facing Backwards*, p. xii.

197 Ignatieff: *Prospect*, October 1999.

198 Ross: *Social Text*, 1996, p. 5.

198–9 Harding: *Is Science Multicultural?*, p. x.

199 Ross: *Social Text*, p. 3.

199 Collins: *Social Studies of Science*, 1981.

199 Barnes and Bloor: 'Relativism, rationalism and the sociology of knowledge', p. 27.

199–200 Harding: *Is Science Multicultural?*, pp. 6, 8; *idem, Whose science?
Whose knowledge?*, p. 10.

200 Young: *White Mythologies*, p. 3.

200 Chatterjee: cited in Nanda, *Prophets Facing Backwards*, p. 151.

200 Spivak: 'Can the subaltern speak?'.

201 Deloria: *Red Earth, White Lies*, p. 7.

201 Watson-Verran and Turnbull: 'Science and the other', p. 115.

201–2 Deloria: *Red Earth, White Lies*, pp. 36, 40, 41.

204 Ubelaker: cited in Turner, *Quarterly Review of Archaeology* 7, 1986, p. 1.

204 Bonnishen and Schneider: *The Sciences*, July/August 2000.

204–5 Minthorn: 'Human remains should be reburied', http://www.
umatilla.nsn.us/kman1.html (last visited 1 November 2007).

205 Tsosie and Huglin: cited in Lee, *Tri-City Herald*, 26 December
1999.

206 Thomas: *Skull Wars*, p. 244.

206 Clark: *Skeptical Inquirer*, May/June 1999.

206 Bonnishen and Schneider: *The Sciences*, July/August 2000.

206 Foley: speaking at a debate 'Human Remains: Objects to Study or Ancestors to Bury?', 2 May 2003; transcript at http://www.instituteofideas. com/transcripts/human_remains.pdf (last visited 1 November 2007).

207 Ruff: cited in Goodhart, *Harvard Magazine*, 16 November 2003.

207 Besterman: speaking at debate on 'Human Remains: Objects to Study or Ancestors to Bury?', 2 May 2003; transcript at http://www.instituteofideas. com/transcripts/human_remains.pdf (last visited 1 November 2007).

207 Hubert and Fforde: 'Introduction' to Fforde, Hubert and Turnbull (eds.), *The Dead and their Possessions*, pp. 10, 1.

207 Thornton: cited in Jenkins, *Human Remains*, p. 14.

208 Chatters: *Ancient Encounters*, p. 60.

208 'Thomas tells a story': *Skull Wars*, pp. 218–9.

208 'lay claim to their own pasts': Jane Hubert, speaking at a debate on 'Human Remains: Objects to Study or Ancestors to Bury?', 2 May 2003; transcript at http://www.instituteofideas.com/ transcripts/human_ remains.pdf (last visited 1 November 2007).

208–9 Hubert and Fforde: 'Introduction' to Fforde, Hubert and Turnbull (eds.), *The Dead and their Possessions*, pp. 11–12.

209 'one advocate of repatriation suggests': Cressida Fforde, 'Collection, Repatriation and Identity', pp. 39, 38.

209 Rhea: *Race Pride and the American Identity*, pp. 10, 11, 15.

209–10 Fforde: 'Collection, Repatriation and Identity', pp. 37, 38.

210 Besterman: speaking at a debate on 'Human Remains: Objects to Study or Ancestors to Bury?', 2 May 2003; transcript at http://www. instituteofideas.com/transcripts/human_remains.pdf (last visited 1 November 2007).

210 Jenkins: *Human Remains*, p. 13.

210 Hooper-Greenhill: cited in Jenkins, *Human Remains*, p. 13.

211 Besterman: speaking at a debate on 'Human Remains: Objects to Study or Ancestors to Bury?', 2 May 2003; transcript at http://www.instituteofideas. com/transcripts/human_remains.pdf (last visited 1 November 2007).

211 Pickering: cited in Jenkins, *Human Remains*, p. 13.

211–12 Moratto: cited in Chatters, *Ancient Encounters*, p. 95.

212 Minthorn: cited in Jeff Benedict, *No Bone Unturned*, p. 197.

212 Boutros-Ghali: 'Foreword' to Ewen (ed.), *Voices of Indigenous Peoples*.

212 Hubert and Fforde: 'Introduction' to Fforde, Hubert and Turnbull (eds.), *The Dead and their Possessions* p. 10.

214 Lee: *Jackdaw*, September 2004.

214–15 MacGregor: 'A Machine to Generate Tolerance'.

216 United Nations report on the protection of cultural and intellectual property: Daes, *Study on the protection of the cultural and intellectual property of indigenous peoples*, pp. 11–3.

216 'Unesco has envisioned': Unesco, *Convention for the Safeguarding of the Intangible Cultural Heritage*; Unesco, 'Cultural diversity in the era of globalisation' (http://portal.unesco.org/culture/en/ev.php-URL_ID=11605&URL _DO=DO_TOPIC&URL_SECTION=201.html); see also Berryman, *Journal of Intellectual Property Law*, 1994.

216 Brown: 'Safeguarding the Intangible'; see also Brown, *Current Anthropology*, 1998.

Chapter 9: Ancient race wars and modern race science

219 'Europeans Invade America: 20 000 BC': *Discover*, February 1999.

219 'When Columbus came to the New World in 1492': *Santa Fe New Mexican*, 10 August 1997.

219–20 'If a Caucasoid Kennewick Man and his tribe': Ponte, 'Politically Incorrect Genocide, Part 2'.

220 Kortright: Chris Kortright, 'The Question of Kennewick Man: Rewriting colonisation' (http://www.geocities.com/anthropologyresistance/ kennewick; no longer available).

220 Hitt: *Harper's Magazine*, July 2005.

221 Chatters: *Ancient Encounters*, p. 20.

221 Armelagos and Gerven: *American Anthropologist*, 2003.

221 Washburn: *Transactions of the New York Academy of Sciences*, 1951.

222 Gill: *Nova Online*.

222 Armelagos: Armelagos and Gerven, *American Anthropologist*, 2003.

223 Chatters: *Ancient Encounters*, p. 176.

223 Kruzynski story: Dayton, *New Scientist*, 23 February 2002.

223 'Others, however, are less impressed by the new techniques': Kosiba, *American Journal of Physical Anthropology*, 2000; Belcher, Williams and Armelagos, *American Journal of Physical Anthropology*, 2002; Leathers, Edwards and Armelagos, *American Journal of Physical Anthropology*, 2002.

224 Hooton: *The Indians of Pecos Pueblo*, pp. 186, 348, 355, 356, 362; see also Giles, 'E.A. Hooton, 1887–1954'; Thomas, *Skull Wars*, p. 113.

226 Sauer: *Social Sciences and Medicine*, 2001.

228–9 multivariate analysis of Kennewick Man: Chatters, *Ancient Encounters*, pp. 220–223; Steele and Powell, *Evolutionary Anthropology*, 1993; *idem*, 'Paleobiological Evidence for the Peopling of the Americas: A Morphometric View'; Neves and Pucciarelli, *Journal of Human Evolution*, 1991; Walter Neves and Blum, *American Antiquity*, 2000; Powell and Neves, *Yearbook of Physical Anthropology*, 1999.

232 Martin's Pleistocene overkill theory: Martin, *Natural History*, 1967.

232 Adovasio: *The First Americans*, p. 93.

232–3 reasons for Pleistocene extinction: More recently archaeologists have suggested that climate change was responsible for the Pleistocene extinctions. This theory too, as Matt Ridley points out, is likely to have been shaped by politics as much as by scientific evidence; see Ridley, 'Ice Age Politics'.

233–4 the debate over Monte Verde: Adavasio, *The First Americans*, pp. 209, 189; Begley and Murr, *Newsweek*, 26 April 1999.

234 Kortright: Chris Kortright, 'The Question of Kennewick Man: Re-writing colonisation' (http://www.geocities.com/anthropologyresistance/kennewick; no longer available).

234 Solutrean theory: Stanford and Bradley, *Discovering Archaeology*, Feb. 2000.

234–5 'It wouldn't take too much for an intelligent person to learn': transcript of video interview with Dennis Stanford at http://www.s2nmedia. com/arctic/html/dennis_stanford.html (last visited 1 November 2007).

235 Deloria: *Red Earth, White Lies*, pp. 69–70, 54.

236 Marks: 'Your Body, My Property', pp. 41, 40.

237–8 Archambault: Affidavit of Joallyn Archambault, http://www. friendsofpast.org/kennewick-man/court/affidavits/oral-tradition-1.html (last visited 1 November 2007).

Chapter 10: The end of Utopia and the return of race

240 Kohn: *Race Gallery*, p. 138.

240–3 Rushton's thesis: *Race, Evolution and Behaviour.*

242 Kohn: *Race Gallery*, p. 140.

243 birthrate figures: Michael Haines, 'Fertility and Mortality in the United States' (http://eh.net/encyclopedia/article/haines.demography; last visited 1 November 2007); see also Foner and Garraty (eds.) *The Reader's Companion to American History.*

244 Brace: *American Anthropologist*, 1996.

244 Barash: *Animal Behaviour*, 1995.

245 Lynn: Richard Lynn's cv (http://www.rlynn.co.uk; last visited 1 November 2007); *Bulletin of the British Psychological Society*, 1977; *Mankind Quarterly*, 1990.

245 Kohn: *Race Gallery*, p. 96.

246 'continues to believe that it remains a "taboo" to talk of racial differences in intelligence': Murray, *Commentary*, September 2005.

247 'Natural History of Ashkenazi Intelligence': Cochran, Hardy and Harpending, *Journal of Biosocial Science*, 2006.

247 Murray on Jewish genius: *Commentary*, April 2007.

247 Kohn: 'It depends what you mean by difference', *Race Gallery*, p. 139.

248 Kohn: *Race Gallery*, p. 88.

249 Darwin: *Origin of Species*, p. 404.

249 'descended by modification from sociobiology': While there are important theoretical differences between sociobiology and evolutionary psychology I will in this chapter, for the purposes of readability, generally use 'sociobiology' to describe all contemporary Darwinian theories of human nature.

250 Pinker: *How the Mind Works*, p. 21.

251 Cosmides and Tooby: Cosmides, Tooby and Kurzban, *Trends in Cognitive Sciences*, 2003.

251 MacDonald: *A People That Shall Dwell Alone.*

252 Shulevitz: *Slate*, 24 January 2000.

252–3 Tooby: http://www.psych.ucsb.edu/research/cep/slatedialog.html (last visited 1 November 2007); for the full exchange between Shulevitz and Tooby see 'How to Deal with Fringe Academics' at http://www.slate.com/id/74139/entry/74419/ (last visited 1 November 2007).

253 'a letter to the *New York Review of Books*': Allen *et al.* Letter, *New York Review of Books*, 13 November 1975.

253–4 Cosmides and Tooby: 'The psychological foundations of culture', pp. 35, 79.

254 Lévi-Strauss: *Structural Anthropology*, vol. 2, p. 63.

254 de Waal: The Ape and the Sushi Master, p. 6.

255 Wilson: *On Human Nature*, p. 1.

255 Pinker: *Blank Slate*, p. 288.

256 Pagel and Mace: *Nature*, 2004; see also Lovgren, *National Geographic News*, 17 March 2004.

258 Trivers: *Quarterly Review of Biology*, 1971.

258 'ethnic nepotism': van den Berghe, *The Ethnic Phenomenon.*

258–60 Frank Salter: *On Genetic Interests*, pp. 24, 26, 303; *idem*, 'Introduction' to Salter (ed.) *Altruism and Welfare*, p. 6; Butovskaya, Salter, Diankoniv and Smirnov, *Human Nature*, 2000.

261 Tooby and Cosmides: *Brain and Behavioural Studies*, 1989.

261 Gray's review of Salter: *Human Ethology Bulletin*, 2005.

262–3 Goodhart: *Prospect*, February 2004.

263 van den Berghe: *Nations and Nationalism*, 2005.

263 Parekh: *Rethinking Multiculturalism.*

264 'An essay on Salter's work in the far-right magazine *American Renaissance*': Taylor, *American Renaissance*, January 2005.

264–5 Leroi: *New York Times*, 14 March 2005.

267 'a famous study of Moscow beggars': Butovskaya *et al.*, *Human Nature*, 2000.

268–9 Governor Eyre incident: see Lorrimer, *Colour, Class and the Victorians*, p. 195.

268 'there are a good many negroes in Southampton': *Daily Telegraph*, 21 August 1866.

269 British working class support for black rights in the American

Civil War: Blackett, *Divided Hearts*, 2001; Foner, *British Labor and the American Civil War*, 1981.

270–1 Putnam's research on diversity: *Scandinavian Political Studies*, 2007.

270 Giddens: 'Debating diversity', http://commentisfree.guardian. co.uk/anthony_giddens/2007/10/debating_diversity.html (last visited 1 November 2007).

271 Kohn: *The Race Gallery*, p. 166.

272 Leroi: *New York Times*, 14 March 2005.

273 Jose Morales: 'Race, Genetics and Human Difference', http://www. pibiotech.org/rg_blog/ (no longer available).

273 Harker: *Guardian*, 14 February 2003.

273–4 Rachel Hunt: quoted in Daniel Menhinnit, 'Couple take a genetic journey', *Croydon Advertiser*, 10 April 2003.

274 Annette Dula: Paper presented to conference on 'African Genealogy and Genetics: Looking Back to Move Forward', University of Minnesota's Centre for Bioethics, June 21–22 2002; transcript at http://www.ahc. umn.edu/bioethics/afrgen/html/TownHallMeeting.html (last visited 1 November 2007).

275–6 Pinker: *Blank Slate*, pp. 287–9, 293–4.

276 Ridley: *Origin of Virtues*, p. 259.

Afterword: Beyond race and unreason

278 'I am inherently gloomy': Grubbe, *Sunday Times*, 14 October 2007.

278 'If I said what I was quoted as saying': Watson, *Independent*, 29 October 2007.

279 Risch: quoted in Gitschier, *PloS Genetics*, 2005.

279 census categories: 'Standards of the Classification of Federal Data on Race and Ethnicity', Office of Management and Budget *Federal Register* (9 June 1994); 'Revisions to the Standards for the Classification of Federal Data on Race and Ethnicity', Office of Management and Budget *Federal Register Notice* (30 October 1997).

279 'Risch himself defines his races in this way': Risch *et al.*, *Genome Biology*, 2002.

280 'Flynn effect': Flynn, *Psychological Bulletin*, 1984; *idem*, Psychological Bulletin, 1987; Neisser (ed.), *The Rising Curve*.

280 Neisser: Neisser, *American Scientist*, September-October 1997.

281 A study by William Dickens and James Flynn: *Psychological Science*, 2006.

281 IQ scores often reflect power relations: Lee, 'Koreans in Japan and the United States'; Lynn *et al.*, *Personality and Individual Differences*, 1984; Verster and Prinsloo, 'The Diminishing Test Performance Gap Between English Speakers and Afrikaans Speakers in South Africa'.

282-3 Duodo: 'Here we go again', *Comment is free*, http://commentisfree. guardian.co.uk/cameron_duodu/2007/10/here_we_go_again_.html.

283 Baggini: 'Binary limitations', *Comment is free*, http://commentisfree. guardian.co.uk/julian_baggini/2007/10/binary_limitations.html.

283 'Australasian Police Multicultural Advisory Bureau published a "religious diversity handbook"': Liam Houlihan, 'Police told to respect traditions', *Herald Sun*, 25 October 2005, http://www.news.com.au/ heraldsun/story/0,21985,17026063-2862,00.html.

284 'Jackie Pascoe Jamilmira ... was given a twenty-four-hour prison sentence': David Fickling, 'Bridging whitefella law and clan justice', *Guardian*, 30 December 2002.

284 'The court agreed that he had to be judged largely by his own cultural standards': Behabib, *The Claims of Culture*, p. 87.

284–5 Nanda: *Prophets Facing Backwards*, pp. 28, 19, xv, xvi, 2.

285 Thomas: *Sunday Telegraph*, 13 March 2005.

285–6 Goodman: 'Two Questions about Race'.

287 Parekh: *Times Literary Supplement*, 25 February 1994.

287 Taylor: 'The politics of recognition'.

287 Modood: 'Introduction' to Modood and Werbner (eds.), *The Politics of Multiculturalism in the New Europe*, p. 20.

BIBLIOGRAPHY

Adavosa, James, *The First Americans: In Pursuit of Archaeology's Greatest Mystery* (New York: Random House, 2002).

Adorno, T. and Horkheimer, M., *Dialectic of Enlightenment* (London: Verso, 1979; first pub. 1944).

Angier, Natalie, 'Do Races Differ?: Not Really, DNA Shows', *New York Times*, 22 August 2000.

Appiah, Kwame Anthony, *The Ethics of Identity* (Princeton, NJ: Princeton University Press, 2005).

Armelagos, George and Gerven, Dennis P. Van, 'A Century of Skeletal Biology and Paleopathology: Contrasts, contradictions and conflicts', *American Anthropologist*, 105, 2003, pp. 51–62.

Augustine, *City of God* (Harmondsworth: Penguin, 1991).

Banton, Michael, *Racial Theories* (Cambridge: Cambridge University Press, 1987).

Barash, David, 'Review of J.P. Rushton: *Race*', *Animal Behaviour*, 49, 1995, pp. 1131–3.

Barkow, Jerome K., Cosmides, Leda and Tooby, John, *The Adapted Mind: Evolutionary Psychology and the Generation of Culture* (Oxford: Oxford University Press, 1992).

Barnes, Barry and Bloor, David, 'Relativism, rationalism and the sociology of knowledge', in Hollis and Lukes (eds.), *Rationalism and Relativism*.

Barry, Brian, *Culture and Equality: An Egalitarian Critique of Multiculturalism* (Cambridge: Polity Press, 2001).

Bauman, Zygmunt, *Modernity and Ambivalence* (Cambridge: Polity Press, 1991).

Beddoe, John, *The Races of Britain: A Contribution to the Anthropology of Western Europe* (Bristol: J. W. Arrowsmith, 1885).

Beddoe, John, *The Anthropological History of Europe* (Paisley: Gardner, 1912; first pub. 1891).

Begley, Sharon, 'Three is not enough: surprising new lessons from the controversial science of race', *Newsweek*, 13 February 1995.

Begley, Sharon and Murr, Andrew, 'The First Americans', *Newsweek*, 26 April 1999.

Belcher, R., Williams, F. and Armelagos, G.J., 'Misidentification of Meroitic Nubiabs Using Fordisc 2.0', *American Journal of Physical Anthropology*, 34, 2002, p. 42.

Bell, Daniel, *Sociological Journeys: Essays 1960–1980* (London: Heinemann, 1980).

Bendyshe, T., 'The History of Anthropology', *Memoirs of the Anthropological Society of London*, 1, 1865, pp. 335–458.

Benedict, Jeff, *No Bone Unturned: The Adventures of a Top Smithsonian Forensic Scientist and the Legal Battle for America's Oldest Skeletons* (New York: Harper Collins, 2003).

Benedict, Ruth, *Patterns of Culture* (Boston: Houghton Mifflin, 1934).

Benhabib, Sayla, *The Claims of Culture: Equality and Diversity in the Global Era* (Princeton, NJ: Princeton University Press, 2002).

Berghe, Pierre van den, *The Ethnic Phenomenon*, (New York: Elsevier, 1981).

Berghe, Pierre van den, 'Review of *On Genetic Interests* by Frank Slater', *Nations and Nationalism*, 11, 2005, pp. 163–165.

Berlin, Isaiah, *Vico and Herder: Two Studies in the History of Ideas* (London: The Hogarth Press, 1992).

Bernasconi, Robert, *Concepts of Race in the Eighteenth Century* (Bristol: Thoemmes Press, 2001).

Bernasconi, Robert and Lott, Tommy L. (eds.) *The Idea of Race* (Indianapolis: Hackett Publishing Company, 200).

Berryman, Cathryn A., 'Towards a more universal protection of intangible cultural property', *Journal of Intellectual Property Law*, 1, 1994.

Blackett, R. J. M., *Divided Hearts: Britain and the American Civil War* (Baton Rouge: Louisiana State University Press, 2001).

Bloche, M. Gregg, 'Race based therapeutics', *New England Journal of Medicine* 351, 2004, pp. 2035–7.

Blumenbach, Johann Friederich, *The Anthropological Treatises of Johann Friederich Blumenbach*, ed. Thomas Bendyshe (London: Anthropological Society, 1865).

Boas, Franz, 'Some Traits of Primitive Culture', *Journal of American Folklore*, 17, 1904.

Bonnichsen, R. and Steele, D.G. (eds.), *Method and Theory for Investigating the Peopling of the Americas* (Corvallis: Centre for the Study of the First Americans, Oregon State University, 1999).

Bonnishen, R. and Schneider, Alan L., 'Battle of the bones', *The Sciences*, July/August 2000.

Boutros-Ghali, Boutros, 'Foreword' to Ewen (ed.), *Voices of Indigenous Peoples*.

Bowker, Geoffrey C. and Star, Susan Leigh, *Sorting Things Out: Classification and its Consequences* (Cambridge, MA: MIT Press, 1999).

Brace, C. Loring, 'Racialism and Racist Agendas', *American Anthropologist*, 98, 1996, pp. 176–7.

Briggs, Asa, 'Middle Class Consciousness in English Politics 1760–1840', *Past and Present*, 9, April 1956.

Brown, Michael, 'Can Culture Be Copyrighted?', *Current Anthropology*, 39, 1998, pp. 193–222.

Brown, Michael, 'Safeguarding the Intangible', http://www.culturalpolicy. org/commons/comment-print.cfm?ID=12 (last visited 1 November 2007).

Brues, Alice, *People and Races* (New York: MacMillan, 1977).

Bruford, W.H., *Culture and Society in Classical Weimar* (Cambridge: Cambridge University Press, 1962).

Buffon, George-Louis LeClerk, Comte de, *A Natural History, General and Particular Containing the History and Theory of the Earth, A General History of Man, the Brute Creation, Vegetable, Minerals, &c.* trans. by William Smellie (London: Richard Evans, 1817; first pub. between 1749 and 1767).

Burchard, Esteban Gonzalez, Ziv, Elad, Coyle, Natasha, Gomez, Scarlett Lin, Tang, Hua, Karter, Andrew J., Mountain, Joanna L., Perez-Stable, Eliseo

J., Sheppard, Dean and Risch, Neil, 'The Importance of Race and Ethnic Background in Biomedical Research and Clinical Practice', *New England Journal of Medicine*, 348, 20 March 2003.

Burke, Edmund, *Reflections on the Revolution in France* (Harmondsworth: Penguin, 1968; first pub. 1790).

Burrow, J.W., *Evolution and Society: A Study in Victorian Social Theory* (Cambridge: Cambridge University Press, 1966).

Butovskaya, Marina, Salter, Frank, Diankoniv, Ivan and Smirnov, Alexey, 'Urban Begging and Ethnic Nepotism in Russia: An Ethological Pilot Study', *Human Nature*, 11, 2000, pp. 157–182 (reprinted in Salter (ed.), *Altruism and Welfare*).

Calixte, Alexandra and Trocha, Eduardo, *Origins of the Aryan Myth* (*The IB Holocaust Project*, 1997: http://cghs.dade.k12.fl.us/holocaust/myth.htm; last visited 1 November 2007).

Cannadine, David, *Ornamentalism: How the British Saw Their Empire* (London: Allen Lane, 2001).

Cavalli-Sforza, Luigi Luca, *Genes, Peoples and Languages* (London: Allen Lane, 2000).

Cavalli-Sforza, Luigi Luca, Menozzi, Paolo, and Piazza, Alberto, *The History and Geography of Genes* (abridged edition) (Princeton, NJ: Princeton University Press, 1994).

Chappey, Jean-Luc, *La Société des Observateurs de l'Homme: Des anthropologues au temps de Bonaparte (1799–1804)* (Paris: Société des études robespierristes, 2002).

Chase, Allan, *The Legacy of Malthus: The Social Costs of the New Scientific Racism* (Chicago: University of Illinois Press, 1980).

Chatters, James C., *Ancient Encounters: Kennewick Man and the First Americans* (New York: Touchstone, 2001).

Clark, Geoffrey A., 'NAGPRA, Science and the Demon Haunted World', *Skeptical Inquirer*, May/June 1999.

Cochran, Gregory, Hardy, Jason and Harpending, Henry, 'Natural History of Ashkenazi Intelligence', *Journal of Biosocial Science*, 38, 2006, pp. 659–63 (available online at http://homepage.mac.com/harpend/.Public/AshkenaziIQ.jbiosocsci.pdf; last visited 1 November 2007).

Collins, Harry, 'Stages in the empirical programme of relativism', *Social Studies of Science*, 11, 1981, pp. 3–10.

Comte, Auguste, *The Essential Comte: Selected from the Cours de Philosophie Positive*, ed. S. Andreski (London: Croon Helm, 1974).

Condorcet, A. N. de, *Sketch for a Historical Picture of the Progress of the Human Mind*, trans. J. Barraclough, (London: Weidenfeld & Nicholson, 1955; first pub. 1795).

Coon, Carleton S., *The Origin of Races* (New York: Knopf, 1962).

Cosmides, Leda and Tooby, John, 'The psychological foundations of culture' in Barkow, Cosmides and Tooby, *The Adapted Mind*.

Cosmides, Leda, Tooby, John and Kurzban, Robert, 'Perceptions of race', *Trends in Cognitive Sciences*, 7, 2003, pp. 173–9.

Crick, Bernard and Malik, Kenan, 'Difference and integration' (an exchange of letters), *JCWI Bulletin* (Winter 2004/2005), pp. 6–7; the exchange can be found online at http://www.kenanmalik.com/debates/crick_jcwi.html

Daes, Erica-Irene, *Study on the Protection of the Cultural and Intellectual Property of Indigenous Peoples* (New York: United Nations Economic and Social Council Commission on Human Rights, 1993).

Darwin, Charles, *The Origin of Species* (Harmondsworth: Penguin, 1968; first pub. 1859).

Darwin, Charles, *The Descent of Man, and Selection in Relation to Sex* (Princeton, NJ: Princeton University Press, 1981; first pub. 1871).

Darwin, Charles, 'Darwin's notebooks on transmutation of species' Part IV, Fourth notebook [E] (October 1838–10 July 1839). Edited by Gavin de Beer, *Bulletin of the British Museum (Natural History). Historical Series 2*, No. 5, September 1960, pp. 151–183.

Dayton, Leigh, 'Return of the Skulls', *New Scientist*, 23 February 2002.

Degerando, Joseph-Marie, *The Observation of Savage Peoples* (Berkley: University of California Press, 1969; first pub. 1800).

Deloria, Vine Jr., *Red Earth, White Lies: Native Americans and the Myths of Scientific Fact* (Golden, Colorado: Fulcrum, 1997).

Diamond, Jared, 'Race Without Color', *Discover*, November 1994.

Dickens, W.T. and Flynn, J.R., 'Black Americans reduce the racial IQ gap: evidence from standardization samples', *Psychological Science*, 17, 2006, pp. 913–20.

Douthwaite, Julia, *The Wild Girl, the Natural Man and Monsters: Dangerous Experiments in the Age of Enlightenment* (Chicago: Chicago University Press, 2002).

Dunkee, Brady, *Sequencing the Trellis: The Production of Race in the New Human Genomics* (Honors thesis, Brown University, 2003).

Dunn, L.C. and Dobzhansky, Theodosius, *Heredity, Race and Society* (Harmondsworth: Penguin Books, 1946).

Editorial, 'Genes, drugs and race', *Nature Genetics*, 29, 2001, pp. 239–40.

Entine, Jon, 'The Straw Man of Race', *World&I*, 16 (9) (1 September 2001), pp. 294–317; reprinted at http://www.jonentine.com/reviews/straw_man_of_race.htm; last visited on 1 November 2007).

Ewen, Alexander (ed.), *Voices of Indigenous Peoples: Native Peoples Address the United Nations* (Santa Fe: Clear Light Publishers, 1994).

Excoffier, Laurent, 'Human Diversity: Our genes tell us where we live', *Current Biology*, 13, 2003, pp. 134–6.

Exner, Derek V., Dries, D. L., Domanski, M. J. and Cohn, J. N., 'Lesser Response to the Angiotensin-Converting-Enzyme Inhibitor Therapy in Black as Compared with White Patients with Left Ventricular Dysfunction', *New England Journal of Medicine*, 344, 2001, p. 1351.

Eze, Emmanuel Chukwudi (ed.), *Race and the Enlightenment: A Reader* (Oxford: Blackwell, 1997).

Ferguson, Adam, *The History of Civil Society* (Cambridge: Cambridge University Press, 1996; first pub. 1767).

Fernández-Armesto, Felipe, *So You Think You're Human?* (Oxford: Oxford University Press, 2004).

Fforde, Cressida, 'Collection, Repatriation and Identity', in Fforde, Hubert and Turnbull (eds.), *The Dead and their Possessions*.

Fforde, Cressida, Hubert, Jane and Turnbull, Paul (eds.), *The Dead and their Possessions: Repatriation in Principle, Policy and Practice* (London: Routledge, 2002).

Finkielkraut, Alain, *The Defeat of the Mind* (New York: Columbia University Press, 1995; first pub. 1987).

Flynn, J.R. 'The mean IQ of Americans: Massive gains 1932 to 1978', *Psychological Bulletin*, 95, 1984, pp. 29–51.

Flynn, J.R. 'Massive IQ gains in 14 nations', *Psychological Bulletin* 101, 1987, pp. 171–91.

Foner, Eric and Garraty, John A. (eds.) *The Reader's Companion to American History* (New York: Houghton Mifflin, 1991).

Foner, Philip S., *British Labor and the American Civil War* (New York: Holmes and Meier, 1981).

Foster, Morris, 'Ethical Issues in Developing a Haplotype Map with Socially Defined Populations', (http://www.genome.gov/10001683; last viewed 1 November 2007).

Foster, Morris and Sharp, Richard, 'Race, Ethnicity and Genomics: Social Classification as Proxies of Biological Heterogeneity', *Genome Research*, 12, 2002, pp. 844–50.

Frederickson, George M., *The Black Image in the White Mind: The Debate on Afro-American Character and Destiny 1817–1914* (New York: Harper & Row, 1971).

Friedman, John Block, *The Monstrous Races in Medieval Art and Thought* (Cambridge, Mass: Harvard University Press, 1981).

Fryer, Peter, *Staying Power: The History of Black People in Britain* (London: Pluto Press, 1984).

Gellner, Ernest, *Relativism and the Social Sciences* (Cambridge: Cambridge University Press, 1985).

Gibbon, Edward, *The Decline and Fall of the Roman Empire*, 7 vols. (New York: AMS Press, 1974; first pub. 1776–1778).

Gibson, Margaret A. and Ogbu, John U. (eds.), *Minority Status and Schooling: A Comparative Study of Immigrants and Involuntary Minorities* (New York: Garland, 1991).

Giles, Eugene, 'E.A. Hooton, 1887–1954' in Spencer (ed.) *History of Physical Anthropology: An Encyclopaedia*, vol.1, pp. 491–501.

Gill, George W., 'Does Race Exist?: A proponent's view', *Nova Online* (http://www.pbs.org/wgbh/nova/first/gill.html; last visited 1 November 2007).

Gitlin, Todd, *The Twilight of Common Dreams: Why America is Wracked by Culture Wars* (New York: Henry Holt, 1995).

Gitschier, Jane, 'The Whole Side of It: An Interview with Neil Risch', *PloS Genetics*, 1, 2005 (available online at http://genetics.plosjournals.org/perlserv/?request=get-document&doi=10.1371/journal.pgen.0010014 &ct=1; last visited 1 November 2007).

Glazer, Nathan, *We're All Multiculturalists Now* (Cambridge, MA: Harvard University Press, 1997).

Goldberg, David Theo, *Racist Culture: Philosophy and the Politics of Meaning* (Oxford, Blackwell, 1993).

Goldstein, David B. and Chikhi, Lounes, 'Human Migrations and Population Structure: What we know and why it matters', *Annual Review of Genomics & Human Genetics*, 3, 2002.

Goodhart, Adam, 'Going Home', *Harvard Magazine*, 16 November 2003.

Goodhart, David, 'Too Diverse?', *Prospect*, February 2004 (available online at http://www.prospect-magazine.co.uk/article_details.php?id=5835; last visited 1 November 2007).

Goodman, Alan, 'Two Questions about Race', http://raceandgenomics.ssrc.org/Goodman/ (last visited 1 November 2007).

Gossett, Thomas F., *Race: The History of an Idea in America* (Oxford: Oxford University Press, 1963).

Gould, Stephen Jay, *The Mismeasure of Man* (London: Penguin, 1981).

Gould, Stephen Jay, 'Morton's ranking of races by cranial capacity: Unconscious manipulation of data may be a scientific norm', *Science*, 200, 1978, pp. 503–9.

Gould, Stephen Jay, 'Human Equality is a Contingent Fact of History', *Natural History* (November 1984), pp. 9–32.

Grant, Madison, *The Passing of the Great Race: Or the Racial Basis of European History* (New York: Charles Scribner's Sons, 1916).

Graves, Joseph L. Jr., *The Emperor's New Clothes: Biological Theories of Race at the Millennium* (New Brunswick, NJ: Rutgers University Press, 2001).

Gray, John, *Two Faces of Liberalism* (New York: New Press, 2000).

Gray, John, *Straw Dogs: Thoughts on Humans and Other Animals* (London: Granta, 2002).

Gray, Peter, 'Misuse of Evolutionary Theory to Advocate for Racial Discrimination and Segregation: A Critique of Salter's *On Genetic Interests*', *Human Ethology Bulletin*, 20, 2005, pp.10–12.

Greene, John C., 'Some Early Speculations on the origin of Human Races', *American Anthropologist*, 56, 1954, pp. 31–41.

Gutman, Amy (ed.), *Multiculturalism: Examining the Politics of Recognition* (Princeton NJ: Princeton University Press, 1994).

Hahn, Robert A., Mulinare, Joseph and Teutsch, Steven M., 'Inconsistencies in Coding of Race and Ethnicity Between Birth and Death in US Infants: A New Look at Infant Mortality, 1983 through 1985', *Journal of the American Medical Association*, 267, 1992, pp. 259–63.

Hall, Stuart, 'The question of cultural identity' in Hall, Held and McGrew (eds.) *Modernity and its Futures*.

Hall, Stuart, McGrew, Tony and Held, David (eds.) *Modernity and its Futures* (Cambridge: Polity, 1992).

Hamilton, W.D., 'The Evolution of Altruistic Behaviour', *American Naturalist*, 97, 1963, pp. 354–6.

Hamilton, W.D., 'The Genetical Basis of Social Behaviour (Parts 1 & 2)', *Journal of Theoretical Biology*, 7, 1964, pp. 1–52.

Hampson, Norman, *The Enlightenment: An Evaluation of its Assumptions, Attitudes and Values* (Harmondsworth: Penguin, 1968).

Hanke, Lewis, *Bartolomé Las Casas: An Interpretation of Life and Writings* (The Hague: Martinus Nijhoff, 1951).

Hanke, Lewis, *All Mankind is One: A Study of the Disputation Between Bartolomé de Las Casas and Juan Ginés de Sepúlveda in 1550 on the Intellectual and Religious Capacity of the American Indian* (Illinois: Northern Illinois University Press, 1974).

Hannaford, Ivan, *Race: The History of an Idea in the West* (Washington: The Woodrow Wilson Centre Press, 1996).

Harding, Sandra, *Whose science? Whose knowledge?* (Ithaca: Cornel University Press, 1991).

Harding, Sandra, *Is Science Multicultural?: Postcolonialisms, Feminisms and Epistemologies* (Bloomington: Indianan University Press, 1998).

Harker, Joseph, 'Back to Africa', *Guardian*, 14 February 2003.

Harris, David R. and Sim, Jeremiah Joseph, 'Who is Mixed Race?: Patterns and Determinants of Adolescent Racial Identity', unpublished manuscript cited in David R Harris, 'Demography's Race Problem', Paper presented to the Annual Meeting of the Population Association of America, March 2000.

Heartfield, James, *The Death of the Subject Explained* (London: Perpetuity Press, 2002).

Herder, Johann Gottfried von, *Reflections on the Philosophy of the History of Mankind* (Chicago: University of Chicago Press, 1968; first pub. 1791).

Herder, Johann Gottfried von, *J.G. Herder on Social and Political Culture*, ed. F.M. Barnard (Cambridge: Cambridge University press, 1969).

Himmelfarb, Gertrude, *The Idea of Poverty: England in the Early Industrial Age* (London: Faber & Faber, 1984).

Hitt, Jack, 'Mighty White of You: Racial Preferences Color America's Oldest Bones and Skulls', *Harper's Magazine* (July 2005).

Hocutt, Max, 'Is the Concept of Race Illegitimate?', *The Independent Review*, VII, no1 (summer 2002), pp115–128.

Hodgen, M.T., *Early Anthropology in the Sixteenth and Seventeenth Centuries* (Philadehphia: University of Pennsylvania Press, 1964).

Hollis, M. and Lukes, S. (eds.), *Rationalism and Relativism* (Cambridge, MA: MIT Press, 1982).

Hooton, Earnest Albert, *The Indians of Pecos Pueblo: A Study of their Skeletal Remains* (Yale University Press, 1930).

Hume, David, *Inquiry Concerning Human Understanding* (Oxford: Oxford University Press, 1994; first pub. 1748).

Hume, David, *Selected Essays* (Oxford: Oxford University Press, 1993.

Hunt-Grubbe, Charlotte, 'The Elementary DNA of Dr Watson', *Sunday Times*, 14 October 2007.

Huxley, Thomas, 'Emancipation: Black and White', in *Lay Sermons, Addresses and Reviews* (http://www.gutenberg.org/etext/16729; last visited 1 November 2007).

Ignatieff, Michael, 'Ascent of Man', *Prospect*, October 1999, pp. 28–31.

Irvine, S.H. and Berry, J.W. (eds.), *Human Abilities in Cultural Context* (Cambridge: Cambridge University Press, 1988).

Israel, Jonathan I., *Radical Enlightenment: Philosophy and the Making of Modernity, 1650–1750* (Oxford: Oxford University Press, 2001).

Israel, Jonathan I., *Enlightenment Contested: Philosophy, Modernity and the Emancipation of Man, 1670–1752* (Oxford: Oxford University Press, 2006).

Jacoby, Russell, *The End of Utopia: Politics and Culture in an Age of Apathy* (New York: Basic Books, 2000).

Jasonoff, S., Markle, G., Petersen, J. and Pinch, T. (eds.), *Handbook of Science and Technology Studies* (Thousand Oaks: Sage Publications, 1995).

Jefferson, Thomas, *The Writings of Thomas Jefferson*, (Washington: Thomas Jefferson Memorial Association, 1904).

Jenkins, Tiffany, *Human Remains: Objects to Study or Ancestors to Bury?* (London: Institute of Ideas, 2004).

Jensen, Arthur, 'How Much can we boost IQ and scolastic achievement?', *Harvard Educational Review*, 39, pp. 1–123, 1969.

Jones, Greta, *Social Darwinism and English Thought: The Interaction Between Biological and Social Theory* (New Jersey: Harvester, 1980).

Juengst, E., 'Identity and Human Diversity: Keeping Biology Straight from Culture', *American Journal of Human Genetics*, 63, 1998, pp. 673–7.

Kahn, Jonathan, 'How a Drug Becomes "Ethnic": Law, Commerce and the production of Racial Categories in Medicine', *Yale Journal of Health Policy, Law and Ethics*, 4, 2004, pp. 1–46.

Kant, Immanuel, 'On the Different Races of Man', in Emmanuel Chukwudi Eze (ed.), *Race and the Enlightenment: A Reader* (Oxford: Blackwell, 1997), pp. 38–48.

Keen, Benjamin, 'The Legacy of Bartolomé de Las Casas', in *Essays in the Intellectual History of Colonial Latin America* (Colorado: Westview Press, 1998), pp. 57–69.

Kemp, Jack, 'Building Blocks of Humanity', *townhall.com*, 21 February 2001, http://www.townhall.com/columnists/JackKemp/2001/02/21/building_blocks_of_humanity (last visited 1 November 2007).

Kenneally, Thomas, 'Schindler has much to tell us', *Times*, 22 March 1994.

Kirk, Russell, *The Conservative Mind* (London: Faber & Faber, 1954).

Kohn, Marek, *The Race Gallery: The Return of Racial Science* (London: Jonathan Cape, 1995).

Kohn, Marek, 'It depends what you mean by difference', in *30: The Turning of the Tide* (London: Commission for Racial Equality, 2006).

Kosiba, Steven, 'Assessing the Efficacy and Pragmatism of "Race" Designation in Human Skeletal Identification: A Test of Fordisc 2.0 Program', *American Journal of Physical Anthropology*, Supplement 30, 2000, p. 200.

Kruks, Sonia, *Retrieving Experience: Subjectivity and Recognition in Feminist Politics* (Ithaca, NY: Cornell University Press, 2000).

Kuper, Adam, *Culture: The Anthropologists' Account* (Cambridge MA: Harvard University Press, 2001).

Kymlicka, W., *Multicultural Citizenship* (Oxford: Oxford University Press, 1995).

Larson, Edward J., *Summer for the Gods: The Scopes Trial and America's Continuing Debate over Science and Religion* (New York: Basic Books, 1998).

Las Casas, Bartolomé de, *The Defence of the Most Reverend Lord, Don Fray Bartolomé de Las Casas, of the Order of Preachers, Late Bishop of Chiapa, Against the Persecutors and Slanderers of the Peoples of the New World Discovered Across the Seas*, trans. and ed. S. Poole (Illinois: Northern Illinois University Press, 1974).

Las Casas, Bartolomé de, *The Devastation of the Indies: A Brief Account* , trans. Herma Briffault (Baltimore: Johns Hopkins University Press, 1992; first pub. 1542).

Lasch-Quinn, Elizabeth, 'Liberation therapeutics: Consciousness-raising as a problem', *Society*, 39, 2002, pp. 7–15.

Leathers, A., Edwards, J. and Armelagos, G.J., 'Assessment of Classification of Crania Using Fordisc 2.0: Nubian X-Group test', *American Journal of Physical Anthropology*, Supplement 34 (2002), pp. 99–100.

LeBon, Gustav, *The Psychology of Peoples* (New York: S.E. Stechert, 1912; first pub. 1894).

Lee, David, 'The First Flowering', *Jackdaw*, September 2004 (http://www.thejackdaw.co.uk/leaders14.html; last visited 1 November 2007).

Lee, Mike, 'Politics of the past', *Tri-City Herald*, 26 December 1999.

Lee, Sandra Soo-Jin, Mountain, Joanna and Koenig, Barbara A., 'The Meanings of "Race" in the New Genomics: Implications for Health Disparities Research', *Yale Journal of Health Policy, Law and Ethics*, 1, 2001.

Lee, Yongsook, 'Koreans in Japan and the United States', in Gibson and Ogbu (eds.), *Minority Status and Schooling*, pp. 139–65.

Leroi, Armand Marie, 'A Family Tree in Every Gene', *New York Times*, 14 March 2005.

Levin, Michael, 'The Race Concept: A Defence', *Behavior and Philosophy*, 30, pp. 21–42, 2002.

Lévi-Strauss, Claude, *Structural Anthropology*, trans. Claire Jacobson and Brooke Grundfest Schoepf, 2 vols. (Harmondsworth: Penguin, 1972; first pub. 1963).

Lewontin, Richard, 'The Apportionment of Human Diversity', *Journal of Evolutionary Biology*, 6, 1972, pp. 381–98.

Lewontin, Richard, *The Genetic Basis of Evolutionary Change* (New York: Columbia University Press, 1974).

Lewontin, Richard, *Human Diversity* (New York: Scientific American Library, 1982).

Lieberman, Leonard, 'The debate over race: A study in the sociology of knowledge', *Phylon*, 39, 1968, pp. 127–41.

Lieberman, Leonard, 'How "Caucasoids" Got Such Big Crania and Why They Shrank', *Current Anthropology*, 42, 2001, pp. 69–95.

Linnaeus, Carolus, *Prelude to the Betrothal of Plants*, ed. Xtina Wootz and Krister Östlund, (Uppsala: Uppsala University Library, 2007; first pub. 1729).

Linnaeus, Carolus, *Systema Naturae* (10th edition) (Stockholm: Laurentii Salvii, 1758).

Locke, John, *An Essay Concerning Human Understanding* (Harmondsworth: Penguin, 1997; first pub. 1690).

Lorrimer, Douglas A., *Colour, Class and the Victorians: English Attitudes to the Negro in the Mid-Nineteenth Century* (Leicester: Leicester University Press, 1978).

Lovgren, Stefan, 'Cultural Diversity Highest in Resource-Rich Areas, Study Says', *National Geographic News*, 17 March 2004.

Lynn, Richard, 'The intelligence of the Japanese', *Bulletin of the British Psychological Society*, 30, 1977, pp. 69–72.

Lynn, Richard, 'Race differences in intelligence: a global perspective', *Mankind Quarterly*, 1, 1990, pp. 255–96.

Lynn, R., Hampson, S., and Magee, M., 'Home Background, Intelligence, personality and Education as Predictors of Unemployment in Young People', *Personality and Individual Differences*, 5, 1984, pp. 549–57.

Lyon, J. and Sloan, P.R., (eds.), *From Natural History to the History of Nature: Readings from Buffon and His Critics* (Notre Dame, IA: University of Notre Dame Press, 1981).

MacDonald, Kevin, *A People That Shall Dwell Alone: Judaism as a Group Evolutionary Strategy* (Praeger, 1994).

Maistre, J. M. de, *Considerations on France* (Cambridge: Cambridge University Press, 1995; first pub. 1797).

Marchant, James, *Alfred Russel Wallace: Letters and Reminiscences*, 2 vols (New York: Cassell, 1916).

Marcuse, Herbert, *Eros and Civilisation* (London: Abacus, 1972).

Margalit, Avishai and Raz, Joseph, 'National Self-Determination', *Journal of Philosophy*, 87, 1990.

Marks, Jonathan, *Human Biodiversity: Genes, Race and History* (New York: Aldine de Gruyter, 1994).

Marks, Jonathan, *What it Means to be 98% Chimpanzee: Apes, People and their Genes* (Berkley: University of California Press, 2002).

Marks, Jonathan, 'Your Body, My Property: The Problem of Colonial Genetics in a Postcolonial World' in Meskell and Pels (ed.), *Embedding Ethics*.

Martin, P.S., 'Pleistocene Overkill', *Natural History*, 76, 1967, pp. 32–8.

Mayr, Ernst, 'Typological versus Population Thinking' in Sober (ed.), *Conceptual Issues in Evolutionary Biology*, pp. 157–60.

McGregor, Russell, *Imagined Destinies: Aboriginal Australians and the Doomed Race Theory, 1880–1939* (Melbourne: Melbourne University Press, 1997).

McKie, Robin and Harris, Paul, 'Disgrace: How a giant of science was brought low', *Observer*, 21 October 2007.

Melbourne, Tapper, *In the Blood: Sickle Cell Anaemia and the Politics of Race* (Philadelphia: University of Pennsylvania Press, 1999).

Meskell, Lynn and Pels, Peter (eds.), *Embedding Ethics* (Oxford: Berg, 2005).

Michael, J.S., 'A new look at Morton's craniological research', *Current Anthropology*, 29, 1988, 349–54.

Michaels, Walter Benn, *Our America: Nationalism, Modernism and Pluralism* (Durham, NC: Duke University Press, 1995).

Milmo, Cahal, 'Fury at DNA pioneer's theory: Africans are less intelligent than Westerners', *Indepenent*, 29 October 2007.

Modood, Tariq and Werbner, Pnina (eds.), *The Politics of Multiculturalism in the New Europe* (London: Zed, 1997).

Montagu, Ashley, *Man's Most Dangerous Myth: The Fallacy of Race* (Cleveland: World Publishing, 1964).

Montagu, Ashley, 'Edward Tyson, MD, FRS 1650–1708 and the Rise of Human and Comparative Anatomy in England', *Memoirs of the American Philosophical Society*, 20, 1943.

Morton, Samuel George, *Crania Americana: Or, A Comparative View of the Skulls of Various Aboriginal Nations of North and South America, to which is Prefixed an Essay on the Varieties of the Human Species* (Philadelphia: John Pennington, 1839).

Mosse, George L., *Towards the Final Solution: A History of European Racism* (London: J.M. Dent & Sons, 1978).

Murray, Charles and Hernnstein, Richard J., *The Bell Curve: Intelligence and Class Structure in American Life* (New York: Free Press, 1994).

Murray, Charles, 'The Inequality Taboo', *Commentary*, September 2005.

Murray, Charles, 'Jewish Genius', *Commentary*, April 2007.

Murray, Charles and Hernnstein, Richard J., 'Race, Genes and IQ: An Apologia', *New Republic*, 31 October 1994.

Muthu, Sankar, *Enlightenment Against Empire* (Princeton: Princeton University Press, 2003).

Nanda, Meera, *Prophets Facing Backwards: Postmodern Critiques of Science and Hindu Nationalism in India* (New Brunswick, NJ: Rutgers University Press, 2003).

Neisser, Ulric (ed.) *The Rising Curve: Long-Term Gains in IQ and Related Measures* (American Psychological Association, 1998).

Neisser, Ulric, 'Rising Scores on Intelligence Tests', *American Scientist*, September-October 1997.

Nelson, C. and Grossberg, L. (eds.), *Marxism and the Interpretation of Culture* (Urbana: University of Illinois Press, 1988).

library

Neves, Walter and Blum, Max, 'The Buhl Burial: A Reply to Green *et al.*', *American Antiquity*, 65, 2000, pp. 191–3.

Neves, W.A. and Pucciarelli, H.M., 'Morphological Affinities of the First Americans: An Exploratory Analysis Based on Early South American Remains', *Journal of Human Evolution*, 21, 1991, pp. 261–73.

Niebuhr, Barthold Georg, *Lectures on the History of Rome*, 3 vols (http://www.efm.bris.ac.uk/het/niebuhr/index.htm; last visited 1 November 2007).

Nott, J.C. and Gliddon, G.R., *Types of Mankind: Or Ethnological Researches* (Philadelphia: Lippincott, 1854).

Nott, J.C. and Gliddon, G.R., *Indigenous Races, Or New Chapters of Ethnological Enquiry* (Philadelphia: Lippincott, 1857).

O'Neil, Dennis, 'Distribution of Blood Types', http://anthro.palomar.edu/vary/vary_3.htm (last visited 1 November 2007).

Pagden, Anthony, *European Encounters with the New World* (New Haven: Yale University Press, 1993).

Pagel, M. and Mace, R. 'The cultural wealth of nations', *Nature*, 428, 2004, pp. 275–8.

Paine, Thomas, *Rights of Man* (Harmondsworth: Penguin, 1984; first pub. 1791).

Parekh, Bhikhu, *Rethinking Multiculturalism: Cultural Diversity and Political Theory* (Basingstoke: Macmillan, 2000).

Parekh, Bhikhu, 'Superior Peoples: The Narrowness of Liberalism from Mill to Rawls', *Times Literary Supplement*, 25 February 1994.

Pick, Daniel, *Faces of Degeneration: A European Disorder, c. 1848–1914* (Cambridge: Cambridge University Press, 1989).

Pinker, Steven, *How the Mind Works* (London: Allen Lane, 1997).

Pinker, Steven, *The Blank Slate: The Modern Denial of Human Nature* (London: Allen Lane, 2002).

Pinker, Steven, 'Psychoanalysis Q & A' (Interview), *Harvard Crimson*, 19 January 2005 (http://www.thecrimson.com/article.aspx?ref=505366; last visited 1 November 2007).

Poliakov, Leon, *The Aryan Myth: A History of Nationalist Ideas in Europe* (New York: Basic Books, 1974).

Pollock, Mica, *Colormute: Race Talk Dilemmas in an American School* (Princeton University Press, 2005).

Ponte, Lowell, 'Politically Incorrect Genocide, Part 2', *Frontpagemag.com*, 5 October 1999 (http://www.frontpagemag.com/Articles/Read.aspx? GUID={C6C553AA-37A0–4A73–815F-743CDD33123B}; last visited 1 November 2007).

Powell, Joseph and Neves, Walter, 'New Cariofacial and Dental Perspectives on Native American Origins', *Yearbook of Physical Anthropology*, 42, 1999, pp. 153–88.

Powell, J.F. and Rose, J.C. *Report on the Osteological Assessment of the "Kennewick Man" skeleton* (CENWW.97.Kennewick) (Archeology & Ethnography Program, National Park Service, United States Department of Interior, 1999) http://www.cr.nps.gov/archeology/kennewick/powell_rose.htm (last visited 1 November 2007).

Putnam, Robert D., '*E Pluribus Unum*: Diversity and Community in the Twenty-first Century', *Scandinavian Political Studies*, 30, 2007, pp. 137–74.

Raven, C.E., *John Ray, Naturalist* (Cambridge: Cambridge University Press, 1986).

Ray, John, *The Wisdom of God: Manifested in the Works of the Creation: Heavenly Bodies, Elements, Meteors, Fossils, Vegetables, Animals* (New York: Arno, 1978; first pub. 1691).

Raz, Joseph, *Ethics in the Public Domain* (Oxford: Oxford University Press, 1995).

Renan, Ernest, *The Future of Science* (Boston: Roberts Brothers, 1891).

Rhea, Joseph Tilden, *Race Pride and the American Identity* (Cambridge, MA: Harvard University Press, 1997).

Ridley, Matt, *The Origin of Virtues* (London: Viking, 1996).

Ridley, Matt, 'Ice Age Politics', *Prospect*, June 1996.

Ripley, W.Z., *The Races of Europe: A Sociological Study* (New York: D. Appleton, 1899).

Risch, Neil, Burchard, Esteban, Ziv, Elad and Tang, Hua, 'Categorisation of humans in biomedical research: genes, race and disease', *Genome Biology*, 3, 2002 (http://genomebiology.com/2002/3/7/comment/2007.1; last visited on 1 November 2007).

Rosenberg, Noah A., Pritchard, Jonathan K., Weber, James L., Cann, Howard M., Kidd, Kenneth K., Zhivotovsky, Lev A. and Feldman, Marcus W., 'Genetic Structure of Human Populations', *Science*, 298, 2002, pp. 2381–5.

Ross, Andrew, 'Introduction', *Social Text*, 46–47, Spring-Summer 1996.

Rushton, J. Phillipe, *Race, Evolution and Behaviour: A Life History Perspective* (New Brunswick, NJ: Transaction Publications, 1995); there is a also an abridged edition available online at http://www.charlesdarwinresearch. org/Race_Evolution_Behavior.pdf (last visited 1 November 2007).

Rushton, J. Phillipe, 'Race, intelligence, and the brain: The errors and omissions of the "revised" edition of S. J. Gould's *The Mismeasure of Man', Personality and Individual Differences, 23*, 1997, pp. 169–80.

Sailer, Steve, 'It's All Relative: Putting Race in its Proper Perspective', a talk given to a conference at the Ronald Reagan Presidential Library, July 2002. There is a transcript at http://www.vdare.com/asp/printPage.asp? url=http://www.vdare.com/sailer/presentation.htm (last visited on 1 November 2007).

Sailer, Steve, 'African Ancestry Inc. traces DNA roots', *UPI*, 29 April 2003.

Salter, Frank, *On Genetic Interests: Family, Ethny, and Humanity in an Age of Mass Migration* (Frankfurt: Peter Lang, 2003).

Salter, Frank Kemp (ed.) *Altruism and Welfare: New Findings in Evolutionary Theory* (London: Frank Cass: 2004).

Sankar, Pamela and Cho, Mildred K., 'Toward a New Vocabulary of Human Genetic Variation', *Science*, 298, 2002, pp. 1337–8.

Sarich, Vincent and Miele, Frank, *Race: The Reality of Human Differences* (Boulder, Colorado: Westview Press, 2004).

Satel, Sally, 'Medicine's Race Problem', *Policy Review*, 49, 2001; http://www. hoover.org/publications/policyreview/3462856.html (last visited 1 November 2007).

Satel, Sally, 'I am a racially profiling doctor', *New York Times*, 5 May 2002.

Sauer, Norman, 'Forensic Anthropologists and the Concept of Race: If Races Don't Exist, Why are Forensic Anthropologists So Good at Identifying Them?', *Social Sciences and Medicine*, 304, 1992, pp. 107–11.

Schwartz, R.S., 'Racial Profiling in Medical research', *New England Journal of Medicine*, 344, 2001, pp. 1392–3.

Shulevitz, Judith, 'Evolutionary Psychology's Anti-Semite', *Slate*, 24 January 2000; http://www.slate.com/id/1004446/ (last visited 1 November 2007).

Sloan, Phillip R., 'The Buffon-Linnaeus controversy', *Isis*, 67, 1976.

Smith, Michael, Lautenberger, James, Shin, Hyoung Doo, Chretien, Jean-Paul, Shresta, Sadeep, Gilbert, Dennis and O'Brien, Stephen, 'Markers for Mapping Admixture Linkage Disequilibrium in African American and Hispanic Populations', *American Journal of Human Genetics*, 69, 2001, pp. 1080–94.

Smith, Roger, *The Fontana History of the Human Sciences* (London: Fontana, 1997).

Smith, Samuel Stanhope, *An Essay on the Causes of the Variety of Complexion and Figure in the Human Species* (Cambridge, MA: Harvard University Press, 1965; first pub. 1787; second edition, 1810), p. 240n.

Sober, Elliott (ed.), *Conceptual Issues in Evolutionary Biology* (Cambridge, Mass: MIT Press, 1995).

Steele, D. Gentry and Powell, Joseph, 'Paleobiology of the First Americans', *Evolutionary Anthropology*, 2, 1993, pp. 138–46.

Steele, D. Gentry and Powell, Joseph, 'Paleobiological Evidence for the Peopling of the Americas: A Morphometric View', in Bonnichsen and Steele (eds.), *Method and Theory for Investigating the Peopling of the Americas*, pp. 79–96.

Sollas, W.J., *Paleolithic Races and their Modern Representatives* (London: reprinted from Science Progress, 1908–1909).

Spencer, I.F. (ed.), *History of Physical Anthropology: An Encyclopaedia* (New York: Garland, 1997).

Spivak, Gayatri, 'Can the subaltern speak?' in Nelson and Grossberg (eds.), *Marxism and the Interpretation of Culture*, pp. 3–34.

Spurzheim, J.G., 'Phrenological Note by Dr. Spurzheim', *Phrenological Journal*, 6, 1829–1830, p. 312.

Stanford, Dennis and Bradley, Bruce, 'The Solutrean Connection – Did Some Ancient Americans Come from Europe?', *Discovering Archaeology*, Feb 2000, pp. 54–56.

Stanton, William, *The Leopard's Spots: The Scientific Attitude to Race in America: 1815–1859* (Chicago: University of Chicago Press, 1960).

Stepan, Nancy, *The Idea of Race in Science: Great Britain 1800–1960* (London: Macmillan, 1962).

Stevens, Jacqueline, 'Racial Meanings and Scientific Methods: Changing Policies for NIH-Sponsored Publications Reporting Human Variation', *Journal of Health Politics, Policy and Law*, 28, 2003, pp. 1033–87.

Stocking, George W. Jr., *Race, Culture and Evolution: Essays in the History of Anthropology* (Chicago: Chicago University Press, 1968).

Sykes, Brian, *The Seven Daughters of Eve* (London: Bantam: 2001).

Taguieff, Pierre-Andre, 'The New Cultural Racism in France', *Telos*, 83, 1990.

Taine, Hyppolite, *History of English Literature*, trans. H. van Laun (Philadelphia: Gebbie Publishing, 1897; first pub. 1864).

Taylor, Charles, 'The Politics of Recognition' in Gutman (ed.) *Multiculturalism*.

Taylor, Jared, 'What we owe our people', *American Renaissance*, January 2005, (http://www.amren.com/store/salterreview.htm; last visited 1 November 2007).

Tench, Watkin, *Sydney's First Four Years, being a reprint of A Narrative of the Expedition to Botany Bay, and A Complete Account of the Settlement at Port*, ed. L.F. Fitzhardinge (Sydney: Library of Australian History, 1979; first published 1789, 1793).

Thomas, David Hurst, *Skull Wars: Kennewick Man, Archaeology and the Battle for Native American Identity* (New York: Basic Books, 2000), p. 42.

Tishkoff, Sarah A., Varkonyi, Robert, Cahinhinan, Nelie, Abbes, Salem, Argyropoulos, George, Destro-Bisol, Giovanni, Drousiotou, Anthi, Dangerfield, Bruce, Lefranc, Gerard, Loiselet, Jacques, Piro, Anna, Stoneking, Mark, Tagarelli, Antonio, Tagarelli, Giuseppe, Touma, Elias H., Williams, Scott M. and Clark, Andrew G., 'Haplotype Diversity and Linkage Disequilibrium at Human *G6PD*: Recent Origin of Alleles That Confer Malarial Resistance', *Science*, 293, 2001, pp. 455–62.

Todorov, Tzvetan, *On Human Diversity: Nationalism, Racism and Exoticism in French Thought*, trans. C. Porter (Cambridge, MA: Harvard University Press, 1993).

Tooby, John and Cosmides, Leda, 'Kin selection, genic selection and information-dependent strategies', *Behavioural and Brain Studies*, 12, 1989, pp. 542–4.

Trivers, R. L., 'The Evolution of Reciprocal Altruism', *Quarterly Review of Biology*, 46, 1971, pp. 35–57.

Turner, Christy, 'What is lost with skeletal reburial', *Quarterly Review of Archaeology*, 7, 1986.

Unesco, World Conference on Cultural Policies: Mexico City, 26 July to 6 August 1982, *Final Report* (Paris: Unesco, 1982).

Unesco, *Cultural Diversity: Common Heritage, Plural Identities* (Paris: Unesco, 2002), p3. This book can be downloaded from http://unesdoc.unesco.org/images/0012/001271/127161e.pdf (last visited 1 November 2007).

Unesco, *Convention for the Safeguarding of the Intangible Cultural Heritage* (Paris, 17 October 2003).

Venter, Craig, *A Life Decoded* (London: Allen Lane, 2007).

Verster, J.M. and Prinsloo, R.J., 'The Diminishing Test Performance Gap Between English Speakers and Afrikaans Speakers in South Africa' in Irvine and Berry (eds.), *Human Abilities in Cultural Context*, pp. 534–60.

Waal, Frans de, *The Ape and the Sushi Master: Cultural Reflections by a Primatologist* (London: Allen Lane, 2001).

Walker, Alexander, *Physiognomy Founded on Physiology and Applied to Various Countries, Professions and Individuals* (London: Smith, Eider & Co., 1834).

Wallace, Alfred Russel, *Natural Selection and Tropical Nature: Essays on Descriptive and Theoretical Biology* (London: Macmillan, 1891).

Wallace, Alfred Russel, 'The Origins of Human Races and the Antiquity of Man deduced from the Theory of "Natural Selection"', *Journal of the Anthropological Society*, 2, 1864, p. clvii–clxxxvii.

Wallace, Alfred Russel, 'Geological Climates and the Origin of Species', *The Quarterly Review*, 126, 1869, pp. 185–205.

Washburn, S.L., 'The New Physical Anthropology', *Transactions of the New York Academy of Sciences* (ser 2), 13, 1951, pp. 298–304.

Watson, James, *Avoid Boring People: And Other Lessons from a Life in Science* (Oxford: Oxford University Press, 2007).

Watson, James, 'To question genetic intelligence is not racist', *Independent*, 29 October 2007.

Watson-Verran, Helen and Turnbull, David, 'Science and the other: Indigenous knowledge systems' in Jasonoff, Markle, Petersen and Pinch (eds.), *Handbook of STS.*

Weber, Eugene, *Peasants Into Frenchmen: The Modernisation of Rural France, 1870–1914* (Stanford University Press, 1976).

White, Leslie, *The Science of Culture: A Study of Man and Civilisation* (New York: Farrar Strauss, 1949).

Wiener, Philip P. (ed.), *The Dictionary of the History of Ideas: Studies of Selected Pivotal Ideas* (New York: Charles Scribner's & Sons, 1973–74).

Williams, David R., 'The Concept of Race in Health Services Research: 1966 to 1990', *Health Services Research*, 29, 1994, pp. 261–74.

Wilson, E.O., *On Human Nature* (Harmondsworth: Penguin: 1995; first pub. 1978).

Wilson, James F., Weale, Michael E., Smith, Alice C., Gratrix, Fiona, Fletcher, Benjamin, Thomas, Mark G., Bradman, Neil and Goldstein, David B., 'Population genetic structure of variable drug response', *Nature Genetics*, 29, 2001, pp. 265–9.

Wright, Richard, 'I Bite the Hand that Feeds Me', *Atlantic Monthly*, June 1940, pp. 827–8.

Wrong, Dennis H., 'Cultural relativism as ideology', *Critical Review*, 11, 1997, pp. 291-300.

Yancy, Clyde, 'Does race matter in heart failure?' *American Heart Journal*, 146, 2003, pp. 203–6.

Yerkes, R.M, and Yerkes, A.W., *The Great Apes. A Study of Anthropoid Life* (New Haven: Yale University Press, 1929).

Young, Iris Marion, *Justice and the Politics of Difference* (Princeton, NJ: Princeton University Press, 1990).

Young, Robert, *White Mythologies: Writing Histories and the West* (London: Routledge, 1990).

Zack, Naomi, *Philosophy of Science and Race* (London: Routledge, 2002).

Zeitlin, Irving, *Ideology and the Development of Sociological Theory* (Englewoods Cliffs, NJ: Prentice-Hall, 1968).

Zebrowitz, Leslie A., *Reading Faces: Window to the Soul?* (Boulder, Colorado: Westview Press, 1998).

INDEX